9780801567780

Take-It-Along Cookbook

Take-It-Along Cookbook

Jacqueline Hériteau

Illustrations by Peter Kalberkamp

A Helen Van Pelt Wilson Book

HAWTHORN BOOKS, INC.
Publishers/NEW YORK

TAKE-IT-ALONG COOKBOOK

Text copyright © 1975 by Jacqueline Hériteau. Illustrations copyright © 1975 by Peter Kalberkamp. Copyright under International and Pan-American Copyright Conventions. All rights reserved, including the right to reproduce this book or portions thereof in any form, except for the inclusion of brief quotations in a review. All inquiries should be addressed to Hawthorn Books, Inc., 260 Madison Avenue, New York, New York 10016. This book was manufactured in the United States of America and published simultaneously in Canada by Prentice-Hall of Canada, Limited, 1870 Birchmount Road, Scarborough, Ontario.

To Helen Van Pelt Wilson
the editor to whom I owe so much

Contents

Acknowledgments	ix
Have Recipe—Will Travel	xi

PART 1
Share the Party — 1

1. Party Plotting — 3
2. The Gilded Lily: Secrets of a French Chef — 9
3. Menus for All Kinds of Parties — 29

PART 2
Snack Parties and Appetizers — 47

4. Smorgasbord — 49
5. Hors D'Oeuvres Specialties — 57
6. Hurry-Up Appetizers — 65

PART 3
Soup Parties — 77

7. Hot Pots — 79
8. Cold Cups for Hot Days — 87

PART 4
Outdoor Parties — 93

9. Beach Partying — 95
10. Hawaiian Luaus — 105
11. Picnic Fare — 117

PART 5
When You Are Bringing the Main Dish   129

12. *French Specialties*   131
13. *Mediterranean Cooking*   149
14. *Rhineland Fare*   161
15. *From the East and Far East*   171
16. *New Orleans and New England Dishes*   181
17. *Holiday Birds*   197

PART 6
When You Are Bringing the Vegetable   203

18. *Portable Side Dishes*   205

PART 7
When You Are Bringing the Salad   217

19. *Salads, Dressings, Garnishes*   219

PART 8
When You Are Bringing the Dessert   233

20. *Whipped Cream and Other Delights*   235

PART 9
When You Are Bringing the Drinks   257

21. *From Café Brûlot to Peach Champagne*   259

Index   267

Acknowledgments

This collection of recipes was finalized under the direction of my father, Marcel Hériteau (who would rather cook than study recipes), with the loving help of my mother, Madeleine Hériteau (who hounded him day and night).

My sincere thanks to Francesca Bosetti Morris, who helped refine the Southern European recipes, such as Paella and Sangria, and handed over her favorite Italian recipe for Risotto; to Sally Larkin Erath, author of *Cooking for Two*, who helped with New England and seashore specialties; and to the many friends who are superb cooks and gave their take-it-along favorites: Joseph Bednerz for his fine Christmas Cake; Walter Ian Fischman for his delicious Spinach-and-Mushroom Salad; and Nona Remos for an Elegant Stew made with wine and brandy.

My thanks also to Maxine Krasnow who patiently typed the manuscript and a special vote of gratitude to Peter Kalberkamp who turned my how-to squiggles into helpful illustrations.

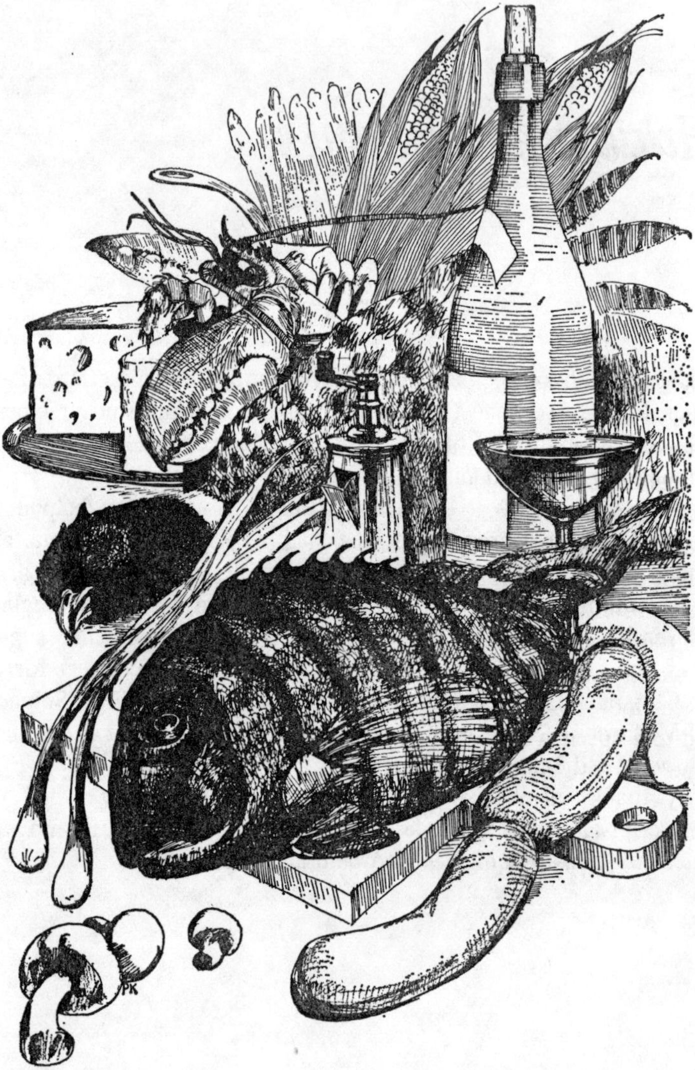

Have Recipe—Will Travel

When you're the one responsible for bringing the vegetable to a bring-a-dish dinner, what do you do? Or the entrée? Or the dessert? After years of taking along the same old casseroles, we finally began to realize that unusual, really good foods will travel if you know a trick or two. We learned you can take a real gourmet dish to a gourmet dinner and a real Oriental dish to an Oriental dinner.

Not all great recipes travel, but the recipes in this book do—and there are enough here to make it possible for you to bring anything from appetizers to desserts to almost any type of take-it-along meal to which you may be asked to contribute. Shared parties, parties to which everyone brings something, mean more parties, so the make-and-tote specials in this collection I call my love-a-party specials. I hope you love parties, too.

—Jacqui

PART 1

Share the Party

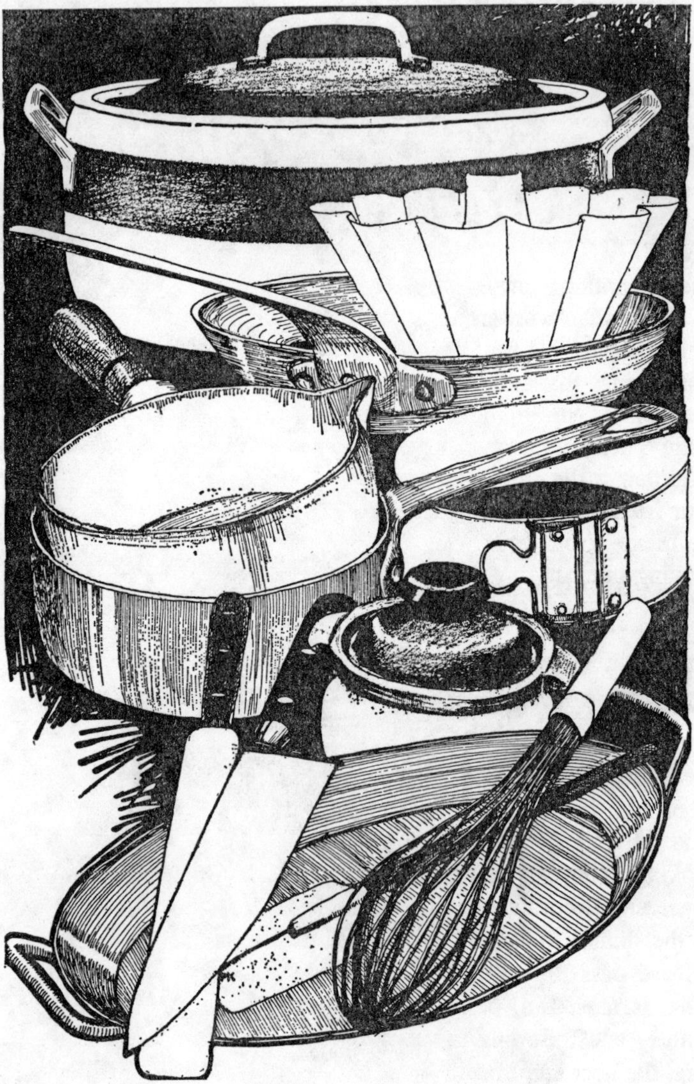

1. Party Plotting

There's nothing new about bringing a cooked dish to a party. We all did it when we were young and broke. And lots of us are still doing it because it's fun, because food and help costs are out of sight, and because that's the way we get together to share meals with other members of the organizations we belong to, from the church to the Little Theatre. One application of bring-a-dish dining that is somewhat new is the dinner club, and if you like to share the cooking with your friends, you would enjoy creating a dinner club. Anything can be the theme, from your vegetable garden to showing off the members' cooking talents.

PARTY THEMES

COUNTRY-OF-THE-MONTH. This is one of the most popular themes for dinner groups of six to ten. Make a list of countries whose food intrigues or appeals to your group, plan the courses, assign the cooking. You can carry the theme to all sorts of extremes—provide music and decorations associated with the country that is the subject of the dinner; hand out mimeographed translations of phrases like "Please pass the salt"; dress in native costumes; plan folk dances. What is most fun, perhaps, is researching the dining customs of a country and following them: In Sweden, for instance, at formal dinners, the host and hostess must toast each guest before the guest may sip his wine. And the gentleman on the right of the hostess must, at the end of the meal, give a formal speech of thanks that refers to each of the guests.

REGIONAL DINNER CLUB. Similar to a country-of-the-month group but based on regional American cooking. This can include Canada and Latin America. Usual size of the group, eight to twelve.

GARDENER'S DINNER CLUB. Monthly dinners planned around the most delicious of the crops due in during the harvest months. In May, for instance, with the first crops of tiny new peas due in, plan a dinner featuring fresh baby peas; in August a corn bake would be in order; in September, a tomato festival. Owners of community gardens will enjoy these. Size of the group can vary from six to thirty, since home-grown foods are low cost.

CALENDAR CLUB. The major holiday of the month dictates the meal from Christmas dinner to George Washington's birthday. Group can be of any size.

GOURMET DINNER CLUB. Another popular theme. Such groups concentrate on the cooking talents of their members. The point is to have only superbly cooked versions of the dishes selected. After the meal, each guest stands and offers a critique on the preparation of the dishes served. The Escoffier Society, whose members generally are professional chefs, enjoy such events with stringent regulations—no women; you must wear a huge French-style dinner napkin tucked into your collar; and there are about twenty-five courses with wines. You can have a lot of pleasure with this idea without going to quite these extremes. Groups are best held to six to ten, since gourmet cooking is most successful in small batches.

COOK-OUT CLUB. The eating version of the Polar Bear Club. Food is casual and the group can be as large as you like. The point is to have one meal outdoors *every* month of the year, and the dinner is usually tied to an activity, swimming or skating, mountain climbing, or berry picking.

BUY-OF-THE-MONTH CLUB. The challenge here is to find the best buy of the month. Each contributor brings a dish made with what he/she has located as the best buy—and somebody wins a prize. The challenge is to see what outrageously good dish can be made with low-cost ingredients. Leftovers count. The group can be a large one.

BIRTHDAY CLUB. Put together a group of twelve and do a yearly round of birthdays—no gifts, otherwise it would be a drain.

HUNT-AND-GAME DINNER CLUB. Meals are based on the seasonal hunting and fishing rounds, and all courses are geared to the game or fish bagged. You can fish in January but there are months when no fish or game is readily available, and you can either be a purist and skip dinner that month, or members can look for inventive ways out (for instance, the Beef en Papilottes) or cook with game purchased from special sources. Magazines for hunters usually have mail-order offerings of game. Groups can be six to twelve. You can't count on enough game for more.

STALKING-THE-WILD-ASPARAGUS DINNER CLUB. A variation on the above, the challenge is to *find* as many as possible of the main ingredients for the club meals—from wild asparagus, to mussels, to dandelions, and berries. Group can be any size. Clamming, berry picking, and many other activities can be considered.

PROGRESSIVE DINNER CLUB. This can be an individual event or a regular monthly feature, since everyone is hostess as well as cook. Guests meet at House No. 1 for appetizers and drinks; House No. 2 for the first course; House No. 3 for the entrée; House No. 4 for dessert and coffee. Transportation is unwieldy in groups of more than twelve.

BAKE-IN CLUB. The purpose is to share the fun of baking. Groups meet casually afternoon-into-evening with a dinner shared by all the families. Goods baked can be for local fund-raising events, or for individual families for Christmas or for freezing. Groups should be small, four to six.

COOK-IN CLUBS. Small groups of working mothers get together one day a month to do advance cooking for the freezer. Again, the cook-in lasts afternoon into evening, with families sharing dinner.

These are only a handful of possibilities.

PARTY PLOTTING

There are lots of ways to organize dinner groups, but the most common is to decide collectively on the theme of the meal, and to assign the responsibility of host. The host then queries each guest to find out what he/she wants to provide. The host can also assign the dishes, but the first method allows those who like to work to do most (which they will anyway), while those who don't like to work won't be made to feel guilty. It also allows someone who is great with desserts to do those, while the casserole expert can do his/her thing, too.

TAKING IT WITH YOU. Some recipes won't travel, notably steaks, grilled meats, most soufflés, and other fast-cooked or flash-cooked foods. The recipes in this collection all do travel, but do not all travel in a completely cooked state; otherwise you'd be limited to casseroles and semiwarm, raw, cold, or very simple foods. Study the recipes here, and you will see ways in which you can adapt many of your own favorites to a take-it-along meal. You *can* contribute a soufflé, providing you prepare it to the point just before ingredients are combined, then combine and cook them at the party. You can take a quiche, you can take a mousse. You can take many other delicate dishes so long as you do three-quarters of the work at home, and plan to complete the cooking at the home of the host.

As a rule of thumb, plan to reheat at the host's home; because if you keep foods scalding hot for an hour you will overcook them. All molded dishes should be unmolded at the host's home; all salads dressed there.

If you are working with a recipe you will complete at the home of the hostess, you should let her know. She may have other dishes coming that will need oven time or broiler time. Have her schedule your dish correctly. If you have one of those marvelous electric warming trays, take it, too, just to make sure there is space to keep your contribution at the right temperature. I like to take my own plates for my course as well; it saves the hostess at the dishwashing end of the evening. And equally important, it guarantees that I have the right kind of plates to serve on, that no one has to wash dishes between courses.

TRAVEL ARRANGEMENTS. Carrying food is usually simple, and may the powers that be bless the inventors of heavy foil, Saran Wrap, and the various brands of plastic bags. Seal your traveling treasures with foil, and wrap in Saran. The recipes in this book have special instructions for travel.

Whenever possible, take your dish in the bowl, casserole, or plate it will be served on, even if this means you'll have to tidy away dollops of stew or sauce from the inner sides of the dish.

Tote bags, insulated and in various sizes, are for sale in department, five-and-ten-cent, and hardware stores. Before you invest in one of these smart little numbers, consider the contents of your attic. I have carried lots of fine party offerings in an insulated plastic bag that used to tote baby food. A big plastic shopping bag set into a sturdy paper shopping bag can transport a lot of goodies, too. Wrap things to be kept warm in several thicknesses of newspaper before you bag them. Newspaper is good insulation.

If you are going to cook at the host's home, you'll find it easier if you bring your own hand-cooking tools—spatula, fork, whip, and other lightweight items. And your own condiments. Measured salt and pepper and herbs can be sealed into twists of foil. Things are apt to be hectic for the hostess anyway, very hectic if three or four cooks are asking where the spoons are, where the basil, where the butter, where the potholders, and does she have any brandy.

2. The Gilded Lily: Secrets of a French Chef

A special look is what party food should have, be it only hamburgers. Once you get into decorating foods for parties, this aspect of the cooking operation becomes almost the most fun. There are lots of ways to trim a fatted calf besides those described in our recipes. Here are some suggestions to get you started.

GARNISHES. A garnish in a color that contrasts with the color of the food is one fast and easy way to create a party mood. Anything from plain pork roast to boiled potatoes looks great turned out onto a bed of crisped watercress tips, curly parsley branches, lettuce or

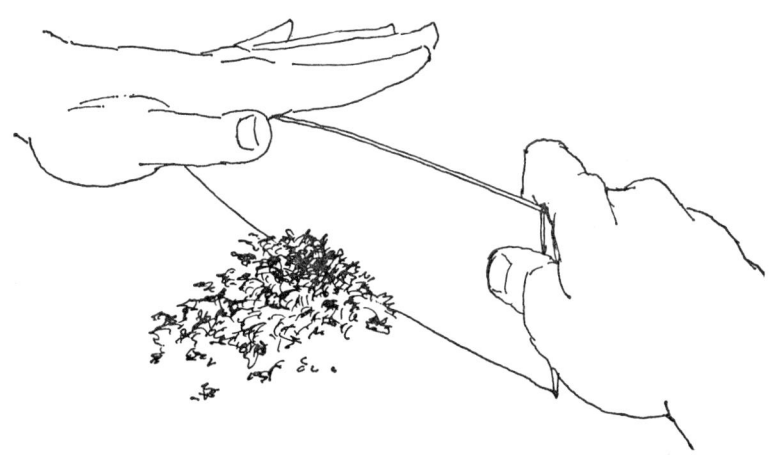

Mincing parsley: To mince parsley very fine for use as a garnish, pile a handful of parsley sprigs together, flatten them, then holding the knife as here, rock the handle up and down with the tip pressed to the board by the fingers of your left hand. With the knife, scrape the minced parsley into a heap, flatten it with the knife, and repeat the mincing process. Mincing parsley is easiest when the sprigs are dry.

raw spinach or dill. A sprig or a leaf or two of any of these set across the top of a casserole, a purée, a fish or a vegetable dish picks it up. Or, mince parsley ever so fine, a whole bunch of it, and ring the dish with it. Hard-boiled egg yolks or egg whites, pressed through a sieve, can be used to pattern a green salad, brighten a dark-brown stew, garnish anything in a bold color from black caviar to red salmon. Strips of pimiento make handsome red garnishes. Strips of carrot or green pepper, cooked limp but removed from the water before their color fades, look good in aspics. So do slivers of green onion, parboiled. You can make flower petals by shaping hard-boiled egg whites; sprigs of parsley, dill, or watercress make the leaves.

Fresh herbs of all sorts make attractive garnishes, but be sure you use an herb appropriate to the dish. Feathery dill in branch or snips is fine on potatoes, sausage, and pork dishes. Basil works with anything (almost) Italian. Parsley with anything (almost) French.

EDIBLE FLOWERS. A surprising number of flowers are edible, including tiny pinks, rose petals, violets, pot marigolds, nasturtiums (delicious whole in salads), squash blossoms, gardenias, the flowers of sweet fennel, chives and dill (with all stems cut off), flowers of borage, tomatoes, and baby dandelions (all stems cut off). They're a delight as a garnish on main courses, in salads, ringing plates of appetizers, floating in soups hot or cold, and they look especially pretty with desserts.

CANDIED FLOWERS. Decorate desserts with candied flowers as violets and rose petals. To candy rose petals, cut away the hard portion at the pointed base. Dip each petal separately in egg white well frothed, then dust it *thoroughly* with superfine granulated sugar. Dry on waxed paper several days, then store away from the light in a tightly sealed box. Candy African violets or true violets and single mint leaves in the same manner, and you can create a whole bouquet to garnish a plain cake top or a creamy mousse.

PASTRY DECORATING. There are many kits. The decorating tips are sold in sets or individually and fit into heavy linen pastry bags. You'll need more than one bag if you plan to work in several colors. Among the most useful sizes are No. 30 for eight-point stars and

Working with a pastry tip: Professionals make pastry roses with a pastry tip and a pastry nail—a small piece of white cardboard held on a nail. When the rose has hardened, it can be slid off its holder onto the cake surface. You can work directly on the surface to be decorated, of course, but a pastry nail makes the process easier.

writing, No. 3 for wide scrolls, No. 16 for six-point stars, No. 21 for large stars, No. 48 for ribbons, No. 67 for leaves, No. 96 to make flowers, No. 104 for small rose petals and No. 124 for large rose petals. Practice using the tips some rainy afternoon. The following recipe is a good one to practice with; it will help you gauge the consistency required to work well with pastry tips.

Young chefs love to work with colored creams and pastry tubes (so do I), and the instructions below offer a few suggestions for beginners.

Pastry Tube Frosting

½ cup shortening
¼ teaspoon salt
1½ cup confectioners' sugar
¼ cup soft margarine
1½ teaspoons flavoring extract

Combine shortening with the salt, beat in one cup of the sugar, then add the margarine, the remaining sugar, and the flavoring.

Fit the tip of the pastry tube in place *before* you put frosting in the bag. Half-fill the bag, then twist the top until it is pressing against

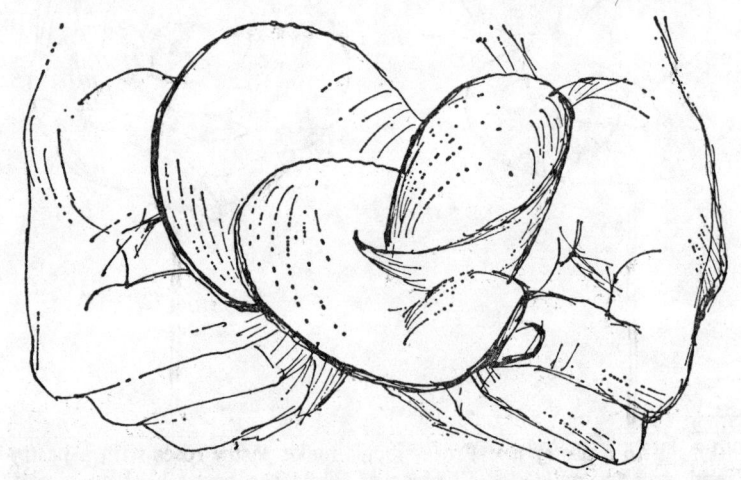

Gumdrop rose: Big, fat gumdrops in many colors rolled out with a rolling pin make flexible rounds which, pressed together, will form a rose for decorating party foods.

the contents. Work with one hand squeezing the bag ever tighter, and the other guiding the tip. The tip is held at a slant for almost all decorating.

Young children love to make dessert decorations with large gumdrops, as in the illustration.

You can dress up main courses with pastry tips, too, with mashed potatoes of about the same consistency as the Pastry Tube Frosting. Mashed carrots or butternut squash, mixed with a little mashed potato, also achieve the right consistency.

Squeeze mashed potatoes into decorative mounds on cookie sheets, dab with melted butter and warm under a medium broiler for 15 minutes before serving. Egg yolks moistened with milk to the consistency of Pastry Tube Frosting are great for decorating appetizers, canapes, and hors d'oeuvre dishes.

CARVED VEGETABLES AND FRUIT. Turn sculptor and decorate party fare with carved vegetables or fruits as do the Japanese. Work with thin round slices of radishes, cucumbers, or carrots, and celery

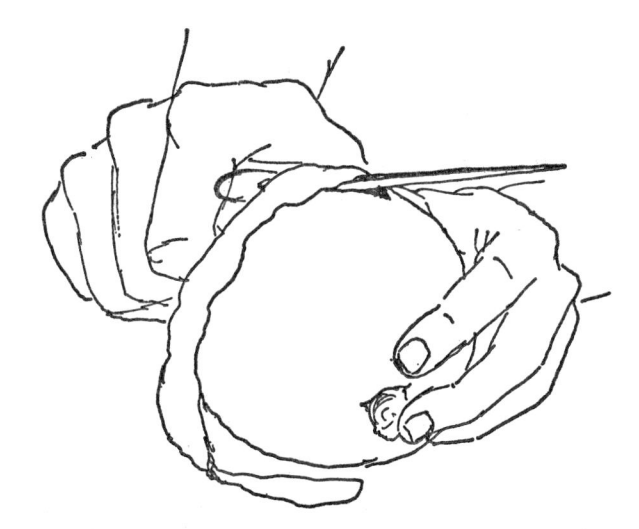

Tomato rose: With a very sharp knife, peel the skin and ¼ inch of flesh from a large, firm tomato, starting at the top and working toward the bottom. The strip must come away in one piece. Move the knife up and down in a sawing motion, and turn the tomato as you work. Curl the bottom of the strip around to make a circle and spear it together with a toothpick. Arrange the rest of the strip around to make a rosette.

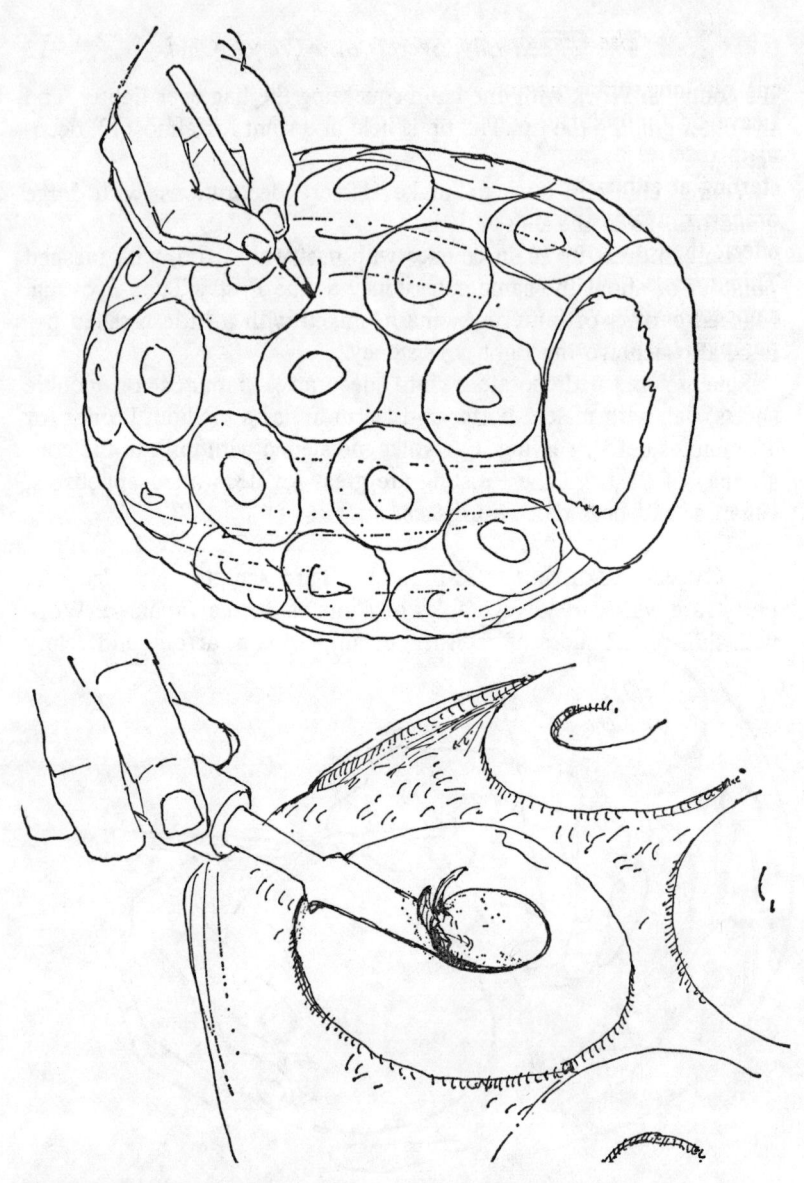

Carving vegetables: Make a decorative container of a pumpkin or any of the edible squashes by carving the surface. Draw the design on the skin of a well-washed pumpkin. Follow the design with a sharp knife, and remove the outer skin to a depth of ⅛ to ¼ inch. The skin that remains will appear as a raised layer of a stronger color. A carved pumpkin makes a super tureen for a harvest buffet.

cut on long, thin diagonals to see what shapes you can achieve. Leave on the colorful skins. When tomatoes are plentiful, make tomato rosettes by paring the whole tomato in a single inch-wide strip, starting at either top or bottom. It's just like using a knife to peel an orange in a single strip. Use a very thin, very sharp knife for the best effect, then curl the tomato ribbon itself around to make a rosette. Thin rounds of lemon, lime, fresh pineapple, and orange with peels snipped at intervals make pretty decorations, too. Try our carved pumpkin trick, to make a decorative "bowl" for soup or punch.

Patterned vegetable pieces: A plate of carved vegetable pieces is easy to make and adds a festive note to any occasion. Here cucumber slices, carrot slices, celery slices, a carved lemon, and roses of raw winter radishes suggest ways to turn everyday foods into decorative accessories.

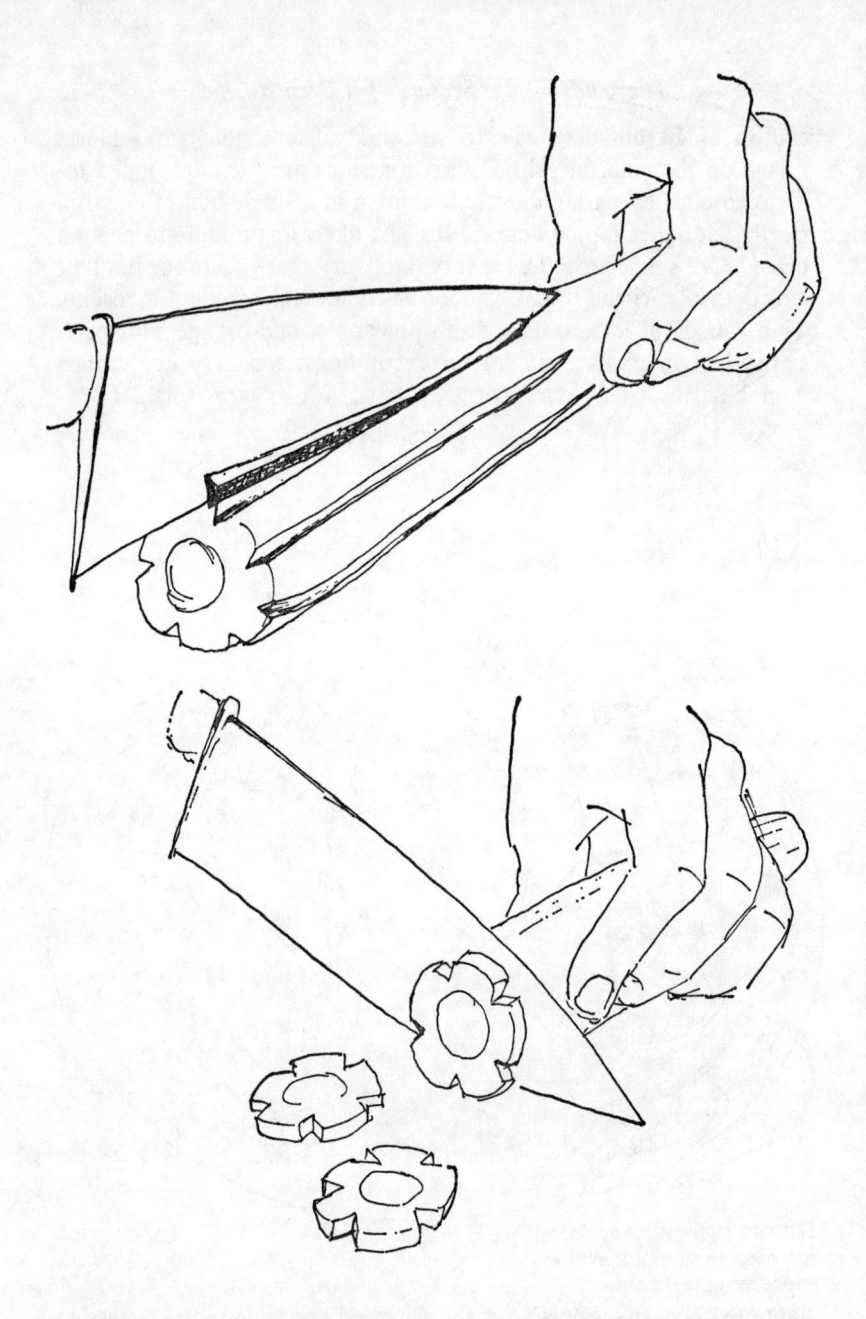

Patterned vegetable slices: These two steps in the process that produces decorative carrot slices suggests the basic method used for patterning all vegetable slices.

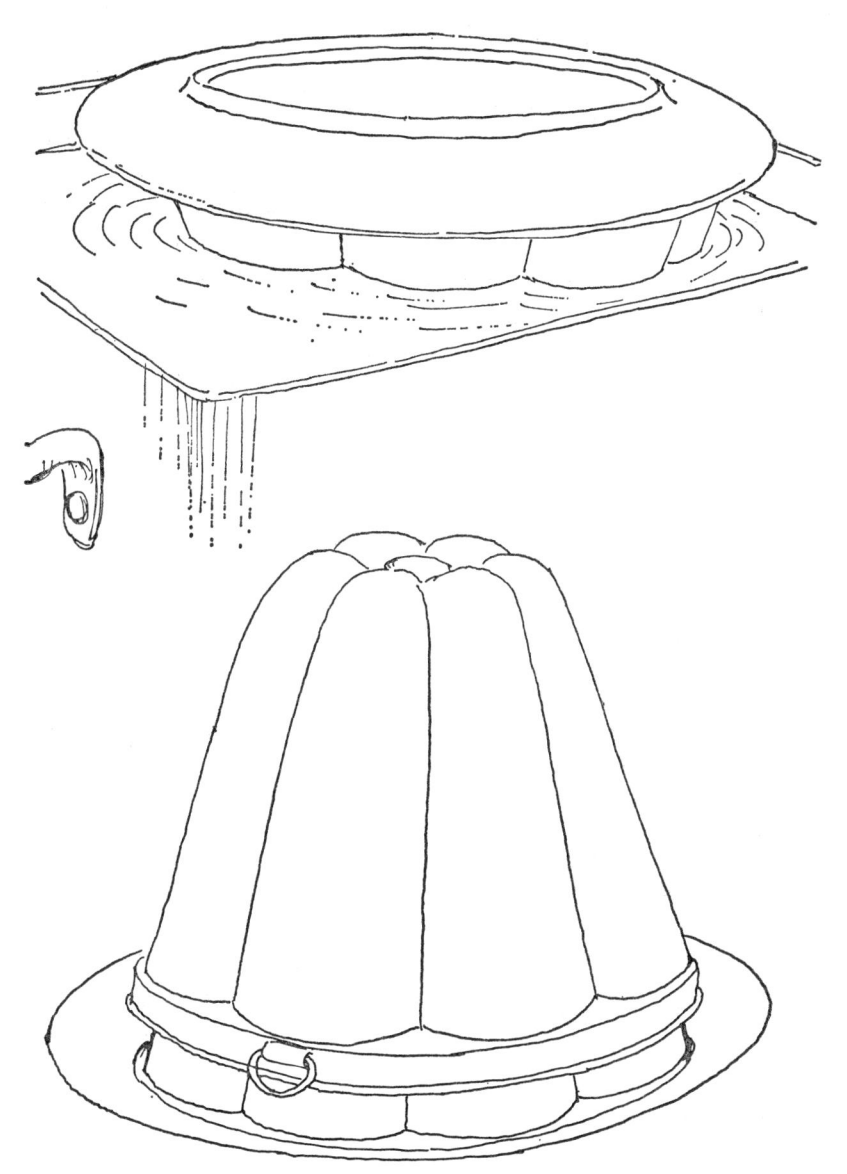

How to unmold: Aspics, jellies of all kinds, custard desserts, and mousses are easy to unmold. Warm the mold briefly, as shown above, in hot water, protecting the contents by placing a plate over the top. Lift the mold from the water, with the plate in place, and invert the mold with the plate still firmly in place. If the contents don't slip out the first time, let the mold rest on the plate, inverted, for a few minutes. If the contents still won't slip out, repeat the process.

MAGIC WITH SHAPES. One of the fastest ways to win a round of applause for the presentation of almost any standard dish is to change the classic shape: serve Crême Caramel in individual pots, make meat loaf in individual custard cups, serve rice in a molded form created by letting the drained cooked rice "set" in the mold for 10 to 15 minutes before serving. You can mold spaghetti and noodles the same way. Set gelatins and jellies, aspics and mousses, pâtés and puddings in elegantly fluted molds. Unmold at the party after setting the bottom of the mold *briefly* in very hot water.

SECRETS OF A FRENCH CHEF

The kinds of pots and pans you cook in govern the distribution of heat and have a lot to do with the success of your recipes. We use very heavy iron skillets for all sautéing and frying, and even for roasts—the gravy is better. Heavy aluminum saucepans and soup kettles of hotel or professional size and quality are our favorites. Dutch ovens of cast iron, some enameled and some not, are our preference for casserole recipes: enameled when milk, cream, or an acid (tomato or wine) is among the ingredients. Cast iron, by the way, generally is not expensive.

Some special equipment that the party-minded cook will find useful are a spring-form cake pan, tube cake pans in various sizes, tube molds and fluted molds, again in various sizes. The small ceramic pots that hold 8 to 12 ounces are a delight for custards and specialties, such as Onion Soup. A blender does for many recipes what press-through-a-sieve used to do, and makes life much easier. A broad-faced spatula knife is my favorite for sautéing, and I find a rubber spatula for turning batter out of bowls indispensable. My father cherishes whips in various sizes for the quick binding of cream sauces. And a big professional carving knife is a must for chopping everything from parsley on.

HERBS AND CONDIMENTS

Among the most important herbs and spices to have handy are: cinnamon, nutmeg, allspice, thyme, bay leaf (imported), parsley, cloves (whole and ground), marjoram, tarragon, celery (or celery salt), onion (or onion salt), garlic (or garlic salt), oregano, basil, saffron, sage for Italian and Mediterranean cooking; cardamom, curry, turmeric, coriander, cumin, ground ginger (or fresh, keep it frozen), soy sauce, paprika, red pepper, black pepper, white pepper, sea or kosher salt. You can give shelf space to a great many other seasonings, especially if you like international cookery, but the ones I've listed will be right for most of the recipes here. Also Worcestershire sauce appears rather often in this book.

Many French recipes call for a combination of herbs the French call a *bouquet garni*.

Bouquet Garni

2 sprigs fresh parsley	¼ teaspoon dried or one
1 bay leaf, dried	sprig fresh thyme

Put all together in a small cheesecloth bag. Tie the top closed with a string that is long enough to hang over edge of saucepan or soup kettle.

BOUILLON, BROTH, CONSOMMÉ, STOCK

The best casseroles, stews, rissotos, and vegetable dishes are made using stock or broth, usually chicken or beef, instead of plain water. Below are two classic recipes for stock from scratch. You can substitute bouillon cubes dissolved in water, or canned consommé. (Some canned consommés never let you forget their origin no matter what you cook them with, so select carefully. I use College Inn clear broths.) When I use bouillon cubes I add a tablespoonful or two of leftover chicken gravy or beef gravy or pork gravy (for dark dishes).

Chicken Bouillon or Broth

Serve the chicken in a cream sauce made with a cupful of the broth.

1 2½-pound chicken	1 teaspoon rosemary
Water to cover	(use only for broth in
1 small onion, peeled	Italian recipes)
1 medium carrot, scraped	Bouquet Garni (omit if
1 parsnip, peeled	using rosemary)
2 cloves garlic, peeled	Salt to taste
6 black peppercorns	

1. Place the chicken in cold water with all other ingredients. When the water boils, lower the heat, cover, simmer four hours, replenishing water occasionally.
2. Strain broth. Chill, skim away most, but not all, of the fat. Store in the refrigerator or freeze in one-cup batches.

Makes about 6 cups.

Beef Bouillon

I save in the freezer bones from roasts and steaks to make this one.

2½ teaspoons salt	2 medium onions, peeled,
1 pound stew beef	stuck with 6 whole cloves
Water	Bouquet garni
2 quarts beef bones and meat	2 medium garlic cloves, peeled
2 medium carrots, scraped	

1. Sprinkle a little salt in a heavy skillet, turn heat to high and brown the beef on all sides. Pour a little water into the skillet, scrape up the pan juices and turn with all the other ingredients and 2 teaspoons of salt into a large kettle. Cover with cold water, and bring the water to a boil. Turn the heat down, cover, and simmer for 6 hours. Taste, and boil down, uncovered, if broth seems insipid.
2. Allow to cool, uncovered; strain, then refrigerate until fat settles; skim away fat and discard. Freeze bouillon in 2-cup lots.

Makes 2 quarts.

MAGIC WITH SAUCES

One of the secrets of good cooking is the use of leftover gravies and pan drippings, the strongly flavored juices that caramelize in the bottom of a cooking dish. One reason the Hériteau clan is addicted to heavy skillets and saucepans is that the juices caramelize in this type of utensil, where they tend to burn in thinner, lighter vessels. A cup of warm water poured into the pan about 20 minutes before a roast is done makes delicious gravy and lots of it, usually, so you'll have some for your secret larder. When fat settles on the top, use the dark, jelled stuff underneath. The recipes in this book do not call for pan drippings, except where drippings are created in the cooking process, but almost any dish you make—from plain boiled rice to a meat casserole—will be a little more delicious if you have even one or 2 tablespoons of a good gravy to add to it.

We collect beef and pork drippings together, and reboil the whole when using a part. Chicken drippings we keep separately, since they go to flavor more delicate dishes. If you use stock made from bouillon cubes, add a spoonful of drippings. This, by the way, is a trick Chinese chefs also know, and it is rumored that one great Chinese chef had in his family drippings that had been continued from generation to generation for 200 years.

BUTTER OR MARGARINE

Some recipes here call for either, but so many people use them as substitutes for each other today, that not all recipes trouble to say so. Butter is less greasy for cooking, finer in flavor, especially when it is really fresh, but so many brands of margarine today have good flavor, it is hard to fault them. You can't brown meats in margarine, but I'm just bored with being uppity about the other uses of margarine in cooking, especially with today's prices and the number of cholesterol counters.

TASTE IT

You can't cook by recipe alone, you have to taste. Recipes are indications, road-maps, but only you know whether you prefer things salty, peppery, bland, rich, thin, what-have-you. *Your* palate is what you should be trying to please, and the only way you know the dish you serve pleases you is by tasting it before you serve it. Because people who don't smoke and those who don't drink cocktails come to the dinner table with more sensitive palates, the recipes here go easy on both salt and pepper; you may want to increase the salt and pepper in many of the recipes. Dishes that may seem insipid often require only a little bit of salt to bring the flavor up to what you consider excellent. Pepper can do the same thing. Many cooks don't use enough.

ACCESSORIES FOR GRAVY

There's no use having a wonderful sauce unless you have bread to soak in it. In this country, sopping up gravy is considered bad form, but in Europe, at all except formal occasions, it is considered *good* form. In fact, if you don't poke a bit of bread into your gravy, your hostess may consider it a criticism of her cooking. Good French and Italian bread is available in most areas.

Wipe the loaf with a cloth soaked in warm water, and pop it into a 375° oven for 10 minutes. Then cut it into big chunks and serve it at once.

Another good gravy-sopper is a hot biscuit. Try this as a substitute for bread, and as an accompaniment for meals consisting of sturdy soups.

Butter Biscuits

2 cups all-purpose flour
2 teaspoons baking powder
2 teaspoons sugar
½ teaspoon salt
6 tablespoons butter
½ to 1 cup milk

1. Preheat oven to 450°.
2. Sift flour, baking powder, sugar, and salt into a mixing bowl.

Cut in the butter as for pie dough. Add milk, omitting the last little bit if the dough is reaching the point where it won't hold its shape.

3. Grease and flour the cookie sheet. Drop the dough on it by the tablespoon and shape into little rounds. Bake 12 to 15 minutes, until golden brown.

Makes 8 to 10 2-inch biscuits.

ON MIXES

Cake, muffin, pie-crust mixes are good. And they save time. Cut 1 tablespoon of cold butter into a pie-crust mix before moistening; it makes a richer pastry. When the crust is for a dessert, add 2 teaspoons of sugar.

INDEX OF SUBSTITUTES

When you are madly cooking away and suddenly you find a vital ingredient missing, stop and think; there usually is a substitute. Here are some I use.

Bouillon or Stock. Dissolve 1½ bouillon cubes in 6 ounces hot water. Canned; use consommé or broth.
Bread Crumbs. Roll out saltines to make cracker crumbs.
Butter for Cooking. Margarine, rendered chicken fat, oil, shortening, or rendered pork fat.
Carrots. Parsnips or baby white turnips.
Cornstarch as a thickener. All-purpose flour.
Light Cream. Use whole milk or heavy cream thinned with milk.
Whipped Cream. Use ice cream.
Croutons. Make your own. Cube crustless white bread and sauté in a little butter until golden.
Curry Powder. Turmeric plus cardamom, ginger powder, and cumin.
Garlic. Garlic salt or garlic powder.
Fresh Ginger. Powdered ginger. One slice equals about ¼ teaspoon, powdered.

Lemon Juice. Vinegar, preferably white, or lime juice, strained, or a bit of white wine.

Lettuce. Usually any leafy green will do.

Fresh Mayonnaise. For each ½ cup mayonnaise use commercial mayonnaise plus ½ teaspoon lemon juice and ½ teaspoon mustard.

Milk. Use powdered milk and water, blended.

Powdered Mustard. Equivalent prepared mustard.

Olive Oil. Use any vegetable oil.

Parsley. Chervil.

Black Pepper. White pepper or paprika.

Pepper Mill. Crush peppercorns with a rolling pin.

Scallions. Green onions, plain onions, onion powder to taste, frozen onions.

Shallots. ⅔ of an onion plus one garlic clove.

Tarragon Vinegar. Heat a pinch of tarragon in wine vinegar for 3 minutes, strain.

Truffle. One tablespoon minced mushroom with ⅛ teaspoon of lemon juice or grated lemon rind.

Wine Vinegar. Cider or red vinegar or white vinegar with a little wine.

EQUIVALENTS

- 1 teaspoon fresh herb = ½ teaspoon dried
- 1 teaspoon = ⅙ ounce
- 1 tablespoon = 3 teaspoons or ½ fluid ounce
- 1 cup = 16 tablespoons
- 16 fluid ounces = 1 pint
- 4 cups = 32 fluid ounces
- 1 pound sliced carrots = about 4 cups
- 2 large celery stalks cut = about 1 cup
- ½ pound mushrooms sliced = about 2½ cups
- 1 medium onion = about ⅓ cup
- 1 pound chopped onions = about 4 cups
- 1 cup raw rice = about 3 cups cooked rice

HINTS AND TIPS

Crusts bake golden brown when brushed with yolk of 1 egg mixed with 1 to 2 tablespoons cold water. Or brush with milk.

Perennial supply of parsley can be grown in pots in a sunny window.

Freeze herbs when harvest time is on you; seal them into Baggies. They won't do as a garnish but they'll be great for flavor.

Grate orange, lemon rinds before juicing your breakfast fruit. Air-dry several days, then store in sealed bottles.

Warm plates before serving your guests. It helps keep the food from cooling too rapidly.

Crisp French bread before serving: brush with a wet cloth or paper towel, and put into an oven at 375° for 10 minutes.

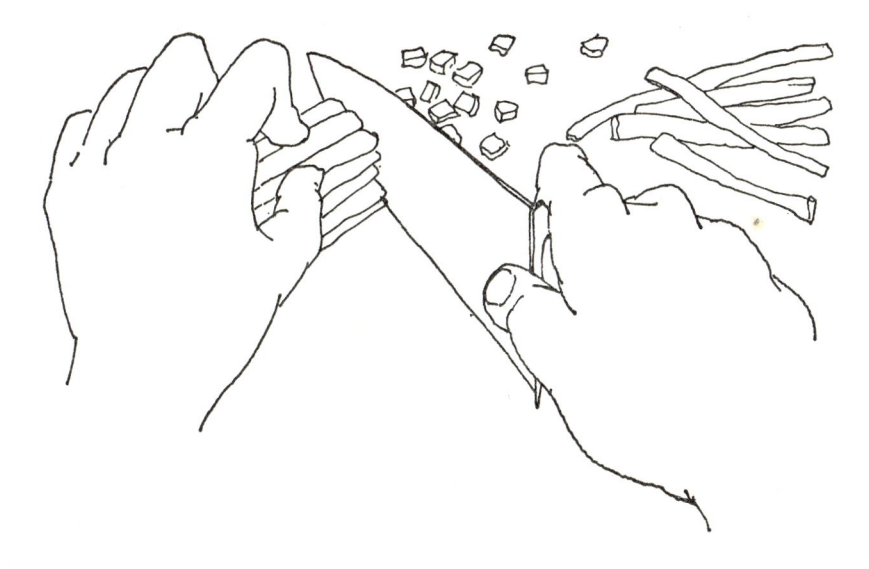

Julienne cubes: To reduce root vegetables, such as carrots, potatoes, and turnips, to small cubes, peel the vegetables, cut them into strips of ½ inch thickness, gather the strips together, as here, and cut across the heap.

Make butter curls from an ice-cold butter stick using a potato peeler; drop curls into cold water, drain, serve.

Frost punch glasses by dipping rims in frothed egg white, then in superfine sugar. Or set in the freezer 10 to 15 minutes.

Crisp greens and garnishes in cold water briefly, then store sealed in plastic in the refrigerator, ready for your salad or garnish.

THE ULTIMATE SECRET OF GOOD COOKING

Smells. That's right. When hungry people smell the delicious aroma of exotic spices being grated, pies baking, casseroles bubbling, they're convinced before they sit down at the table that it's going to

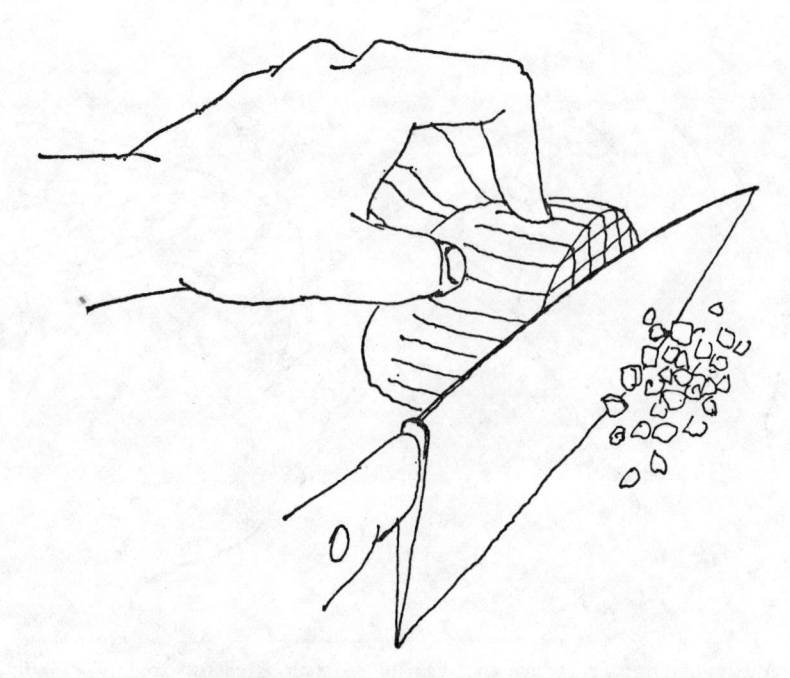

Mincing onions: Make a checkerboard pattern of cuts from the top of the onion to within ½ inch of the base, then slice across.

be divine. So—make sure the sweet scents of your take-it-along dish communicate a message of fine food to come: open the kitchen door, lift the lid on a simmering stew, and invite a sniff from the crowd before they become engrossed in the seating arrangements and their dinner neighbors.

Pleasure in food is the other great secret to its success. The fun of a party you share is the chance to let your joy in cooking shine through. Cooking is one of the most creative of the arts of living —don't be afraid to cook, and don't be afraid of recipes. They are road guides to your creativity, maps to the pleasure of good food. Toss them together—innovate, taste, add dill no matter what the author says if you like it, have fun, and your guests will, too.

3. Menus for All Kinds of Parties

The dishes for a take-it-along menu can be left to the inventiveness of the individual contributors, but most often they are coordinated by the planners. (It's safer that way. I went to a dinner once where everybody, including me, had done chicken.)

In planning a menu, it's a good idea to keep in mind the rules that once governed those elaborate dinners called Cordon Bleu and Escoffier: The main rule was that each cold dish was followed by a hot dish, each heavy dish by a light one, each roast or grilled meat by a creamy dish or a mélange of some kind. If you plan cold appetizers or hors d'oeuvres, then follow them with a hot course if you can.

Like all rules, these are meant to be broken, or rather you can't help breaking them often. However, do abide by the principle: Variety in flavor, texture, and palate sensation is what makes a meal exciting, and should govern menu planning.

Try to avoid an excess of rich, heavy cooking. A rich meat course should have a light vegetable course to go with it, and a cool green salad to follow. The dessert should be as light and cool as possible, too. If you want a rich dessert, then plan a light meal to precede it; otherwise, no one will have room for the dessert, and the guests will be annoyed with themselves for over-eating.

Here are a number of interesting and varied menus for memorable meals. Note that the selections in italics are recipes featured in this book.

NEW YEAR'S EVE SMORGASBORD

Aquavit; Cold Beer

Scandia Herring
Chilled Black Caviar on Black Bread with Lemon Wedges
Danish Open Sandwiches
Poached Salmon with Sauce Verte
Janson's Temptation
Red Cabbage Salad
Plate of Assorted Cheeses, served with Crackers
Fruit
Pastries
Roasted Nuts

Coffee

CHRISTMAS BUFFET FOR TEN OR TWELVE

Cocktails

Carousel of Stuffed Delights

FIRST COURSE
Littleneck Clams on the Half Shell with Lemon Wedges

ENTRÉE
Christmas Goose with Chestnut Stuffing, served with Cold Duck Wine
Baby Peas in Butter Sauce
Iceberg Lettuce Salad with *Green Goddess Dressing*

DESSERT
Cherries Jubilee

Café Brûlot Diabolique

CHRISTMAS BUFFET

Cocktails

Mushroom Caps
Cheese Straws

ENTRÉE
Christmas Duck with Cherries, served with a Red Burgundy Wine
Mashed Yams
Green Beans in *Lemon Butter Sauce*
Green Salad with *Oil and Vinegar Dressing*

DESSERT
Joe Bednerz' Christmas Cake, served with Chilled Champagne

Coffee

CHRISTMAS DINNER FOR EIGHT

Rhubarb Rum Punch

FIRST COURSE
Shrimp in Tomato Aspic, served with Hot Dinner Rolls and Butter

ENTRÉE
Partridge in a Pear Tree
Buttered Baby Beets
Green Beans Lyonnaise
Green Salad with *Herb Dressing*

DESSERT
Fruit in Champagne

Café Filtre

SHARE THE PARTY

EASTER MENU

Cocktails

Cheese Puffs

FIRST COURSE
Asparagus in Lemon Butter Sauce

ENTRÉE
Cider Baked Picnic Ham with Chilled Rosé Wine
Corn Pudding
Spinach-and-Mushroom Salad

DESSERT
Cheesecake with Strawberry Sauce

Coffee

Tea

THANKSGIVING DINNER

Cocktails

Plate of Chilled Celery, Olives
Dry Roasted Nuts

FIRST COURSE
Oysters on the Half Shell

ENTRÉE
Roast Turkey with Cold Duck Wine and Cranberry Sauce
Maple-Candied Butternut Squash
Mashed Turnips
Green Salad with *Thousand Island Dressing*

DESSERT
Pumpkin Pie with Whipped Cream

Coffee

Tea

BOEUF BOURGUIGNONNE DINNER FOR EIGHT

Chilled Apéritif Wine over Ice, served with Lemon Peel

FIRST COURSE
Artichokes and Mushrooms, served with Dinner Rolls and Butter

ENTRÉE
Boeuf Bourguignonne Marcel's Way with Châteauneuf-du-Pape Wine, served with Hot, Crisp French Bread and Butter
Riced Potatoes
Green Salad with *Herb Dressing*

DESSERT
Chilled Fruit Mousse

Café Filtre

EASY GOURMET DINNER FOR EIGHT

Chilled Apéritif Wine, served over Ice with Lemon Peel

Dry Roasted Nuts

FIRST COURSE
Cold Shrimp with Fresh Mayonnaise, served with Crisp, Warm Dinner Rolls and Butter

ENTRÉE
Blanquette de Veau, served with Chilled Mateus Wine
Plain Boiled Rice
Iceberg Lettuce Salad with *Parsley Dressing*

CHEESE COURSE
Plate of Brie, Swiss, and Roquefort Cheese, served with Light Bordeaux and French Bread and Butter

DESSERT
Fruit Salad, dressed with Cointreau Liqueur

Café Filtre

Liqueurs

FIVE-COURSE GOURMET DINNER FOR EIGHT

Cocktails or Chilled Apéritif Wine

Cheese Mousse, served with Crackers

FIRST COURSE
Coquille St. Jacques, served with Chilled Blanc de Blanc Wine

ENTRÉE
Roast Beef, served with Châteauneuf-du-Pape Wine
Green Beans Lyonnaise

SALAD COURSE
Spinach and Mushroom Salad, served with *Green Goddess Dressing*

DESSERT
A Charlotte from the Isles

Café Filtre

Liqueurs

SIX-COURSE GOURMET DINNER FOR EIGHT

Apéritif Wine, such as Lilet, Chilled, served over Ice, with Lemon Peel

FIRST COURSE
Pâté Maison, served with chilled dry Sherry

SOUP COURSE
Consommé of Beef Stock, garnished with Minced Parsley

ENTRÉE
Coq au Vin, served with Red Burgundy Wine
Diana Walton's Mushroom Pie
Green Salad with *Garlic Dressing*

Plate of Cheeses, served with French Bread and Butter and a Light Red Bordeaux Wine

DESSERT
Crème Caramel

Café Filtre

BUFFET FOR SIXTEEN GOURMETS

Cocktail, or Apéritif Wine, such as Lilet Red or White, Chilled

Brandied Cheese Spread
Cold Shrimp with Fresh Mayonnaise
Pâté Maison Marcel, served with Crisp French Bread and Butter

ENTRÉE
Navarin Printanier, served with Chilled Rosé Wine
Boeuf Bourguignonne Marcel's Way, served with Room-Temperature Red Bordeaux Wine
Spinach and Mushroom Salad with *Oil and Vinegar Dressing*

DESSERT
Crème Caramel

Salted, Roasted Nuts and Chocolate Mints

Café Brûlot Diabolique

Tray of Liqueurs

MEAT PIE PARTY FOR A CROWD

Cocktails

Carousel of Stuffed Delights

ENTRÉE
Beef-and-Kidney Pie
Tourtière Canadienne
Cold Vegetable Salad
Carrot-and-Raisin Slaw

DESSERT
Cheesecake with Strawberry Sauce

Coffee

Tea

MEAT PIE PARTY FOR A CROWD

ENTRÉE
Creamy Chicken Pie
Lamb Pie
Stuffed Baked Tomatoes
Green Salad with *Parsley Dressing*

DESSERT
Sour-Cherry Ribbon

Coffee

Tea

HOT POT SKATING PARTY

Green Pea Soup with Ham Bone, served with Hot Rolls and Butter
Cold Vegetable Salad

Sour-Cherry Ribbon

Coffee

Tea

HOT POT FOR A MULTITUDE

Sausage Roll

Onion Soup, served with Hot Rolls and Butter

Stuffed Baked Apples

Coffee

Tea

COLD CUP LUNCHEON

Garden Rhubarb Soup, served with Hot Rolls and Butter

Lettuce Hearts with *Roquefort Dressing*

Mayonnaise au Chocolat des Sables

Coffee

Tea

LUNCHEON PARTY 1

Mussels Clemence
Hot Butter Biscuits

Basket of Fresh Fruit

Coffee

Tea

LUNCHEON PARTY 2

Jellied Gazpacho, served with Hot Rolls and Butter Curls

New Orleans Pecan Pie

Coffee

Tea

LUNCHEON PARTY 3

Chef's Salad, served with Hot Rolls and Butter

Dick Engelbretsen's Carrot Cake

Coffee

Tea

GOURMET PICNIC

Cocktails

Pâté Maison on Crackers

ENTRÉE
Chicken Breasts Chaud Froid, served with Cold White Wine
Italian Rice Salad

Pear Slices Stuffed with Brandied Cheese Spread

Coffee

Tea

CLAMBAKE FOR TWENTY-FIVE

Clambake for Twenty-Five, served with Cold Beer
Mediterranean Salad

Chilled Watermelon

SEASHORE DINNER

FIRST COURSE
New England Clam Chowder

ENTRÉE
Sea Bass with *Lemon-Butter Sauce the Fast Way,* served with Chilled Blanc de Blanc
Green Salad with *Oil and Vinegar Dressing,* served with French Bread and Butter Curls

DESSERT
Angel-Food Shortcake

Coffee

GAME CATCHER'S DINNER

FIRST COURSE
Mussels Clemence

ENTRÉE
Marinated Venison, served with a Red Burgundy Wine
Vegetable Casserole
Green Salad with *Garlic Dressing*

DESSERT
Basket of Fresh Fruit

Coffee

TRY-THESE PARTY MENU

FIRST COURSE
Peanut-Butter Soup

ENTRÉE
Paupiettes of Beef
Diana Walton's Mushroom Pie
Salade de L'Île Barbe

DESSERT
Dick Engelbretsen's Carrot Cake

Café Brûlot Diabolique

INFLATION DINNER PARTY

First Course
Borscht

Entrée
Hamburger Wellington
Casserole of Root Vegetables
Green Salad with *Thousand Island Dressing*

Lime Meringue Pie
Coffee

NEW ENGLAND PICNIC FOR A CROWD

Baked Beans the New England Way
Hot Frankfurter Sandwiches
Potato Salad
Cole Slaw

Berry Ice Cream

Coffee

Tea

NEW ENGLAND DINNER

Cocktails

Relishes with Crackers

First Course
New England Clam Chowder

Entrée
Chicken Breasts Vermont Style
Buttered Parsnips
Iceberg Lettuce Salad with *Thousand Island Dressing*

Dessert
Indian Pudding

Coffee

Tea

NEW ORLEANS DINNER

Cocktails

Baby Shrimp, served with Hot Horseradish Sauce

ENTRÉE
New Orleans Fresh Crab Gumbo, served with Chilled Chablis
Boiled White Rice
Iceberg Lettuce Salad with *Oil and Vinegar Dressing*

DESSERT
New Orleans Pecan Pie

Café Brûlot Diabolique

PAELLA DINNER

Sangria Cup

Chopped Chicken Livers

ENTRÉE
Paella Valenciana, served with *Sangria Cup*
Escarole Salad with *Oil and Vinegar Dressing*

DESSERT
Fruit from the Sangria

Café Filtre

EASY GREEK DINNER

Cocktails

Dolmas

ENTRÉE
Moussaka
Lamb Kabobs
Green Salad with *Oil and Vinegar Dressing*

Saffron Fruit Cream, or Greek Pastries

Café Filtre

ORIENTAL DINNER FOR SIX

Cocktails

Shrimp Toast

ENTRÉE
Malaysian Chicken Curry, served with Warmed Rice Wine or Cold Beer
Chinese Mushrooms, Snow Peas, and Bamboo Shoots
Boiled White Rice
Raita

DESSERT
Chilled Canned Mandarin Oranges

Chinese Tea

HAWAIIAN LUAU FOR SIXTEEN

Cocktails

Shrimp Toast

ENTRÉE
Sweet-Sour Spareribs—Hawaiian Style
Luau Pungent Turkey
Fish Baked in Ti Leaves
Baked Yams
Boiled Rice
Salad for a Luau

DESSERT
Fruit Mix for a Luau

Long Bamboo Drink for a Luau

INDIAN BUFFET

ENTRÉE
Eggplant Relish, served with Indian Hard Bread
Lamb Korma, served with Cold Beer
Pineapple Chutney
Chicken Pulao with Shrimps
Raita
Onion Sambal

Saffron Fruit Cream

Black Tea

ITALIAN DINNER FOR A CROWD

Cocktails

Bagna Cauda

ENTRÉE
Lasagna with Red Chianti Wine
Mediterranean Salad

DESSERT
Plate of Cheeses
Basket of Fresh Fruit

Café Filtre

ITALIAN GOURMET DINNER FOR A FEW

Cocktails or Apéritif

Bagna Cauda

ENTRÉE
Francesca Bosetti Morris's Risotto alla Milanese, served with Cold White Chianti Wine
Spinach-and-Mushroom Salad

DESSERT
Fruit in Champagne

Café Filtre

MEDITERRANEAN DINNER

Cocktails

Quick Pissaladière

ENTRÉE
Bouillabaisse, served with French Bread and Butter and Chilled Chablis Wine
Green Salad

DESSERT
Chilled Fruit Mousse

Café Filtre

GERMAN SPECIALTIES

Cocktails

ENTRÉE
Hasenpfeffer, served with Chilled Rhine Wine
Potato Dumplings
White Cabbage

DESSERT
Cheesecake with Strawberry Sauce

Tea

Coffee

RHINELAND DINNER

Cocktails

Fiddler's Herring, served with Crackers

ENTRÉE
Bratwurst in Sour Cream, served with Chilled German Beer
Noodles
Lettuce Salad with *Thousand Island Dressing*

DESSERT
Stuffed Baked Apples

Coffee

Tea

PART 2
Snack Parties and Appetizers

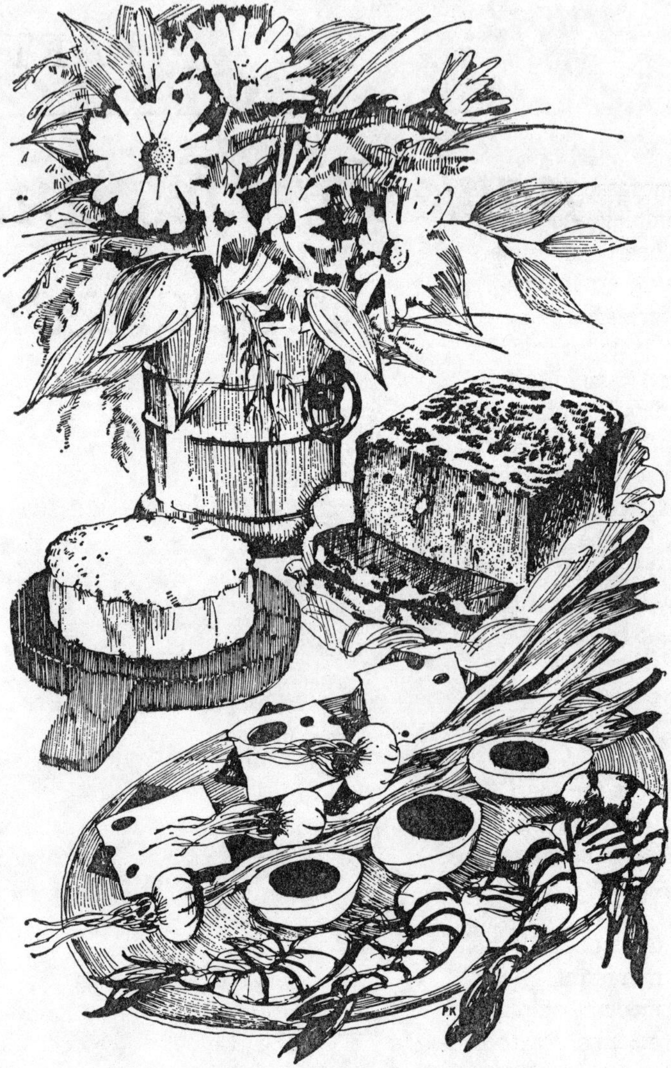

4. Smorgasbord

A smorgasbord in the Scandinavian countries that I know is either a complete meal composed of all sorts of odds and ends or else it is a hearty predinner course of appetizers, usually served with iced aquavit, a caraway-flavored vodka.

For a smorgasbord meal, almost anything goes. In Scandinavia, it often includes cold, boiled lobster served with fresh mayonnaise, and several casseroles from other lands. Classic smorgasbord recipes are Janson's Temptation, Danish Open Sandwiches, Scandia Herring, and the others included in this chapter. However, any of the appetizers in Part 2 are suitable for inclusion.

As take-it-along fare, appetizers are ideal. Most of them travel very well, can be prepared ahead of time, and present few problems in preparation to the cook. And because most of us love to investigate many flavor sensations at one sitting, smorgasbord parties are always a great success.

Janson's Temptation

This is the most delicious version of scalloped potatoes I've ever tasted and belongs with a smorgasbord. Make it ahead and reheat just before serving in a 375° oven for 15 minutes at home or at the party.

- 3 tablespoons butter or margarine
- 3 medium onions, peeled
- 8 medium potatoes, peeled
- 12 anchovy fillets
- 2 tablespoons bread crumbs
- 1 cup heavy cream
- Dill for garnish

1. In a heavy skillet over low heat, melt the butter, add the onions and cook until translucent. Do not brown them.

2. Cut the potatoes into long, thin, matchstick strips. Butter a glass baking dish. Make a layer of potatoes, scatter a few anchovies over them, a layer of onions on top, and sprinkle with bread crumbs. Repeat the layers until all the ingredients are used. Finish with bread crumbs.

3. Bake in an oven preheated to 425° for 20 minutes. Pour the cream over all and cook 20 to 35 minutes more. Garnish with snips of fresh dill.

Serves 8 to 10.

Take-It-Along Tips: Wrap the casserole securely in foil; wrap dill separately and garnish the dish just before serving.

Danish Open Sandwiches

Always try and get as much variety as possible into Danish sandwiches; serve them with a knife and fork.

1. Sliced hard-boiled egg, tomato, and crisp bacon
2. Creamed liver pâté, topped with red cabbage and orange
3. Thick slices of Danish Camembert, topped with cherries and parsley
4. Slices of Danish luncheon meat or salami with lemon, cucumber, tomato, potato salad and watercress
5. Slices of Danish Samsoe, garnished with a radish flower
6. Curls of Danish salami on soft cream cheese
7. Shrimps on a bed of lettuce with mayonnaise and twists of lemon
8. Potato salad on a bed of lettuce with diced cooked potatoes in a cheese-flavored mayonnaise with pieces of orange and grape
9. Twists of salami, garnished with raw onion
10. Liver pâté, garnished with raw mushroom, gherkin, and tomato
11. Danish Blue cheese with a flower made of thin pieces of carrot and grape
12. Danish luncheon meat, topped with salad, tomato, and cucumber
13. Soft Danish cream cheese, grapes, and walnuts rolled into soft balls, served on toothpicks

Smorgasbord

Take-It-Along Tips: Arrange closely on a large serving platter. Sprinkle sandwiches with soft surfaces with a coat of finely minced parsley, then wrap the dish in a very, very large piece of heavy foil. Bring the ends of the foil together several inches above the tops of the sandwiches and fold firmly together so the foil won't touch the tops of the sandwiches. You'll have to carry this on your lap in the car to keep the platter straight.

Scandia Herring

1 12-ounce can kippered herring	3½ teaspoons lemon juice
1 teaspoon powdered mustard	2½ teaspoons sugar
	¾ cup olive oil
¼ teaspoon white pepper	1 medium onion, minced
¼ cup water	½ cup minced parsley

1. Drain herring and arrange in shallow serving bowl.
2. Mix mustard, sugar, lemon juice, pepper, oil, and water and pour over herring.
3. Marinate overnight in refrigerator. Serve chilled, sprinkled with onion and parsley.

Serves 6 to 8.

Take-It-Along Tips: Place in a decorative bowl and overwrap with Saran Wrap for traveling.

Fiddler's Herring

1 5- to 6-ounce can matjes herring, or delicatessen equivalent	½ cup chopped chives or minced onion
1 cup sour cream	3 hard-boiled eggs, chopped
	3 tablespoons minced parsley

1. Drain herring and arrange pieces on serving plate.
2. Cover with sour cream and garnish in diagonal, alternating strips with chives, eggs, and parsley.

Serves 6 to 8.

Take-It-Along Tips: Place in serving bowl and overwrap with Saran Wrap for traveling.

Red Eggs

- 4 hard-boiled eggs
- 1 small can tiny peas
- Salt
- ⅔ cup mayonnaise
- ½ cup heavy cream, whipped
- 2 tablespoons chili sauce
- 1 can tiny shrimp, drained, chilled

1. Halve the eggs, slice a bit from the bottom so they will sit, and arrange, yolk-side up, on a bed of well-drained peas, salted to taste.
2. Mix mayonnaise and cream and blend in chili sauce. Spoon dressing over eggs and garnish with shrimp.

Serves 8.

Take-It-Along Tips: Complete step 1. Pack sauce into a jar with a lid. Wrap egg dish in foil, sealing firmly to hold eggs in place. Wrap shrimp in foil. Complete the dish at the party.

Pickled Cucumbers the Old Way

- 2 medium cucumbers
- Salt
- 2 cups white vinegar
- 3 tablespoons minced parsley
- ½ cup sugar
- ¼ teaspoon fresh ground pepper

1. Peel cucumbers and, with a potato peeler, slice thinly into a bowl and sprinkle each layer lightly with salt. Cover with Saran Wrap and place a weight on top. Refrigerate half a day, pouring off cucumber juice as often as you think of it.
2. Mix vinegar, sugar, pepper, and parsley with remaining liquid. Toss cucumbers in dressing and refrigerate at least two hours before serving.

Serves 8 to 10.

Take-It-Along Tips: Place in a small serving bowl and cover with foil for traveling.

Stuffed Onion Rolls

2 large yellow onions
1 tablespoon butter
1 pound ground veal
1 tablespoon all-purpose flour
1 egg, slightly beaten
Salt
Pepper
1 cup heavy cream

1. Peel onions, scald in a lot of boiling water until onion leaves separate, about five to ten minutes. Cut in half crosswise so the leaves form small cups.
2. Brown butter and remove from heat. Dip outer sides of onion leaves in butter and set cup sides up.
3. Mix together veal, flour, egg, salt, pepper, cream. Place a little of this stuffing into each onion cup. Fold onions around the stuffing to make bobbin-shaped rolls and place edges downward on a buttered baking dish.
4. About 40 minutes before the buffet, heat oven to 425°, bake rolls 20 to 30 minutes, basting. Serve very hot.
Serves 8 to 10.

Take-It-Along Tips: Place unbaked rolls in baking dish, cover with foil for traveling, and bake at the home of the host.

Red Cabbage Salad

4 cups shredded red cabbage
1 lemon
2 tablespoons honey
Salt
¼ cup water

1. Place all the ingredients in a heavy 2-quart kettle and cover the kettle.
2. Bring to a simmer over low heat, increase heat slightly and simmer tightly covered for about one hour, until cabbage is tender.
3. Chill several hours before serving.
Serves 8 to 10.

Take-It-Along Tips: Place in a small serving dish to chill, cover with foil for traveling.

Eggplant Relish

This is great as part of a smorgasbord, as a dip with crackers or Melba toast, or as part of a first course of varied hors d'oeuvres.

1 medium eggplant	3 tablespoons minced parsley
½ cup diced celery	½ teaspoon oregano
½ cup canned pimiento strips	¼ cup olive oil
2 cloves garlic, peeled, minced	⅓ cup white wine vinegar
3 tablespoons chopped capers	¼ teaspoon paprika
⅓ to ½ teaspoon salt	

1. Wash and stem the eggplant. Simmer in boiling water 15 to 20 minutes, or until a fork goes through it easily. Cool, peel, and cut into ½-inch cubes.
2. While the eggplant is cooling, measure all the remaining ingredients into a large serving bowl and mix well. Fold in the cubed, cooled eggplant. Cover and refrigerate for a day before serving.
3. Serve in a bowl with crackers on the side; or serve individual portions on a small leaf of lettuce.

Serves 6 to 8 as a first course; 10 to 14 as a dip.

Take-It-Along Tips: Cover with foil or Saran Wrap for traveling. If you are serving this with lettuce, prepare lettuce cups and take them along in a plastic bag.

Sausage Roll

This disappears as quickly as it is served. It is very filling, so make the servings *small*. A quick way to make it is to use packaged piecrust mix and sausage meat.

1 cup all-purpose flour	8 ounces sausage meat
½ teaspoon salt	1 teaspoon caraway seed
½ cup shortening	Bunch of watercress (optional)
1 teaspoon lemon juice	
2 to 2½ tablespoons cold water	

1. Sift the flour and salt together. Cut the shortening into the flour, using 2 knives. Work until mixture is like coarse oatmeal. Sprinkle with lemon juice and 2 tablespoons of water, and press the mixture to the side of the bowl with a fork to create a lump of stiff dough. If the mixture isn't damp enough to form dough, add ½ tablespoon of water.

2. On a lightly floured board, roll the dough into a long strip. Fold in thirds. Seal the ends. Give the pastry a half turn, roll out again. Repeat 3 times.

3. Flour the board again and roll the pastry into one long, rectangular strip. On the floured board, roll out the sausage meat into a strip as long as, but half as narrow as, the strip of dough. Set the sausage strip on one half of the pastry strip, fold the other pastry half over the sausage strip, press the pastry edges together to seal them. Sprinkle with caraway seeds.

4. Place the roll on an ungreased baking tray and cut crosswise into 12 to 16 pieces. Cover with foil and refrigerate.

5. To serve, preheat oven to 450°. Bake sausage roll 10 minutes, reduce heat to 375°, bake 10 minutes more. Serve on a bed of watercress.

Makes 8 to 10 servings. Make 2 rolls to serve twice as many.

Take-It-Along Tips: Take unbaked roll to your party on its baking tray, covered with foil, and bake at the party.

5. Hors D'Oeuvres Specialties

Originally, the hors d'oeuvres table was rather like the smorgasbord, an offering of flavorful specialties served before the real meal began. Today, in French homes and in little restaurants, the hors d'oeuvres course often consists of a tasty little dish of vegetables in a seasoned sauce, like the Vegetable Marinade, eggs served with Fresh Mayonnaise, artichokes in Lemon Butter Sauce, or some of the more elaborate recipes here.

Pâté Maison is one of the classic hors d'oeuvres offered in French restaurants. They're all called Pâté Maison—meat loaf as prepared in this restaurant, is what it means—but each is different. Try the recipe given for it here, and change the flavorings to suit your own palate. Then you'll be able to call it Pâté Maison, meaning, as prepared in your house.

The hors d'oeuvres recipes here, served in small portions, make good appetizers to offer with drinks. They can also be treated as gourmet luncheon dishes. A tableful of hors d'oeuvres makes a very elegant meal: Serve with them cold white or rosé wine, champagne spiked with a few drops of brandy, or iced tea.

Most of the hors d'oeuvres recipes *cannot* be doubled without losing texture or flavor; it is best to make them in two batches.

Pâté Maison Marcel

To make this pâté, buy rendered chicken fat or save up chicken fat skimmed from the drippings of a roasted chicken cooked with a bit of garlic. Covered, in the refrigerator the pâté will keep 2 weeks; sealed in plastic and frozen, it will keep for up to 6 months. The texture is slightly changed by freezing, but the flavor remains excellent.

1 pound chicken legs	6 whole cloves
1 pound pork shoulder	2 cups cold water
1¾ teaspoons salt	¾ pound chicken livers
½ teaspoon pepper	1 cup chicken fat
1 bay leaf	3 small cloves garlic, peeled, crushed
1 teaspoon thyme	
⅛ teaspoon allspice	½ bunch parsley, minced fine
1 teaspoon savory	
1 small onion	

1. In a large soup kettle, place chicken legs, pork, salt, pepper, bay leaf, thyme, allspice, savory, onion stuck with cloves, and water. Over medium heat, bring to a boil. Cover lightly and simmer for 2 hours. Do not add more water.

2. Remove meat, reserving the liquid. Pick meat from bones and chop fine.

3. Place the chicken livers in the cooking liquid and simmer over low heat 10 minutes. Remove and chop livers.

4. Discard bay leaf and onion. Add chicken fat to remaining cooking liquid and boil rapidly for 5 minutes.

5. Put meat and liver through an electric blender, a cup at a time, adding to each batch a little of the cooking liquid. Place meats in a large bowl and mix well with garlic and parsley. Taste, and add salt and pepper as needed.

6. Pour into a one-quart mold, or into 3 8-ounce molds. Chill overnight before serving. Unmold onto a bed of parsley and serve with crackers.

Makes 20 to 30 servings as an appetizer; 16 to 24 servings as a first course.

Take-It-Along Tips: Take this to the party in its mold, wrapped in foil, and unmold at the host home. Garnish after unmolding.

Quiche with Cream and Cheese

The custard pie called a quiche can be chilled after cooking and served cold at a picnic, or as an appetizer with drinks, but it *isn't* as mouth-watering as a golden puffed-up quiche straight from the oven. Serve it hot as a first course.

1 8-inch pie shell	¾ cup finely grated Swiss cheese
1 egg white	
2½ tablespoons soft butter	½ teaspoon salt
8 slices bacon	⅛ teaspoon pepper
3 whole eggs	⅛ teaspoon nutmeg
1½ cups half and half, cream and milk	1 small onion, grated
	2 teaspoons flour

1. Bake the pie shell 10 minutes. Let cool.
2. Brush the cooled pie shell with the egg white, then line with one tablespoon of the soft butter. Turn the oven to 375°. Set rack in upper third of oven.
3. Sauté the bacon slowly until crisped, turning often. It should be lightly browned when done. Drain on paper towel, then place in bottom of pie shell.
4. Beat the eggs until thick and lemon colored. Beat in the half and half, cheese, salt, pepper, and nutmeg.
5. In a small saucepan, sauté the onion in butter until translucent. Mix in the flour, simmer 2 minutes, stirring. Beat into the egg mixture. Turn the egg mixture into the pie shell and dot with bits of butter.
6. Bake 25 to 30 minutes without opening the oven door. Insert a silver knife in the center; if it comes out clean, the quiche is done. If not, bake another 10 to 15 minutes. Serve at once before it sinks.

Makes 6 portions as a first course, 8 to 10 as an appetizer.

VARIATIONS. A variety of other cheeses, including Camembert, Gruyère, and Roquefort can be used.

MUSHROOM QUICHE. For cheese, substitute 2 cups chopped mushrooms, sprinkled with one teaspoon lemon juice, sautéed in butter and dredged with 2 tablespoons of dry sherry and 2 teaspoons flour.

SEAFOOD QUICHE. For cheese, substitute one cup shredded or minced crab, lobster, or shrimp.

Take-It-Along Tips: There are two ways to take this to a party. One is to freeze it after cooking (quiches freeze well enough), take it along still frozen, reheat, and serve. The other is to take the egg mixture in its mixing bowl and the pie shell in the baking tin, and bake at the party. I prefer the latter, but a homemade quiche that has been frozen then reheated is still delicious.

Coquille St. Jacques

To serve as a first course, present in the large scallop shells sold in shops specializing in kitchenware. Or, serve as a finger appetizer in small, fluted scallop shells gathered from the beach (and thoroughly washed).

1½ cups water	3 tablespoons flour
1 teaspoon salt	1 pinch nutmeg
1 bay leaf	1 tablespoon lemon juice
½ pound scallops	⅛ teaspoon pepper
1 cup mushrooms, wiped	¼ cup light cream
1 pound raw shrimps	6 to 12 scallop shells, washed, dried
3 tablespoons softened butter	½ cup grated Swiss cheese

1. In a small saucepan, bring the water to a boil with the salt and bay leaf. Cut the scallops in half or in quarters to make uniform sizes and poach them and the mushrooms in the water for 2 minutes. Remove the scallops and mushrooms to a small bowl.

2. In the liquid, simmer the shrimps for 5 minutes, then turn off the heat and let the shrimps rest in the liquid 10 minutes more. Peel the shrimps, devein them, chop coarsely and set aside. Bring the liquid to a boil.

3. In the top of a double boiler, stir the softened butter and the flour into a paste, then whip in 1½ cups of the boiling liquid, stirring rapidly. Add the scallops, mushrooms, shrimps, nutmeg, lemon juice, and pepper.

4. Half fill the bottom of the double boiler, bring the water to a boil, set the top of the boiler with its contents in place, cover, lower the heat. Keep the sauce hot but not boiling for 10 minutes.

5. To serve, thin the scallop mixture with cream, reheat. Fill the

shells with the mixture, sprinkle with grated Swiss cheese, and put under a hot broiler until the mixture bubbles and browns.

Makes 12 to 16 servings in tiny scallop shells, or serves 6 as a first course.

Take-It-Along Tips: Take the scallop shells you'll serve this in, the seafood sauce ready to go, the cream, and the Swiss cheese to the party, fill the shells with sauce, as in step 5, and heat and serve.

Mussels Clemence

This is my French grandmother's recipe, a creamy concoction with an exquisite flavor. If you're lucky enough to have a place at the ocean where you can gather mussels, it will become a favorite in your family, too. We make it from leftover steamed mussels.

3 quarts mussels, in the shell	½ teaspoon salt
1 cup dry white wine	⅛ teaspoon pepper
1 cup milk	½ cup soda-cracker crumbs
1 medium onion, peeled, sliced	⅓ bunch parsley, chopped fine
1 carrot, peeled, sliced thinly	3 garlic cloves, peeled, minced
1 bay leaf	
2 sprigs parsley	½ cup light cream
7 tablespoons butter	1½ cups cooking liquid

1. Check mussels, discarding any that are not tightly closed. Scrub very thoroughly under cold running water to remove sand, seaweed, and barnacles. Use stiff brush or steel wool. With a sharp knife, trim the beard from the edges of the mussels. Place mussels in a large bowl, cover with cold water, and let stand one to 2 hours. Drain.

2. Place the mussels in a large kettle with the wine, milk, onion, carrot, bay leaf, parsley, 3 tablespoons of butter, salt, and pepper.

3. Cover tightly and bring to a boil over high heat. Continue cooking until all mussels open, about 4 minutes. Shake the pot often to get mussels on the bottom up to the top. Don't overcook.

4. Drain mussels; reserve cooking liquid. Remove the empty half shell of each mussel.

5. For the next step, use two large frying pans, and have all remaining ingredients measured and ready to use. Over a high flame, melt 4 tablespoons of butter until white, add mussels, stir 2 minutes; add crumbs, chopped parsley, and garlic. Cook one minute, turning the mussels so they are coated. Add the cream, turn once more, add ½ cup of cooking liquid and let simmer 3 minutes. If you are dining at home, serve the mussels as soon as ready. If not, stack in an ovenproof serving dish and warm 2 to 3 minutes before serving.

6. Serve with paper napkins—this is messy finger food.

Serves 6 as a main course, 12 to 16 as an appetizer.

Take-It-Along Tips: Follow the recipe through step 4, take the ingredients to the party, along with two large frying pans, and finish the recipe there: This is a delicacy and must be handled with care, but it's worth the effort.

Shrimp in Tomato Aspic

A cool, pretty molded jelly served on a bed of unpeeled, thinly sliced cucumbers.

1 pound raw shrimps	2 envelopes unflavored gelatin
1 carrot, scraped, sliced thin	
1 stalk celery with leaves, minced	2 10-ounce cans condensed tomato soup
1 large slice onion, minced	¼ cup dry sherry
1 bay leaf	1 cucumber, sliced thin
6 peppercorns	2 lemons

1. Rinse the shrimps; place in a saucepan with just enough water to cover. Add the carrot, celery, onion, bay leaf, and peppercorns. Bring to a boil; lower the heat and simmer 5 minutes. Strain ¾ cup cooking liquid and chill.

2. Shell and devein shrimps. Reserve 10 whole shrimps for garnish. Chop the remaining shrimps coarsely. Return to cooking liquid.

3. Soften the gelatin in the chilled shrimp liquid. Dissolve over low heat; stir in the soup and sherry. Chill until slightly thickened. Drain chopped shrimps. Remove the bay leaf and peppercorns. Fold in the drained shrimps. Pour into either 10 small molds or one large mold. Garnish with whole shrimps. Refrigerate until set.

4. To serve, set the mold for one minute in hot water. Turn onto a platter or onto plates of sliced cucumbers.

Take-It-Along Tips: Take the mold and prepared cucumbers and lemon to the party, unmold and garnish at the host home.

Dolmas

These are Turkish stuffed vine leaves. Always greeted with applause, they are exotic but easier to prepare than you think. Serve the dolmas hot as a main course, or cold as part of a many-dish party meal. They are served without forks. Squeeze several drops of lemon juice on the dolma before eating.

- 3 tablespoons olive oil
- 1 large onion, peeled, chopped
- 6 tablespoons raw converted rice
- 4 tablespoons pine nuts or slivered almonds
- 12 ounces raw ground beef
- ½ teaspoon freshly chopped mint, or ¼ teaspoon dried mint
- ⅛ teaspoon cinnamon
- Salt
- Pepper
- 30 vine leaves, canned
- ½ cup dry white wine
- Water as needed
- 2 lemons, sliced into thin wedges

1. Over low heat in a large heavy saucepan, heat the oil and sauté the chopped onion for 4 minutes, then add the rice and sauté until pale gold. Add pine nuts, or slivered almonds, and sauté for one minute.
2. Remove from the heat. Combine the meat, mint, and cinnamon, add salt and pepper to taste. Mix well.
3. Soak the vine leaves for one minute in very hot water to soften them. Remove with a slotted spoon. Spread the vine leaves out flat and put a tablespoon of the meat mixture in the center of each. Fold in the ends and roll into finger-shaped bundles. Arrange rolls in a small ovenproof dish, pour on the wine, and add enough water to cover the leaves. They must not be left dry at the start of cooking. Simmer, covered, for 25 minutes over low heat, then remove lid and cook until the liquid is absorbed.
4. Serve with lemon wedges.

Makes 8 to 10 generous portions.

Take-It-Along Tips: Take the finished dolmas and the lemon wedges, wrapped in foil, to the party and arrange on a serving platter there.

Cheese Mousse

This is a beautiful molded dish to pass with crackers or serve as a first course. Take it to the party in the mold—unmold it when you are ready to serve.

¾ pound blue cheese or Roquefort (at room temperature)	6 medium egg yolks
	6 tablespoons heavy cream
1½ envelopes unflavored gelatin	1½ cups heavy cream
	3 medium egg whites
¼ cup cold water	Watercress
	Melba toast

1. Mash the cheese and force through a sieve. Set aside. Soften gelatin in the cold water.
2. In the top of a double boiler, beat the egg yolks with the 6 tablespoons of cream for one minute with a mixer at high speed. Then stir the mixture over simmering water until it has thickened enough to be creamy. Add the gelatin and stir until it is completely dissolved. Remove from the heat.
3. Stir in the cheese. Set aside to cool. Whip the cream. Beat the egg whites until stiff.
4. Fold the whipped cream and egg whites into the cooled cheese mixture.
5. Pour the mousse into an oiled mold. Chill for at least 2 hours, or until the mixture is firm.
6. To serve warm the mold one minute in hot water, then unmold onto a serving plate. Garnish with watercress. Offer with rounds of Melba toast.

Serves 16 to 20 as an appetizer; 8 to 10 as a first course.

Take-It-Along Tips: Take this to the party in its mold, wrapped in foil, and unmold onto a serving dish there.

6. Hurry-Up Appetizers

When you're the one who is bringing the appetizers, and you're not going to have much time to make them, try these recipes. Most are intended to be made ahead of time, stored or frozen, and toted to the dinner in that state.

If you haven't time to cook ahead, then bring a collection of any of these: giant ripe olives; stuffed giant green olives; nuts; slices of salami or bologna wrapped around tiny gherkin pickles; a plate of cheeses with crackers.

Or you can buy two pints of sour cream, divide them into lots in small, ornate dishes, and flavor each dish with one of your favored powdered herbs; a crushed slice of onion; a crushed garlic clove; a small tin of minced clams, drained; or a small can of shredded crabmeat, drained.

Most of the appetizers here can be doubled without spoiling the recipe.

Carousel of Stuffed Delights

A gala plateful of varied tidbits to serve at a smorgasbord or with cocktails. The shrimp-stuffed eggs make a good first course. (You will need all these ingredients for the various stuffings.)

3 cherry tomatoes
6 hard-boiled eggs
6 stalks celery, cleaned
½ cup canned crabmeat
1 tablespoon mayonnaise
½ teaspoon lemon juice
½ teaspoon curry powder
8 ounces canned shrimp, drained
1 tablespoon lemon juice
2 tablespoons mayonnaise
Salt and pepper

1 cup Roquefort or blue cheese
1 tablespoon minced celery
1 tablespoon sour cream
¼ teaspoon black pepper
1 cup finely diced cooked ham
1 tablespoon mayonnaise
½ teaspoon Dijon mustard
2 tablespoons minced fresh dill
½ cup minced dill

1. Slice off the ends of the tomatoes about ⅛ inch below the stems, and scoop out the insides with a demitasse spoon. Halve the eggs lengthwise and remove the yolks. Reserve. Cut the celery into 2-inch chunks. After you have finished the stuffing, on a large round plate make a wheel with tomatoes as the outer ring, eggs as the hub, celery as the spokes.

CRABMEAT STUFFING

2. Shred crabmeat and mix with mayonnaise, lemon juice, and curry.

SHRIMP STUFFING

3. Combine mashed yolks of all the hard-cooked eggs, 6 minced shrimps, lemon juice, mayonnaise, and salt and pepper to taste.

CHEESE STUFFING

4. Mix together Roquefort or blue cheese, minced celery, sour cream, pepper.

HAM STUFFING

5. Mix chopped ham with mayonnaise, Dijon mustard, minced dill.

6. Fill eggs with shrimp stuffing, and top with whole shrimps. Fill tomatoes and celery with other stuffings. Garnish all with minced dill.

Serves 12 to 16.

Take-It-Along Tips: Arrange the finished delights on a big platter covered with sprigs of parsley to keep them from sliding. Wrap in a

Guacamole

A creamy avocado dip from Mexico to serve with crisp potato or corn chips, crackers, or raw vegetable chunks. Or serve it as part of a smorgasbord, with individual portions in lettuce-leaf cups. It is important that the avocado be really ripe.

- 1 ripe avocado
- 1 teaspoon crushed onion
- 1 small garlic clove, peeled, crushed
- 1 dash Tabasco sauce, optional
- Paprika
- 1 tablespoon finely minced, celery leaves
- ½ teaspoon lemon juice, strained
- Salt
- ⅓ cup Fresh Mayonnaise (page 222) or commercial mayonnaise plus ⅛ teaspoon mustard

1. Halve the avocado. With a teaspoon, scoop the meat into a small bowl. With a fork, mash in the onion; mix in the garlic, Tabasco sauce, paprika, minced celery leaves, lemon juice, and salt to taste.
2. Spread the mayonnaise over the mixture, covering completely, so no air reaches the avocado. Cover the bowl and chill.
3. Just before serving, beat the layer of mayonnaise and the avocado mixture together. Serve immediately.

As a first course, this serves 4 to 6; as a dip it serves 8 to 12.

Take-It-Along Tips: Wrap the chilled Guacamole in foil and take to the party; do not mix in the mayonnaise until ready to serve.

Bagna Cauda

A hot, pungent Italian dip for raw vegetables. The key to its success is a good olive oil. You'll need a fondue dish and a Sterno flame for this one. Make the sauce just before you leave for the party.

8 cups raw cut vegetables	½ pound (2 sticks) butter
6 cloves garlic	or margarine
12 anchovy fillets in oil	1 cup light olive oil
	Black pepper

1. For this recipe cauliflower, zucchini, celery, fennel, fresh mushrooms, small summer squash, cut into ¾- to 1-inch pieces, are all suitable. Ice the vegetables and arrange on a serving tray with toothpicks or fondue forks.
2. Mash the garlic and anchovies to a paste in the mortar or in the bottom of a bowl.
3. Turn into a fondue dish and set over low heat, stirring until the mixture thickens. Stir in butter and oil, a little at a time. Cook for 3 minutes, then remove from heat and keep warm.
4. To serve, sprinkle with black pepper and set over the Sterno flame, and stir until the mixture bubbles. Place iced vegetables beside the sauce.

Makes 2 cups of sauce, enough for dipping a large bowlful of raw vegetable pieces.

Take-It-Along Tips: Follow the recipe through step 2, wrap the ingredients, and take to the party. Finish the recipe there.

Artichokes and Mushrooms

This is one of the most luxurious of smorgasbord tidbits. You can also serve with cocktails or on a leaf of iceberg lettuce as part of a plate of hors d'oeuvres.

2 cups large, fresh mushrooms	1 medium clove garlic, peeled, minced
1 package frozen artichoke hearts	1 teaspoon salt
⅓ cup olive oil	2 teaspoons fresh, or 1 teaspoon dried, tarragon
2 tablespoons lemon juice	
2 tablespoons wine vinegar	⅛ teaspoon black pepper

1. Stem mushrooms, rub caps clean with paper towel. Save stems to make Mushroom Soup.
2. Cook, drain, dry the artichokes as directed on the package, and set in a small serving bowl with the mushrooms.
3. Place the remaining ingredients in the blender, and blend at high speed for 2 minutes. In a small saucepan, over medium heat, bring this sauce to simmering heat. Pour at once over the artichokes and mushrooms.
4. Marinate at room temperature for 3 to 6 hours. Cover, then chill, preferably 2 to 3 days, before serving.

Serves 12 as a cocktail appetizer; 6 as hors d'oeuvres.

Take-It-Along Tips: Wrap in foil in a serving dish to take to the party.

Stuffed Mushroom Caps

Serve these at a smorgasbord dinner, or as an appetizer at a gala party, or as a hot first course for a gourmet dinner. For a smorgasbord, plan on 4 to 6 mushrooms per guest, probably 2 pounds of mushrooms for 6 to 8 guests, depending on the size of the mushrooms, about as big around as a half-dollar.

1 pound large mushrooms	2 tablespoons grated Parmesan cheese
¼ cup olive oil	
¼ cup minced onion	1 egg
1 garlic clove, peeled, minced	1 tablespoon chopped dill
½ cup finely chopped ham	½ teaspoon oregano
½ cup fine dry bread crumbs	½ teaspoon salt
	Freshly ground pepper

1. Wipe the mushrooms clean. Remove stems. Chop enough of the stems to make ½ cup.
2. Heat the oil in a skillet. Toss the mushroom caps in the oil just long enough to coat them. Remove caps from the skillet and set aside.
3. To the skillet, add the chopped stems, onion, and garlic. If the mixture seems dry, add another tablespoon of oil. Simmer for 10 minutes, or until mixture has cooked almost to a pulp. Remove the

skillet from the heat and stir in the ham, bread crumbs, cheese, egg, dill, oregano, salt, and pepper.

4. Set the caps upside down in an ovenproof serving dish; spoon the mixture into the caps. Drizzle a little oil over them.

5. Before serving, preheat the oven to 325° and bake for 30 minutes. Serve hot.

Makes 8 to 10 portions as an appetizer. Serves 4 as a first course.

Take-It-Along Tips: Follow the recipe through step 4, wrap the baking dish in Saran Wrap or foil; take to the party and finish there.

Chopped Chicken Livers

Chopped chicken livers done this way and served with Melba toast rounds is one of the most popular of all appetizers. It also makes a delicious first course served with crusty French bread, and it takes very little time to make. Use fresh chicken livers for the best results. Instead of chicken fat, you can use soft pork fat skimmed from the drippings of a roast cooked with a bit of garlic.

⅛ pound butter
¾ cup soft chicken fat
2 Bermuda onions, peeled, chopped
½ pound chicken livers
1 clove garlic, minced
2 large hard-boiled eggs, shelled
¼ cup chopped parsley
Bunch of fresh dill, or parsley
Melba toast

1. Place the butter and 2 tablespoons of chicken fat in a heavy frying pan and sauté onions over medium heat until golden.

2. Remove all but 2 tablespoons onion and let remaining onion get quite brown, almost burned. Remove browned onion. Place chicken livers and garlic in the fat and over medium-high heat, sauté covered for about 5 minutes, shaking the pan frequently to keep the livers from sticking.

3. On a cutting board, chop the livers, hard-boiled eggs, onions, and parsley along with the juices remaining in the pan.

4. Scoop the mixture into a medium bowl and whip in as much chicken fat as the mixture will absorb.

5. Turn into a mold rinsed in cold water and chill for 3 to 4 hours.

Unmold onto a bed of dill or parsley edged with rounds of Melba toast.

Makes 12 to 16 servings as an appetizer; serves 6 to 8 as part of a smorgasbord.

Take-It-Along Tips: Take the mold to the party wrapped in foil; unmold and garnish at the host home.

Brandied Cheese Spread

This is a delicious, sharply flavored spread to serve with cocktails. If possible, make it 4 or 5 days ahead to allow the flavor to ripen. Because it keeps refrigerated for weeks, it also makes a dandy gift packed into a pretty, covered jar.

4 tablespoons butter	16 ounces Roquefort or blue cheese
16 ounces cream cheese	¼ cup brandy or Cognac

1. In electric mixer at low speed, beat butter and cheeses together until soft and completely blended. Beat in brandy.
2. To store, refrigerate, covered. Allow it to reach room temperature before serving. Serve with Melba toast or bland crackers.

Serves 12 to 16.

Take-It-Along Tips: Take to the party in its container and serve in the container or turn onto a serving dish.

Shrimp Toast

Crisp, rich little appetizers that can be made ahead and reheated in a medium oven. They can be frozen and reheated, but won't be quite as crisp.

1 cup raw shrimp, shelled, deveined	½ teaspoon salt
4 water chestnuts, rinsed	¼ teaspoon black pepper
1 egg, slightly beaten	10 slices bread, crusts removed
1 tablespoon dry sherry	3 cups oil for deep frying
¼ teaspoon ground ginger	

1. Mince shrimp and water chestnuts in blender at low speed.

2. In a medium bowl, mix shrimp and water chestnuts with the egg, sherry, ginger, salt, pepper.

3. Cut the bread into triangles, and spread firmly with the shrimp mixture. Make sure the paste is really stuck to bread edges so it won't separate.

4. Deep-fry at 350°, or until a bit of bread sizzles when it hits the oil. Lower 3 to 4 slices at a time into the oil, shrimp side down. When the edges brown, flip and brown on other side. Remove with a slotted spoon, and drain on paper toweling. Place on a cookie sheet ready to reheat or freeze, sealed in plastic.

5. When ready to serve, reheat at 350°. Serve hot.

Makes 6 to 8 servings.

Take-It-Along Tips: If these are going to a party, freeze them, take them frozen and wrapped in foil to the host home, and warm them there just before serving in a 350° oven for 10 minutes.

Cheese Toast

These hot cheese snacks are always a sure-fire success, and are easy to make ahead and broil just before serving. If you can't buy bread rounds, use a cookie cutter to create shapes from a large sliced loaf. The onion slices won't quite fit, but cover the bread right to the edges with the cheese and mayonnaise mixture and they'll still be delicious.

2 Bermuda onions	1 package fresh sesame or rye bread rounds
¼ pound butter, at room temperature	1 cup grated Parmesan cheese
	½ cup mayonnaise

1. Peel onions and slice paper-thin to create rounds the size of the bread rounds.

2. Butter a package of sesame or rye rounds. Cover each round with an onion ring.

3. Mix cheese and mayonnaise; cover onion and bread to the edges with a low mound of the cheese-mayonnaise mixture.

4. Freeze, covered until ready to use.

5. Heat broiler and broil rounds until topping bubbles and turns golden brown, 4 to 5 minutes. Serve piping hot.

Makes 10 to 12 portions.

Take-It-Along Tips: Carry these ready to bake on cookie sheets covered with foil and finish at the host home.

Cheese Puffs

These tiny olive-stuffed pastries always win applause. Make and freeze them days or weeks ahead.

½ pound sharp Cheddar cheese, grated	½ teaspoon salt
¼ cup butter	½ teaspoon paprika
½ cup sifted all-purpose flour	1 small bottle of small stuffed olives (about 30), wiped dry

1. In a small bowl, with the beater at low speed, beat the cheese into the butter. Add flour, salt, and paprika. Mix at low speed. Gather dough into a ball, wrap in wax paper, and refrigerate for 3 hours.
2. Pinch off one teaspoon of the mixture, flatten it with your fingers, and wrap it around a stuffed olive, with the ends of dough open. Roll gently in the palms of your hands until the sides of the dough adhere. Freeze, sealed in plastic, until party time.
3. Bake at 400° for 15 minutes, or until golden brown, and serve at once.

Makes about 30 balls.

Take-It-Along Tips: Freeze these after step 2 and take them to the party in their freezer bag. Follow step 3 after you get to the host home.

Cheese Straws

Homemade cheese straws are a treat, and they're easy to make. For a gala touch, offer them set into rings made of baked cheese-straw dough. One caution—they are fragile.

1 cup all-purpose flour	5 ounces butter
½ teaspoon salt	4 ounces firm Cheddar cheese, finely grated
⅛ teaspoon pepper	
⅛ teaspoon dried mustard	2 egg yolks, beaten
⅛ teaspoon celery salt	1 egg white, slightly beaten

1. Sieve together flour, salt, pepper, mustard, celery salt. Cut the butter in bits and, with your fingers, crumble the butter into the flour mixture until it resembles fine bread crumbs. Toss the cheese lightly with this mixture.
2. Work the egg yolks into the flour mixture. Roll out firmly but gently on a well-floured board until about ¼-inch thick. Cut into fingers ¼-inch wide, 3- to 4-inches long. Gather up any pastry left, roll out again, and cut into rings with a doughnut cutter. Lay fingers and rings on lightly greased baking trays. Brush with egg white.
3. Set in preheated 425° oven. Bake 12 to 15 minutes or until golden brown.
4. Cool completely before removing from trays. Gently lift straws with a spatula as they are fragile and break easily when fresh.

Serves 8 to 10.

Take-It-Along Tips: Take these to the party on their baking trays to make sure they travel whole. Or freeze in the trays and heat at 350° for 10 minutes before serving.

Hurry-Up Appetizers

Cheese Dip

This basic dip recipe can also be flavored with almost any herb and served with any crisp tidbit or cracker or with raw vegetable sticks.

2 tablespoons butter	½ teaspoon anchovy paste, or other flavoring
6 ounces cream cheese	
½ small onion, minced	3 tablespoons, or more, sour cream

1. At low speed, in an electric mixer beat butter and cream cheese until blended. Beat in finely minced onion and anchovy paste. Blend well, and add enough of the sour cream to create a mixture of dipping consistency.
Serves 6 to 8.

GARLIC OR HERB CHEESE DIP. Substitute for the anchovy paste ½ clove garlic, minced, or one tablespoon minced dill, tarragon, or parsley, or any other herb you like.

Take-It-Along Tips: Take to the party in its serving bowl wrapped in foil.

Quick Pissaladière

A robust, flavorful appetizer from the south of France for a hungry crowd.

1 package hot roll mix	2 cans anchovy fillets
3 pounds onions, peeled, sliced	1 bottle pitted black olives
2 garlic cloves, peeled, minced	½ teaspoon ground thyme
1 cup olive oil	Cold milk

1. Prepare the dough as directed on the package, and roll out on a floured board to a thickness of ⅛ inch and a length of about 18 inches. Press the edges upward to make a raised border that will hold the filling. Set on a cookie sheet.
2. In a large, heavy skillet over low heat, simmer the onions

and garlic in the oil until golden brown. With a slotted spoon, remove the onions and the garlic from the oil and spread evenly over the dough.

3. Drain the anchovy fillets, cut in strips lengthwise, and lay in a lattice pattern over the onions. Place a pitted black olive in the center of each square. Sprinkle with ground thyme. Wipe dough with a pastry brush dipped in cold milk. Cover with foil and refrigerate until party time.

4. To serve, bake in a 350° oven for 15 minutes or until the edges of the crust are pale brown. Set under a medium-hot broiler, until crust has turned a rich brown. Cut into squares the size of the lattice sections and serve at once.

Serves 10 to 16.

Take-It-Along Tips: Follow through step 3, take the cookie sheet to the party, and finish there.

PART 3
Soup Parties

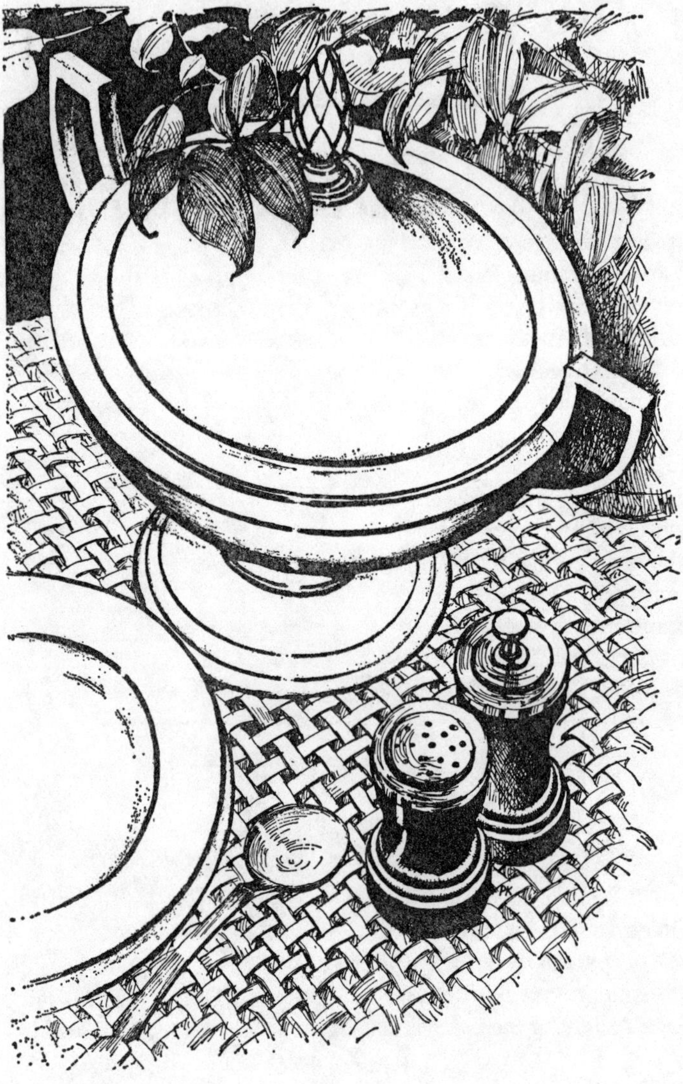

7. Hot Pots

Soup has become a much neglected delight, and inflation being the way it is and soups being as economical as they are, it's a good time to reverse that trend. You can feed a multitude with pennies-worth of dried split peas and a leftover ham bone—the two, with a few spices, make a thick, rich, delicious soup to serve as a main course for a snack party or an after-ski get-together. Add hot French bread with butter and a dessert and I promise the food will really be a hit.

In this chapter there are many other hearty soups to serve as a main course, along with a few, such as Cream-of-Celery, Cream-of-Mushroom, and Leek-and-Potato Soup to serve as luncheon fare or as the soup course for a gourmet meal. These three soups are all inexpensive.

Some mouth-watering seafood stews such as New England Clam Chowder, Deer Island Lobster Stew, and the Mediterranean seafood soup called Bouillabaisse you will find in Chapter 9.

All of the soup recipes can be doubled to serve twice as many.

Onion Soup Gratinée

Onion soup is usually served in individual ovenproof ceramic soup bowls. They are easy to find in kitchen-supply shops. A bowlful of onion soup, a green salad, cheese with bread, and a sweet for dessert make a delightful meal for midday or late evening.

Note that the ingredients listed below are for one portion. Multiply by the number of guests expected to get the amount of ingredients required.

FOR ONE SERVING:

1 medium onion, peeled, sliced thin	Salt
	Pepper
½ tablespoon butter	¼ ounce Swiss cheese, slivered
½ beef bouillon cube, dissolved in 1 cup hot water	1 small slice stale French bread
½ tablespoon dry white wine (optional)	1 tablespoon grated Swiss cheese

1. Over medium heat in a heavy kettle, simmer the onion in the butter until *lightly* browned.
2. Stir in the beef bouillon and wine. Simmer for 30 minutes. Season with salt and pepper to taste.
3. Put the Swiss cheese slivers and bread slice broken into 2 or 3 one-inch chunks into 8- or 10-ounce ovenproof soup bowls.
4. Pour the soup into the bowls; the bread will float to the surface; sprinkle with grated Swiss cheese. Bake in a preheated 325° oven about 20 minutes. Then set under a broiler at high heat till top browns. Serve hot.

Take-It-Along Tips: Make the bouillon and take it to the party in its kettle, along with the remaining ingredients. Finish the soup there, starting at step 4.

Green Pea Soup with Ham Bone

A favorite in French Canada, this is another one-dish meal recipe. Save your next ham bone in the freezer and try it.

2 tablespoons butter	1 ham bone or smoked ham hock
1 cup minced onion	
12 cups cold water	1 cup finely chopped celery
2 cups (1 pound) green split peas, washed	1 cup diced carrot
	⅛ teaspoon savory
4 whole cloves	⅛ teaspoon marjoram
1 bay leaf	1 tablespoon salt
	¼ teaspoon pepper

1. Over low heat, melt the butter in a large soup kettle; add the onion and simmer until translucent. Add water and all other ingredients. Bring to a boil, cover, reduce heat, simmer four hours, or until peas have disintegrated. When soup has thickened after the second

hour of cooking, stir occasionally. Add water if soup begins to stick to bottom or becomes too thick.

2. Remove the ham bone, bay leaf, and cloves. Trim ham from bone, cut into dice, and return to soup. Add pepper if needed and salt. Amount of salt needed will vary depending on saltiness of the ham.

3. To serve, reheat.

Makes 10 to 12 portions.

Take-It-Along Tips: Take this with you in its cooking kettle, and turn into a soup tureen when ready to serve.

Leek-and-Potato Soup

A wonderful blending of flavors makes this hot thick soup a favorite. The expensive, dressed-up variation is called Vichyssoise. Serve with hot Butter Biscuits or ham sandwiches.

6 large or 8 small leeks	3 cups *old* potatoes, peeled, diced
2 tablespoons butter	1 tablespoon salt
1 small onion, peeled, minced	1 tablespoon butter
3 quarts water	½ cup heavy cream, optional

1. Cut away root tips and tough green tops of leeks and slice lengthwise down the center. Separate the stalks, wash carefully, and cut into long thin strips.

2. In a medium soup kettle over low heat melt the butter, add the onion, and simmer until translucent.

3. Add the water to the onion, add the potatoes, raise the heat, and bring to a boil. Boil rapidly until potatoes are tender. Add leeks, boil rapidly, uncovered, until the soup begins to thicken. It should cook 40 to 60 minutes in all.

4. Remove from heat and mash the vegetables with a potato masher. Leeks will be stringy. Add more salt, if desired.

5. To serve, reheat the soup, stir in the butter and cream, and pour into large soup plates.

Makes 8 to 10 portions.

Take-It-Along Tips: Take this to the party in its cooking kettle, along with the butter and cream, then follow step 5.

Vegetable Soup

A thick hearty soup that makes a meal all by itself—and costs pennies. Serve it with warm, crusty French bread.

1 cup dried white or lima beans	2 large onions, minced
1 medium green cabbage	1 large clove garlic, peeled
2 quarts boiling water	¼ teaspoon thyme
3 to 4 large potatoes	1 tablespoon salt
2 large carrots	¼ teaspoon black pepper
1 medium rutabaga or turnip	Water, about 2½ quarts
2 large leeks, cut up	1 pound salt pork
	¼ cup minced parsley

1. Soak the beans in water to cover overnight, then drain.
2. Clean the cabbage and cut away the tough part of the stalk. Quarter the cabbage and put it into the boiling water for 4 minutes. Drain off the water. Put the cabbage into a large soup kettle. Add the beans and potatoes, peeled and sliced; the carrots, scraped and thickly sliced; the rutabaga or turnip, peeled and diced; the leeks, onions, garlic, thyme, salt, and pepper. Add water and cover. Simmer gently, for 1½ hours. Add the salt pork and simmer, covered, another hour or until the pork is thoroughly cooked. If the water boils down, add another cupful.
3. Serve in large soup plates with cut up pieces of salt pork. Garnish with a sprinkling of parsley.

Makes 8 to 10 generous portions.

Take-It-Along Tips: Take this to the party in its cooking kettle, along with the parsley, and follow step 3 once you get there.

Thick Chicken Soup

This is another hearty, meal-in-one soup to serve with hot French bread, or with thin, light sandwiches made with sliced cucumbers or tomatoes. An economical version of this can be made from saved-up frozen chicken necks, backs, wing tips, liver and gizzards. If you have a bit of chicken gravy to add, it picks up the flavor.

Hot Pots

1 4-pound chicken	⅛ teaspoon pepper
3 quarts cold water	½ teaspoon savory
2 cubes chicken bouillon, or 2 tablespoons chicken gravy	1½ cups carrots, peeled, cubed
1 medium onion, peeled, sliced	1½ cups celery, diced
	½ cup peas (fresh or frozen)
1 small bay leaf	2 tablespoons butter
2 sprigs parsley	2 tablespoons flour
1 teaspoon salt or more	

1. Wash chicken and cut into individual portions. Be sure to use liver and gizzards.

2. In a 5-quart kettle, bring the chicken and water to a boil. Skim off scum, add bouillon cubes, onion, herbs, and seasonings, simmer uncovered ½ hour. Add vegetables, simmer covered for ¾ hour. Taste to check seasonings. You may want more salt.

3. Over low heat, melt the butter in a saucepan, stir in the flour, mixing until smooth. Quickly stir in 3 cups of chicken broth. Return to the soup kettle, bring to a boil. Simmer 5 minutes more.

4. To serve, reheat over low flame, serve in large soup plates, dividing meat and vegetables among guests.

Makes 10 to 12 portions. Double the ingredients to serve 20 to 24, except for the salt. Bouillon cubes are salty, so taste the soup before doubling the salt.

Take-It-Along Tips: Take this to the party in its cooking kettle and follow step 4 when you get there.

Scotch Broth

A hearty cold-weather soup to serve with crusty hot bread and butter. Can be made using leftover lamb leg instead of the shoulder cut. With a salad and dessert, this makes a complete meal.

3 pounds lamb shoulder, bone in	1½ teaspoons salt
	⅛ teaspoon pepper
3½ quarts cold water	1 cup barley
1 bay leaf	2 tablespoons butter
1 cup diced carrots	2 tablespoons flour
1 cup diced celery	2 tablespoons finely chopped parsley
1 cup leek, washed, sliced	
1 cup turnips, peeled, diced	

1. Cut the meat into 2-inch cubes; retain bones.
2. In a 4-quart kettle, place water, meat bones, meat, bay leaf, and bring to a boil. Over medium heat, cook ¾ hour, skimming froth often. Add vegetables, salt, pepper, and barley; cover and simmer one hour, or until meat is tender. Taste and adjust seasonings.
3. In a small saucepan over a low heat, melt the butter, stir in the flour, and mix until smooth. Pour one cup of soup into the flour, stir smooth. Mix this back into the soup. Simmer 5 minutes more.
4. To serve, reheat over low flame and divide into large soup bowls, with meat and vegetables in each. Sprinkle with chopped parsley.

Makes 12 to 14 portions.

VARIATION. Substitute veal for lamb. When the soup is ready, mix one tablespoon of strained lemon juice with one beaten egg yolk, stir in one cup of hot broth; then stir the mixture into the soup. Reheat to serve, but do not boil.

Take-It-Along Tips: Take this to the party in its cooking kettle and follow step 4 when you get there.

Cream-of-Celery Soup

Inexpensive and delicious, offer it as the first course of a gourmet meal, or serve it with meat or cheese sandwiches for a quick portable lunch.

2 tablespoons butter	2 teaspoons salt
2 medium onions, peeled, minced	¼ teaspoon curry powder (optional)
4 cups celery, peeled, minced	¼ teaspoon pepper
1 small potato, peeled, diced	Paprika
2 tablespoons flour	
4 cubes chicken bouillon, dissolved in 4 cups boiling water	

1. Over low heat, melt the butter in a 4-quart saucepan. Add the onions and simmer, uncovered, until translucent. Add the celery and potato. Cook 5 minutes, stirring. Add the flour; stir until smooth.

Add the chicken bouillon, stirring quickly as you pour to keep the mixture smooth. Add salt, curry powder, and pepper. Simmer 20 minutes, or until celery is tender.

2. Put in blender and blend thoroughly for 2 minutes.
3. To serve, reheat, but do not boil. Garnish with paprika.

Makes 8 to 10 servings.

VARIATION. To serve cold, add ½ cup cream and chill 10 minutes in the freezer.

Take-It-Along Tips: Take this to the party in its cooking kettle and follow step 3 when you get there.

Cream-of-Mushroom Soup

Nice hot with sandwiches or cold with hot biscuits.

2 tablespoons butter	2 cups milk, heated
2 medium onions, peeled, minced	1 teaspoon salt
	¼ teaspoon pepper
2 cups fresh mushrooms, wiped, minced	4 tablespoons light cream (optional)
2 tablespoons flour	2 tablespoons parsley, minced
2 chicken bouillon cubes, dissolved in 2 cups boiling water	

1. Melt the butter in a 4-quart saucepan over low heat. Add onion. Simmer until translucent. Add mushrooms. Simmer 2 minutes, stirring. Add flour; stir until smooth. Add bouillon, then milk, stirring quickly as you pour to keep the mixture smooth. Add salt and pepper. Simmer 20 minutes.
2. Put in the blender and blend at low speed for 2 minutes.
3. Reheat before serving, over low heat. Do not boil. Add cream and garnish with parsley.

Makes 8 to 10 servings.

VARIATION: To serve cold, stir in ½ cup light cream and chill 10 minutes in the freezer.

Take-It-Along Tips: Follow recipe through step 2, take the soup to the party in its cooking kettle, and proceed with recipe.

Peanut-Butter Soup

Served with bacon or ham sandwiches, this is an inexpensive and unusual cold-weather snack.

- 2 teaspoons minced onion
- 4 tablespoons butter
- ⅔ cup peanut butter
- 4 tablespoons flour
- 3 cups chicken broth
- 3½ cups milk
- 1 cup heavy cream
- Salt
- Pepper

1. Over low heat in a heavy kettle, sauté the onion in butter until golden.
2. Remove from heat and stir in the peanut butter and flour.
3. Return to the heat and slowly stir in the chicken broth mixed with the milk and cream. Simmer, stirring constantly, until smooth and slightly thickened, about 10 minutes. Season to taste with salt and pepper.
4. To serve, reheat over low heat, stirring often.

Serves 12.

Take-It-Along Tips: Follow the recipe through step 3, take the soup to the party in its cooking kettle, and proceed with recipe.

8. Cold Cups for Hot Days

When you are asked to supply the main course for a light meal on a hot day, think of soup. Not steaming hot soups, not clear consommé soups, but rich, thick taste treats like Vichyssoise and Borscht. Too often these soups, hot or cold, are offered as an extraneous course in a big meal: Treated as the mainstay of an after-theatre party or poolside luncheon, they completely satisfy everyone and get the kind of attention they deserve.

With a cold soup, serve hot biscuits or hot rolls or warmed, crackly French bread slices, with butter, a tossed salad, and a dessert.

Soup recipes can be doubled without affecting flavor.

Vichyssoise

The most elegant of cold soups, vichyssoise is also delicious hot. Serve it hot as a rich first course for a gourmet dinner or cold for a light lunch. Use old potatoes; they thicken the soup.

2 tablespoons butter
1 large onion, peeled, minced
4 cups minced leeks
2 medium potatoes peeled, sliced thin
2 cups milk
2 cups light cream
2 teaspoons salt
1½ teaspoons pepper
¼ teaspoon nutmeg
2 tablespoons fresh chives, chopped

1. Melt the butter over low heat in a large kettle. Add the onion. Simmer until translucent and golden. Add leeks. Sauté 5 minutes, stirring. Add the potatoes, then stir in the milk and cream. Simmer 20 minutes. Add salt, pepper, nutmeg.
2. Put through a blender.
3. To serve, reheat without boiling. Serve sprinkled with chives. *Makes 8 to 10 portions.*

VARIATION: If you serve this cold, add ½ cup heavy cream and chill 15 minutes in the freezer beforehand.

Take-It-Along Tips: If the soup is to be served hot, take it to the party in its cooking kettle and finish there, as described in step 3. If to be served cold, follow instructions in the variation, take to the party in a decorative soup tureen sealed with Saran Wrap. Garnish with chives just before serving.

Borscht

Hot, or cold, this thick, rich, beet-red soup garnished with sour cream is heaven. I serve it cold as a first course for cold summer luncheons, or hot as a first course for a light supper.

2 16-ounce cans whole beets, or 6 large cooked beets, peeled	1 teaspoon salt
	1 teaspoon light brown sugar
8 cups beef stock or canned bouillon	1 tablespoon white vinegar
	10 to 12 tablespoons sour cream
1 tablespoon butter	

1. Grate the cooked beets into the stock. Place in a large kettle and simmer 5 minutes. Add butter, salt, sugar, and vinegar, and simmer 10 minutes. Put through the blender at low speed.
2. Serve in deep soup bowls; top each portion with one tablespoon fresh sour cream.

Makes 10 to 12 portions.

Take-It-Along Tips: If the Borscht is to be served hot, take it to the party in its cooking kettle, and reheat there. If it is to be served cold, turn it into a soup tureen, seal the tureen in Saran Wrap, and take it to the party. As each portion is served, top it with sour cream. Or take the sour cream in a decorative sauce boat and pass it among guests.

Chilled Cream-of-Shrimp Soup

A bowlful of this pretty pink soup with a few whole shrimp as garnish makes an elegant first course.

- 3 cups water
- 1 bay leaf
- 2 to 2½ teaspoons sea or table salt
- 1 pound unshelled fresh or thawed frozen shrimp, washed
- 2 tablespoons butter
- 1 small onion, peeled, minced
- 2 tablespoons flour
- ⅛ teaspoon white pepper
- Pinch nutmeg
- ½ teaspoon lemon juice
- 1 cup light cream

1. In a medium kettle, place water, bay leaf, and 1 to 1½ teaspoons salt. Cover and bring to a rapid boil. Add shrimp and simmer 10 minutes. Let shrimp stand in the cooking liquid 10 minutes.
2. Peel and devein the shrimp. Reserve the cooking liquid, but discard the bay leaf. Chop all but a quarter of the shrimp.
3. Over low heat, melt butter in the kettle, add the minced onion, and simmer until translucent. Stir in the flour. Gradually stir in the cooking liquid, keeping the mixture smooth by rapid, constant stirring. Simmer 5 minutes. Add salt, pepper, nutmeg, lemon juice, and chopped shrimp.
4. At low speed, blend until smooth. Pour into a soup tureen, stir in cream and the reserved whole shrimp.
5. Serve well chilled.

Makes 8 portions. Double ingredients, except the bay leaf, to serve 16.

Take-It-Along Tips: Chill, take to the party in a tureen, covered with Saran Wrap.

Jellied Gazpacho

A glamorous variation on the cold tomato-flavored soup called gazpacho, these delicious little jellied cubes are lovely piled into your favorite tureen or punch bowl.

1 15-ounce can tomato juice	½ cucumber, peeled, slivered
1½ cups water	2 tablespoons corn oil
1 beef bouillon cube	2 tablespoons wine vinegar
1 package unflavored gelatin, dissolved in 3 tablespoons cold water	1 teaspoon salt
2 large ripe tomatoes, peeled	¼ teaspoon freshly ground black pepper
½ green pepper, cored	1 lemon, sliced thinly

1. In a medium saucepan, heat the tomato juice, water, and beef cube. Add the softened gelatin to the stock mixture. Heat, stirring, until gelatin dissolves. Set aside.
2. Chop the tomatoes and pepper and sliver the cucumber. Pour the oil and vinegar over them and season with salt and pepper. Let stand 20 minutes.
3. Stir the vegetables into the tomato-juice mixture; pour into a large, shallow, glass pan, and allow to set, covered, in the refrigerator.
4. To serve, cut into cubes and pile into a tureen. Garnish with slices of lemon.

Makes 4 to 6 servings.

Take-It-Along Tips: Take this to the party in its glass pan and take along a small tureen. Follow step 4 at the host home.

Garden Rhubarb Soup

This is a sweet soup popular in Sweden. It makes a delicious lunch on a hot day. Serve it with freshly made biscuits.

4 cups fresh or frozen rhubarb, diced	2 tablespoons cornstarch, dissolved in ½ cup cold water
4 cups water	
1 cup sugar	1 teaspoon vanilla extract
1 teaspoon grated orange rind	½ cup dry white wine, optional
1 stick cinnamon	
2 whole cloves	8 to 10 thin orange slices

1. Combine first 6 ingredients in a large kettle. Over medium heat, bring to a boil. Reduce heat, cover, and simmer for 20 minutes.

2. Stir dissolved cornstarch into rhubarb mixture. Bring to a boil, remove immediately from heat. Discard cinnamon stick and cloves. Mix in the vanilla. Chill overnight or for several hours.

3. When ready to serve, if desired, add a tablespoon of wine to each portion and garnish with an orange slice.

Makes 8 to 10 servings. Double ingredients to serve 16 to 20, but not the cinnamon.

Take-It-Along Tips: Take this to the party in a serving tureen and follow step 3 at the host home.

PART 4

Outdoor Parties

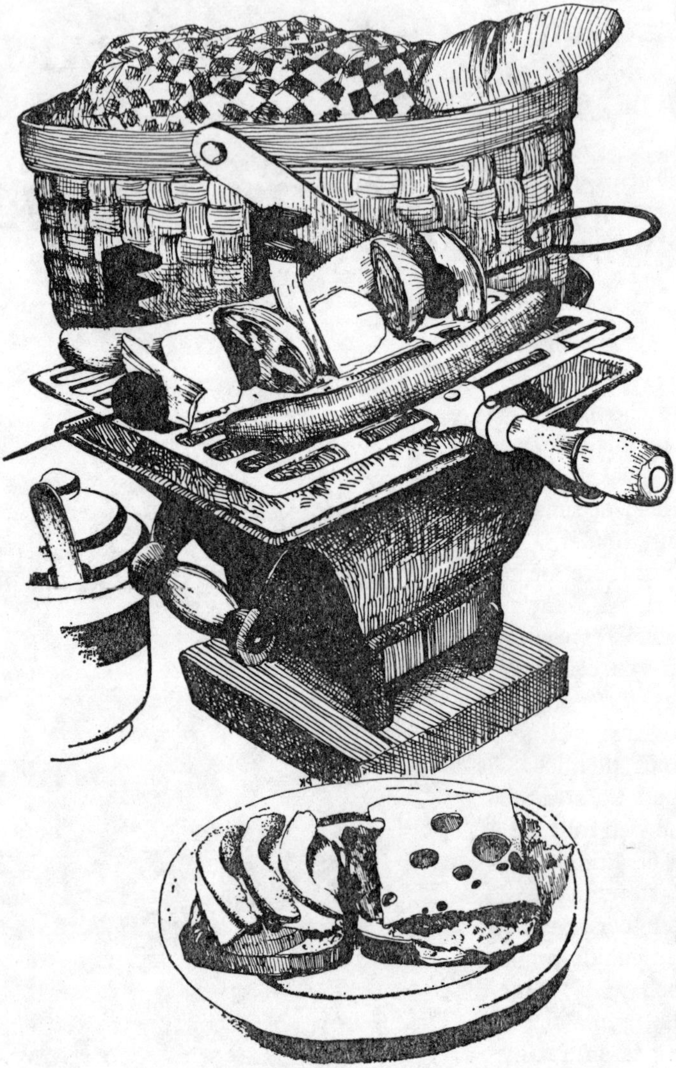

9. Beach Partying

The clambake is the traditional share-the-work party. There's a pit to be dug, firewood to collect, seaweed to gather, lobster and clams and chicken to wrap and cook, watermelon to distribute, and singing to lead at sunset as the fire dies down and the sound of the waves grows louder.

But there are beach parties that require less organization and less effort. A Country Corn Roast set by the lake, or the sea, has almost as much appeal as a clambake, and corn is such an all-purpose flavor that you can serve anything with it, from barbecued chicken to hot dogs.

Simpler yet are the beach parties whose food is toted in a wide-mouth thermos. Classic seashore fare such as Oyster Stew, Deer Island Lobster Stew, and New England Clam Chowder, served with sandwich rolls are easier to carry and taste very good.

The European counterpart of the clambake is Bouillabaisse, a big fish stew. In the old days, the bouillabaisse was made from the day's catch, whatever it was, from shellfish to sea bass, and cooked in a big open cauldron above a beach fire. When you're in the mood to do a beach party that's different, try it. Serve with it rolls and butter, wine (white or rosé), fruit for dessert, and you'll be duplicating parties peasant families along the Mediterranean still hold on its shores.

When you are planning a beach party involving a fire for cooking or ornamental purposes, be aware that many public beaches require that permits be issued for the building of fires and the serving of alcoholic beverages.

Best Clambake Ever—for Twenty-Five

A clambake on the beach can be a great community party. It takes organizing—a pit has to be dug, 6 to 7 bushels of seaweed gathered with enough kindling and split logs to make a roaring fire. Use paper plates and serve the melted butter in paper cups. The traditional clambake beverage is beer; the dessert, great chunks of cold watermelon—both kept chilled in tubs of ice. If you want to hold your clambake in the backyard, build a "pit" on top of the ground, using cinder blocks, and set the food on a sheet of metal (any old, paintless car hoods handy?) large enough to cover the pit. You'll need about a quarter cord of dry, split logs. Protect your hands with work gloves while removing the cooked food from the pit.

- 2 packages cheesecloth
- 1 bushel softshell clams
- 25 white baking potatoes
- 4½ dozen ears of corn
- 25 live 1-pound lobsters, and/or broiler chickens, halved
- 3 pounds butter, melted, hot

1. Cut the cheesecloth into 10-inch squares. Scrub the clams to remove *all* sand and tie them into the cheesecloth squares, about 8 to a bundle.
2. Scrub the potatoes and tie each one in a cheesecloth square.
3. Shuck the corn, removing the coarse outer leaves and the silk: let the thin inner husks remain.
4. About 4 hours before mealtime, start the fire. Dig a shallow pit about 2 feet deep by 5 feet square and line it with brick or large flat stones. Lay kindling covered with logs on the rock bed. Light the fire and let it burn down completely. By the time the fire dies down, the rocks should be red-hot. Then you begin the cooking.
5. Rake away the embers and logs that haven't burned, then spread a 3-inch layer of wet seaweed on the hot rocks. Place a layer of clams on the seaweed, then a layer of corn, and then a layer of potatoes. Arrange the live lobsters on top of the pile. If you are using chicken, season then seal each half in foil before you lay it in the pit.
6. Cover these layers with a 2-inch layer of seaweed, and seal the pit with a large canvas cover, anchored securely on all sides so that

no steam can escape. Set the butter in a covered kettle in the center of the canvas where it will melt while the food cooks.

7. Cook for about one hour. Then roll back the cover, rake off the seaweed, and using tongs, help the guests to help themselves. Serve melted butter in paper cup to each guest.

Serves twenty-five.

Take-It-Along Tips: Everything travels to the beach uncooked, preferably cut up, wrapped, and ready to go, however, or you'll get sand in the chicken.

Country Corn Roast

Fresh corn and chicken on the outdoor grill are a treat—try them this way. Start the fire half an hour before cooking time, and set the rack 4 to 6 inches above the coals. A green salad is just right with this.

FOR EACH GUEST:

2 ears of fresh corn	½ broiler chicken
3 teaspoons softened butter or margarine	Pepper
	Pinch rosemary
Salt	Pinch marjoram, crushed (optional)

1. Shuck the corn. Place each ear on a piece of foil, spread with 2 teaspoons softened butter, and sprinkle generously with salt and pepper. Wrap foil securely around each ear of corn. Don't seal seam, but fold or twist foil around ends (that way the corn will roast instead of steam). Spread one teaspoon butter on each piece of chicken; sprinkle with herbs.

2. Place the chicken on the hot grill and, turning twice, roast over the hot coals for 15 to 20 minutes. Add corn and roast till corn is tender, turning the ears frequently. Serve with more butter, salt, and pepper.

Take-It-Along Tips: Follow step 1 indoors, take everything to the cooking site ready to go on the fire.

Oyster Stew

With a green salad on the side, this makes a complete meal. Serve with crisp, warmed crackers or hot French or Italian bread and butter curls.

1 pint shucked oysters with liquor	⅛ teaspoon mace, powdered
	1 small bay leaf
1 tablespoon onion, thinly sliced	⅓ cup butter
	⅓ cup flour
4 cups milk	½ cup light cream, scalded
2 stalks celery or ¼ teaspoon celery salt	½ tablespoon minced parsley

1. In medium saucepan, place the oysters with their liquor and the onion. Over low heat, bring to a boil and simmer 5 minutes. Set aside.
2. In a medium saucepan, scald the milk with the celery, mace, and bay leaf. Strain into a bowl.
3. Over low heat, melt the butter in a large kettle. Stir in the flour and mix smooth. Then stir in the milk and cream. Adjust seasoning to taste. Remove from heat. Add oysters and juice.
4. When ready to serve, reheat *briefly,* and serve at once, garnished with parsley.

Makes 6 generous servings. Double quantities to serve 12, but use only one bay leaf.

Take-It-Along Tips: Take this to your beach party in big, wide-mouthed thermos bottles, ready to serve. Don't put it into the thermoses boiling hot—or the oysters will continue to cook and come out leathery; instead, put the stew into the thermoses at a temperature a little above lukewarm. Or, take the recipe through step 3, pour very hot into thermoses, take the oysters to the party uncooked, and add to the thermoses 5 minutes before serving. Close the thermoses, and let the oysters cook in the boiling hot soup before serving.

Deer Island Lobster Stew

Chunks of lobster in a creamy broth. An elegant way to begin a gourmet dinner, this also makes a meal by itself.

3 pounds live lobster or 28 ounces frozen lobster meat	2 cups raw potatoes, peeled, diced
½ cup butter	2 cups water, boiling
1½ teaspoons salt	2 cups whole milk, heated
Pinch of pepper	Paprika
1 medium onion, minced	

1. If you have live lobsters, place them in boiling water, cover, and when the water returns to a boil, simmer 10 minutes. Cook frozen lobster half the time directed. Remove meat from lobster shells and cut into ½-inch chunks.

2. In a small saucepan, melt ¼ cup butter. Add the lobster meat. Sauté over medium heat with ½ teaspoon of the salt and the pepper for 3 minutes.

3. In a medium soup kettle, melt 2 tablespoons butter. Add the onion and simmer until translucent. Add the potatoes, one teaspoon salt, and 2 cups of boiling water. Simmer over medium heat for 15 minutes, or until potatoes are cooked; add the lobster meat and milk, remove from heat.

4. To serve, reheat and pour into serving bowls with a dab of the remaining butter. Garnish with a sprinkling of paprika in each bowl.

Makes 6 to 8 good-sized portions.

Take-It-Along Tips: Take this to the party in big, wide-mouthed thermoses, as described in the "Take-It-Along Tips" in the preceding recipe. Pour into thermoses at a temperature between lukewarm and hot; if the stew is boiling hot, the lobster will cook too tough during its traveling time.

New England Clam Chowder

This tastes best when it is made hours before serving.

1 quart shucked steamer clams	½ teaspoon salt
¼ pound salt pork, diced	⅛ teaspoon pepper
1 large onion, peeled, finely sliced	Hot water
	4 cups milk
3 medium-sized potatoes sliced thin	6 split, large, hard crackers
	2 tablespoons butter

1. Remove the tough neck portion of each clam. Separate the belly or soft part from the firm part. Reserve the soft parts, and chop the firm parts coarsely. Strain the clam liquor.

2. In a kettle over medium-high heat, fry salt pork until crisp; add and sauté the onion slices until golden. Add potatoes, salt, and pepper, and sauté slowly, stirring often, for 10 minutes.

3. Add the chopped portion of the clams and liquor and hot water to cover. Simmer 20 minutes.

4. Add the cleaned soft parts and cook 3 minutes more. Skim off any scum. Remove from heat and add milk.

5. When ready to serve, add crackers, reheat briefly; do not boil. Serve in bowls and add a dab of butter to each.

Makes 6 generous servings.

Take-It-Along Tips: Take this to the party in its cooking kettle and reheat over coals that have burned down. Then follow step 5.

Bouillabaisse

Fish for bouillabaisse should be very fresh. On the Mediterranean coast of France, where the dish originated, it is the custom to spend the day fishing for the ingredients, and to make this fish soup with whatever the day's catch of fish and shellfish brings. The most suitable fish available here are cod, flounder, haddock, red snapper, sea bass, or perch. Clean the fish, cut away the fillets (meat), and save the heads and bones. Suitable shellfish are crab, lobster, and scallops. Serve with rosé wine or a dry white wine. This is a complete meal.

4 pounds fish fillets of several kinds	2¼ quarts water Fish heads, bones
2 pounds lobster, crab, scallops	1 medium carrot, peeled, halved
16 to 24 mussels, optional	1 bay leaf
½ cup olive oil	1 tablespoon salt
½ cup chopped leeks, white parts only, or green onions, or onion	⅛ teaspoon black pepper
	⅛ teaspoon saffron
	1 tablespoon chopped parsley
2 large tomatoes, peeled, seeded, or 1 cup canned whole tomatoes, drained	6 to 8 slices stale or toasted French bread
2 cloves garlic, peeled	

1. Cut large fish fillets into crosswise slices, 2 inches wide. Split the lobster, lift the tail flap from the crab. Wash scallops. Scrape mussel shells until clean and rinse thoroughly to remove *all* sand. If using frozen shellfish meat, thaw while preparing bouillabaisse.

2. In a large soup kettle over low heat, heat the olive oil. Add leeks and simmer 5 minutes without browning. Add tomatoes, garlic, and simmer 5 minutes more. Add water, fish heads, bones and trimmings, carrot, bay leaf, salt, pepper, and saffron. If using fresh shellfish, add now. Bring to a boil and simmer, uncovered, skimming off scum, for 20 minutes. Remove shellfish and set aside. Strain bouillon; discard fish heads and bones. Correct seasonings.

3. About 20 minutes before serving, bring the broth to a boil, re-

turn lobster and crab meat to the kettle. Add firm fish (snapper, bass, perch), bring quickly to a boil and keep boiling rapidly, uncovered, for 5 minutes. Then add the soft-fleshed fish (cod, flounder, haddock), scallops, and mussels. Return to a boil and cook exactly 5 minutes more.

4. Serve the bouillabaisse in large soup bowls. In each bowl, place a slice of French bread and a portion of each type of fish and shellfish; cover with broth.

Makes 8 to 10 generous servings.

Take-It-Along Tips: Follow this recipe through step 2, then pack the cooked lobster and crab with raw fish fillets for the trip, and set scallops and mussels on top. Carry broth in its cooking kettle. Then follow steps 3 and 4.

Cod of the Sea

1 10-pound Cod or Striped Bass	3½ cups water
1 tablespoon salt	2 tablespoons butter
1 small onion	3 tablespoons flour
1 bay leaf	3 cups water celery cooked in
⅓ teaspoon dried thyme	Salt
1 small carrot	Pepper
3 cups celery, in 2-inch strips	Minced parsley

1. Set to boil enough water to cover the fish, and add to it salt, onion, bay leaf, thyme, and carrot.
2. Place celery, cut into thin strips 2 inches long, in 3½ cups boiling, unsalted water and cook rapidly until tender. Drain, shake dry over heat.
3. Wrap fish in cheesecloth, lower into boiling water and bring back to the boil. Poach for 20 minutes. Lift from water and drain. Break meat into boneless chunks and place in a heated serving dish.
4. Melt butter in a saucepan, stir in flour, add hot water celery cooked in. Stir and simmer for 5 minutes. Put some of the cream sauce with the cooked celery into a blender and whip smooth. Or rub through a sieve. Return to heat, simmer a few minutes, and season with salt and pepper. Pour over fish chunks and serve hot.

Serves 6 to 8.

Take-It-Along Tips: Follow recipe through step 3, but after you have removed the fish from the water, place it in a warmed, long serving platter. Do not remove it from its cheesecloth wrap. Finish the recipe and take sauce and fish to the party wrapped in heavy foil and overwrapped in newspaper to keep it warm. At the host home, unwrap the fish, turn it onto its serving platter, garnish with parsley, and place before the guests. With each portion, serve the sauce, which has been reheated: Though the fish will be lukewarm, the sauce will be hot enough to compensate.

10. Hawaiian Luaus

How to organize a luau? In the islands, where they have ti leaves, to wrap and bake in, and all the Oriental ingredients necessary for this special brand of cooking, it's easy. In mainland America, you have to improvise. And not too many will criticize your lack of authenticity.

The main ingredient of a luau is the food, and a slow fire to bake things over, or in. You can wrap things in heavy foil, doubled, instead of using ti leaves.

Or, you can light a pretty fire, play Hawaiian music, deck the guests in giant marigold leis, bring most of the food to the party cooked, and finish off, or rewarm it all over the embers when the fire dies down.

Don't double the recipes here. Instead, have each guest bring one of several different dishes, and mix and match flavors, as you do at a Chinese restaurant.

In the dessert chapter, Chapter 20, you'll find a recipe for a luau dessert, and in Chapter 21 there's drink especially appropriate for a luau.

Hawaiian Duck with Bananas

An exotic duck done with bananas, pineapple, and orange. Serve it with baked sweet potatoes or yams.

1 5- to 6-pound duck, fresh or thawed	4 bananas
	1 tablespoon vegetable oil
1 8-ounce can pineapple chunks, drained, chopped	Juice ½ lemon, strained
	1 orange
1 cup red wine	1 tablespoon cornstarch
Salt	1 cup warm water
Pepper	

1. Preheat oven to 400°.
2. Cut the duck into 8 pieces and arrange these in a roasting pan. Pour the pineapple syrup and the wine over the duck. Season with salt and pepper and bake 40 minutes, basting frequently. Remove and keep warm.
3. Lay the unpeeled bananas on an ovenproof dish and brush the skins with oil. Sprinkle with lemon juice and bake in the oven at 400° for 10 minutes. Half peel each when done.
4. Grate the rind from the orange, and reserve. Juice the orange and strain the juice. Blend the cornstarch with the juice. Remove the duck to a serving platter. Keep warm. Scrape the juices from the roasting pan, mixing with one cup of water over low heat. Mix in the orange juice. Bring to a boil and cook, stirring, until thickened, adding the grated rind of the orange and the pineapple at the end.
5. Serve the duck surrounded with the bananas and pour the sauce over the duck.

Makes 6 to 8 servings.

Take-It-Along Tips: Follow the recipe through step 4 and take the duck to the party on its serving dish, surrounded by bananas. Wrap in heavy-duty foil, and overwrap in newspapers to keep warm. Take the sauce in its cooking kettle, reheat at the host home, and pour simmering hot over each portion of duck as it is served.

Sweet-Sour Spareribs—Hawaiian Style

This is a luau dish to be cooked indoors, taken to the party, and finished off over a grill outdoors.

4 pounds pork spareribs cut into 3-inch pieces	2 tablespoons butter
Salt	2 tablespoons cornstarch
Pepper	1 clove garlic, peeled, minced
1 20-ounce can pineapple chunks	⅓ cup vinegar
⅓ cup chopped celery	2 tablespoons soy sauce
⅓ cup seeded, shredded green pepper	1 tablespoon sugar
	½ teaspoon ground ginger
	½ teaspoon salt

1. Arrange ribs, meaty side down, in a shallow roasting pan. Season with salt and pepper. Roast at 450° for 30 minutes. Drain off excess fat. Turn ribs meaty side up. Reduce oven temperature to 325° and continue roasting for one hour.
2. Meanwhile, drain pineapple, reserving syrup. In saucepan, cook celery and green pepper in butter until tender. Combine cornstarch and reserved pineapple syrup, add to pepper mixture; cook and stir until mixture thickens and bubbles. Stir in pineapple bits, garlic, vinegar, soy sauce, sugar, ginger, and the salt. Pour over ribs.
3. Place pan over very hot coals and cook ribs 30 minutes more, basting occasionally.

Makes 6 to 8 generous portions.

Take-It-Along Tips: Follow the recipe through step 2 and carry the ribs to the party in their roasting pan, sealed in heavy-duty foil. Then follow step 3.

Luau Pungent Turkey

For a spur-of-the-moment luau dish, try your turkey leftovers in this sauce. Offer with plain boiled rice or with mashed yams.

- 2 cloves garlic, peeled, minced
- 1 tablespoon soy sauce
- 2 cups tomato juice
- 1 tablespoon vinegar
- ½ cup dark brown sugar
- ½ fresh pineapple, diced or 1 (13¾-ounce) can pineapple bits
- ½ cup minced sweet pickles
- ½ cup sliced cauliflower
- 1 cucumber peeled, seeded, sliced
- 1 green pepper, seeded, chopped
- 12 slices cooked turkey breast

Over low heat, in a large saucepan simmer the garlic in the soy sauce for one minute. Add the tomato juice and vinegar. Cook, uncovered, over moderate heat for 15 minutes. Add the remaining ingredients, cover, simmer another 15 minutes.

Serves 6 to 8.

Take-It-Along Tips: When this dish is meant for a take-along party, complete the making of the sauce but do not include the turkey slices, which are cooked. Take the sauce and the turkey slices separately to the party, reheat the sauce at the party, with the turkey slices in it.

Chicken Livers Islander

Liver, mushrooms, and green peppers roasted on small skewers and served with a pungent sauce. Guests dip chunks of meat and vegetables in the communal sauce bowl before eating.

- 2 pounds fresh chicken livers
- 16 large mushroom caps, wiped
- 2 large green peppers, seeded
- ½ cup chicken bouillon
- 1 tablespoon soy sauce
- ½ cup prepared mustard
- ⅓ cup tomato juice
- ⅛ teaspoon garlic powder, or 1 small clove, peeled, minced

1. Cut chicken livers and mushrooms in half. Cut green peppers into strips ½ inch wide. Thread on small skewers, alternating chicken livers and vegetables.
2. Combine chicken bouillon and soy sauce. Brush mixture over chicken livers and vegetables.
3. Broil about 4 inches from the coals, or the broiler, for 8 minutes, or until livers are cooked. Brush with bouillon mixture several times during broiling; turn skewers once.
4. Blend remaining ingredients and heat in a small saucepan. Serve the skewers on a platter with sauce in a bowl on the side.

Serves 8 to 10.

Take-It-Along Tips: Take the livers and vegetables, raw, threaded on skewers to the party. Prepare the bouillon, step 2, and the sauce, step 4. Take all to the party and finish the recipe there.

Luau Riblets

Breast of lamb, which is often a bargain meat, is excellent for a party prepared this way. We do it in a roaster that has a revolving spit, but it can be roasted on an outdoor grill with the rack set 5 to 6 inches above hot coals. Cook 45 minutes. Or bake it in the oven at 325° for about one hour.

2½ pound breast of lamb in one piece, with fat trimmed off	½ cup soy sauce
	1 tablespoon prepared horseradish
½ cup lemon juice, strained	1 teaspoon prepared mustard
½ cup beef bouillon	

1. Place lamb in a large bowl; blend the other ingredients and pour over the meat. Marinate at room temperature several hours or overnight.
2. Thread the meat onto a spit, reserving the marinade. Roast about 1½ hours or until the meat begins to pull away from the bones. Baste *frequently* with reserved marinade as the meat cooks.
3. To serve, cut into individual riblets.

Makes 6 servings. Double the meat and make ¼ more sauce to serve twice as many guests.

Take-It-Along Tips: Follow step one, take the meat to the party in its marinade dish, sealed in Saran Wrap, then finish the recipe.

Fish Baked in Ti Leaves

Ti leaves are available in some specialty shops but the thin inner husks of corn can be substituted. In a pinch, use foil to wrap the fish. The ti is a palmlike plant sometimes called cabbage tree.

3 pounds whole butterfish, mullet, bass, or halibut fillets	6 ti leaves or corn husks, or strips of foil
1½ tablespoons coarse salt	½ lemon, sliced

1. Rub both sides of fish with salt. If you have ti leaves, use a sharp knife to remove the fibrous center part. Divide the fish fillets among the 6 leaves. Arrange the lemon slices over the fish. Wrap fish and tie with thread or string.

2. Set the fish packages in a shallow pan and bake at 350° for 40 minutes. Or bury the fish in a bed of dying coals and bake for one hour.

Makes 6 servings.

Take-It-Along Tips: Take the wrapped fish to the party in their cooking pan, wrapped in Saran Wrap, and finish there.

Fish Adobo

This dish is a little more difficult to tote than other luau recipes.

- 3 pounds sole or bass fillets
- ½ cup water
- 1½ teaspoons salt
- ¼ cup cider vinegar
- ½ teaspoon paprika
- 2 cloves garlic, peeled minced
- ¾ teaspoon black pepper
- 1 teaspoon chopped fresh ginger, or ½ teaspoon ground ginger
- ¼ cup dry sherry
- 2 tablespoons ginger ale
- 1½ pounds fresh spinach

1. Place fish fillets in a bowl.
2. Combine water, salt, vinegar, paprika, garlic, pepper, ginger, sherry, and ginger ale, and pour over the fish fillets. Marinate at room temperature one hour, turning twice.
3. Transfer to a medium skillet and simmer over low heat, covered, for 20 minutes. Remove the fish from the skillet with a slotted spoon. Set on a warm serving platter; cover and keep warm.
4. Add spinach to the hot marinade in the pan, cover, and simmer 5 minutes. Remove the spinach with a slotted spoon and garnish the fish platter with it; then pour the remaining sauce over all and serve as soon as possible.

Makes 4 generous portions.

Take-It-Along Tips: If the dish is to travel, take the finished fish to the party in a serving platter wrapped in foil, and overwrapped in newspaper to keep warm. Take the sauce in its cooking kettle, reheat at the party, and serve very hot over the fish portions.

Roast Pork Loin with Honey-Baked Bananas

A pungent dish that usually is a big hit.

1 5-pound pork loin	6 bananas, peeled
Salt	12 tablespoons butter or
Pepper	margarine, melted
1 12-ounce jar pineapple	Juice ½ lemon
preserves	¼ cup honey
⅓ cup horseradish mustard	

1. Place the pork loin on a rack in a shallow roasting pan; season with salt and pepper.
2. Bake, uncovered, at 325° for 2½ hours or until a meat thermometer registers 170°. Pour off the drippings.
3. In a small saucepan, heat together the pineapple preserves and horseradish mustard. Baste the roast with a little of this sauce during the last 15 minutes of roasting; reserve the remaining sauce to serve hot with the roast.
4. Arrange the peeled bananas around the pork. Brush 2 tablespoons melted butter over each and the lemon juice mixed with the honey. Bake at 325° for 15 minutes, turning the bananas twice.

Makes 12 to 14 portions. Serve ½ or ⅓ of a banana with each portion.

Take-It-Along Tips: Take the pork, cooked through step 3, to the party along with the prepared bananas, and the lemon juice mixed with honey. Finish step 4 at the party.

Hawaiian Rump Roast

This is a casserole, luau style.

- 1 4-pound rolled beef rump roast
- 2 tablespoons shortening
- 1 medium onion, peeled, sliced thin
- 3 tablespoons soy sauce
- ¼ teaspoon ground ginger
- ⅛ teaspoon pepper
- ¼ cup water
- 1 8-ounce can pineapple chunks
- ¼ cup sliced celery
- ½ cup cold water
- ¼ cup all-purpose flour

1. In a large Dutch oven over low heat, brown the roast on all sides in hot shortening. Add onions, soy sauce, ginger, pepper, and water. Cover tightly; simmer for 2½ hours, or until tender. Add pineapple and juice and celery. Continue cooking, covered, for 20 minutes, or until celery is tender. Remove meat to a platter and keep warm.
2. Lift out the pineapple and celery.
3. Pour the pan juices into a measuring cup and skim off the fat. Return 1½ cups of juice to the pan. Blend ½ cup cold water with the flour, stir into the juices. Simmer, stirring constantly, until thickened and bubbly; cook one minute more. Season with salt and pepper. Add reserved pineapple and celery. To serve slice beef and ladle this sauce over each serving.

Makes 8 to 10 servings.

Take-It-Along Tips: Make this the day before and take to the party with the sauce. Reheat in the sauce at 325° before serving.

Salad for a Luau

½ medium head lettuce
2 pounds endive
1 7-ounce jar pimientos, drained
1 2-ounce jar pimientos

1 cup chicken bouillon
¼ teaspoon dry mustard
1 teaspoon parsley flakes
½ teaspoon tarragon leaves

1. Line a bowl with washed, crisped lettuce leaves. Cut bottom from each stalk of endive flat so that it will stand upright. Gently separate the tops of the leaves. Stand endive in the bowl.

2. Cut all pimientos in strips. Coil one strip around the tip of each endive. Crowd the endives together with more lettuce leaves.

3. Combine remaining pimientos and all other ingredients in a blender at medium speed for about 4 minutes, or until pimientos are puréed and dressing is well mixed. Chill.

4. Just before serving, pour the dressing over the salad.

Makes 8 to 10 servings.

Take-It-Along Tips: Prepare all the ingredients at home, including the sauce, but do not follow step one till you get to the party. The trip will joggle the standing endives.

11. Picnic Fare

The trick when you're asked to bring a dish to a picnic is to find something different from potato salad and cold chicken. Not that there's anything wrong with either, but everybody else will think of them.

This small group of recipes are ones I've found most people didn't bring. In addition, they go well with potato salad and cold chicken, are easy to prepare ahead and tote.

The Cider-Baked Picnic Ham is meant for a really big crowd and is also a delicious way to do your ham for Easter dinner.

Any of these recipes are suited to a gourmet picnic, except the young-people specials made with hot dogs; but a number of the recipes in Parts 2 and 5 make glamorous picnic fare, too, especially Chicken Breasts Chaud Froid and Cold Salmon with Green Mayonnaise.

The recipes in this chapter can be doubled or tripled for serving a really big crowd.

Mrs. Fearon's Ham Loaf

This is the king of meat loaves and is delicious cold. The recipe serves 8. For larger groups it may be doubled. Make the loaf longer and bake for the same time.

1 pound cooked ham	1 teaspoon salt
½ pound boneless pork shoulder	¼ teaspoon pepper
	½ cup water
½ pound beef chuck	4 slices canned pineapple
2 eggs	Maraschino cherries
1½ cups cornflakes, crushed	Watercress or parsley, washed
½ cup pineapple juice	
½ cup milk	

1. Heat the oven to 350°.
2. Put the ham, pork, and beef through the grinder together on the fine blade.
3. In a large bowl, mix the ground meats. Make a well in the center; break the eggs into it. Add the cornflakes, pineapple juice, milk, salt, and pepper. Blend the meat thoroughly and form a loaf.
4. Pour water into the bottom of an 8-inch by 4-inch loaf pan, and place the meat in the pan.
5. Arrange the pineapple slices decoratively over the top of the loaf; poke toothpicks stuck with cherries into the center of the slices.
6. Bake 1½ hours in a 350° oven. Remove from oven; pour off fat. Serve cold or warm on a bed of watercress.

Makes 8 to 10 portions.

Take-It-Along Tips: Wrap a wooden board the size of the loaf with heavy-duty foil, cover with watercress, set the cooled loaf upright on it, close and seal in more foil.

Cider-Baked Picnic Ham

A wonderfully sweet ham to serve lukewarm or cold at a picnic. If you decide to serve this ham hot, turn the cider drippings into a sauce: Skim the fat from the drippings, then thicken the sauce by stirring in one tablespoon of cornstarch dissolved in one tablespoon of cold water, and allow mixture to simmer 3 minutes, stirring constantly. I use Tobin's Holiday hams.

1 10- to 12-pound ham	2 teaspoons dry mustard
3 quarts sweet cider	1 teaspoon powdered cloves
2 cups maple sugar	2 cups raisins

1. In a big kettle over low heat, simmer the ham in the cider for 2 hours. Remove and skin the ham. Reserve the cider.
2. Make a thick paste with the maple sugar, mustard, cloves, and ¼ to ½ cup of the hot cider. Smear the ham with the paste.
3. Place the ham in the baking pan, pour the cider liquor over it, add the raisins, and bake 1½ hours at 325°. Baste often.

Makes 20 to 24 portions.

Take-It-Along Tips: Remove the ham from the baking pan 15 minutes before it is done, and place on a carving platter. At once, wrap the platter and the ham in heavy-duty foil, then overwrap in several layers of newspapers. It will finish cooking during the trip.

Ham in Wine Jelly

Diced ham in a rich, chicken-and-wine-flavored jelly. A hint of tarragon and the chopped parsley make it special. This is a dish for a gourmet picnic, and so easy and pretty to serve.

- 3 cups chicken bouillon or consommé
- 1 cup dry white wine
- 2 shallots, or green onions, minced
- 1 teaspoon minced fresh tarragon, or ½ teaspoon dry
- 2 envelopes unflavored gelatin
- 1 tablespoon tarragon vinegar
- 4 cups cooked ham, diced small
- 5 tablespoons minced parsley

1. Over low heat in a medium saucepan, simmer the chicken bouillon, wine, shallots, and tarragon for 20 minutes. Strain through cheesecloth, and allow 20 minutes to cool.
2. Dissolve the gelatin in ½ cup cooled stock; mix back into the stock. Stir in the vinegar.
3. Place the diced ham in a glass serving bowl and pour over enough stock to half cover it.
4. Chill the remaining stock in the refrigerator; when it begins to thicken, stir the minced parsley into it. Pour this over the ham.
5. Chill until the gelatin is set, or overnight, and serve in wedges cut directly from the bowl.

Makes 8 portions.

Take-It-Along Tips: Take to the party in its bowl and serve from the bowl, as described in step 5.

Galantine De Porc Marcel

The French make wonderful dishes using portions of meat we often overlook. Try this pork preserve. It's as popular as the pâté at my parties and great picnic fare. It will keep for 2 weeks in the refrigerator and up to 6 months in the freezer.

2½ pounds boneless shoulder of pork	¼ teaspoon savory
1½ pounds pork hocks	¼ teaspoon thyme
1 onion, stuck with 8 cloves	⅛ teaspoon nutmeg
3 cups water	3 small garlic cloves, peeled
2½ teaspoons salt	1 tablespoon minced parsley
¼ teaspoon pepper	

1. In a heavy saucepan, combine meats, onion, water, salt, pepper, savory, thyme, and nutmeg. Bring to a boil and simmer slowly until meat is thoroughly cooked, 1½ to 2 hours. Remove the meat. Reserve the cooking liquid.

2. Remove the rinds from the pork hocks, and blend the rinds in the electric blender with the garlic, parsley, and one cup of the cooking liquid. Remove the pork hock meat from the bones, and chop coarsely. Turn it into a large bowl and stir in the blended rind mixture. Check the seasonings and correct to your taste.

3. Pour into a 4-quart mold that has been rinsed in cold water. Refrigerate overnight before serving. Unmold onto a large platter.
Serves 12 to 15.

Take-It-Along Tips: For picnics, serve directly from the mold.

Aspic of Tongue

A sharply flavored sauce, such as horseradish or mustard, is delicious with this elegant aspic. Or make Vinaigrette Sauce. Serve the tongue with French bread and butter curls and a green salad.

1 4½-pound smoked tongue	1 tablespoon unflavored gelatin
Cold water	¼ cup water
1 carrot, peeled, sliced	Lettuce or parsley
2 stalks celery	Mustard or horseradish sauce
1 large onion, stuck with 6 cloves	
1 large bay leaf	

1. In a large kettle, place the tongue and enough water to cover, along with the carrot, celery, onion, and bay leaf. Bring to a boil and simmer 45 minutes to the pound, or according to instructions on the tongue wrapper. Lift the tongue from the stock and let it cool for several hours.
2. While the tongue cools, boil the stock, uncovered, until there are only 2 cups left.
3. Remove and discard the skin of the tongue and any of the tiny bones. Place the tongue in a round mold that is a fairly tight fit.
4. Dissolve the gelatin in water, stir into the 2 cups of hot cooking liquid, and pour it over the tongue. Place a small plate with a weight on top of the tongue to hold it down in the liquid. Refrigerate overnight or until set. Remove the weight.
5. To unmold, dip the mold in very hot water for half a minute to loosen the gelatin; then turn out upside-down onto a serving platter lined with lettuce or parsley. Serve tongue, thinly sliced, with mustard or horseradish sauce.

Makes 12 to 16 portions.

Take-It-Along Tips: You can serve this at a picnic from its mold, but it's more fun to unmold it. Just before you leave the house, dip the mold for half a minute in very hot water, then take to the party, and unmold there. It may be a little harder to get out of the mold than it would be the minute after it was dipped in hot water, and may not come out perfectly. But it's worth a try.

Smoked Haddock Salad

A hearty and inexpensive picnic dish that also makes a good hot-weather lunch. If you can find ripe red peppers, this dish will be prettier.

8 medium potatoes	4 fresh sweet peppers, seeded, cut into thin strips
2 long narrow cucumbers, peeled	¾ cup olive oil
Salt	4 tablespoons white wine vinegar
2 pounds smoked haddock	¼ teaspoon pepper
⅔ cup milk	

1. Boil the potatoes in their skins until tender. Do not overcook; you want them intact. Peel and slice crosswise.
2. Cut the cucumber into very thin slices and sprinkle all over lightly with salt. Allow to rest 30 minutes. Rinse and dry on a paper towel.
3. Over low heat, poach the haddock in the milk for 15 minutes. Strain and break it into large flakes with a fork.
4. In a serving bowl, place the flaked fish, the potatoes, cucumber slices, peppers, olive oil, vinegar, and pepper. (Do not salt; the haddock is already salty.) Mix well.

Makes 8 portions. To serve 16, double the ingredients but use only 1¼ cups of oil.

Take-It-Along Tips: Take the recipe through step 4, but do not mix till you get to the party.

Cold Meat Salad

A hearty salad that makes a complete lunch or picnic meal; serve with French bread and butter, and cold rosé wine.

¼ cup Oil-and-Vinegar Dressing	2 cups cooked meat, diced
	1 small onion, peeled
½ cup Fresh Mayonnaise, or commercial mayonnaise	4 cups leftover vegetables
	1 head lettuce, washed

1. Prepare the Oil-and-Vinegar Dressing (with garlic or without) in the bottom of a large wooden salad bowl. Beat in the mayonnaise. Toss the meat in the dressing. Sliver the onion on a potato peeler into the meat and toss together. Dice almost any combination of vegetables into the meat and toss again. Tear the lettuce into bits and pile over the meat. Do not toss. Chill.
2. Just before serving, stir the lettuce into the meat mixture.
Makes 8 to 10 portions.

Take-It-Along Tips: Follow the recipe through step one, take the salad to the party wrapped in Saran Wrap, and mix there.

Chef's Salad

A meat-and-cheese salad to serve as a main course.

2 cups cubed, cooked chicken	1 small head iceberg lettuce
1½ cups cubed, cooked ham	½ cup radish slices
1 cup cubed Swiss cheese	½ cup Fresh Mayonnaise or Roquefort Dressing
1 celery stalk, minced	
¼ cup Oil-and-Vinegar Dressing	

When ready to serve the salad, toss the meats, cheese, and celery, in the Oil-and-Vinegar Dressing. Taste and add more salt if desired. Arrange the lettuce in a frilly ruffle around the outer edge of a bowl. Pile the meat mixture inside, and arrange the radish slices on top. Serve with Fresh Mayonnaise or Roquefort Dressing on the side.

Makes 4 to 6 portions.

Take-It-Along Tips: Complete the recipe, and take it, wrapped in Saran Wrap, to the party. Serve dressing on the side.

Hot Frankfurter Sandwiches

Kids usually love franks this way. Bake them in an oven or take them to a cookout, and bake them in the dying embers of a fire; they are delicious.

2 cups finely chopped frankfurters	3 tablespoons chili sauce
	2 tablespoons pickle relish
⅓ cup shredded sharp process American cheese	1 teaspoon prepared mustard
2 hard-boiled eggs, chopped	¼ teaspoon celery seed
	8 frankfurter buns, split

1. Combine all ingredients except buns.
2. Butter the inside of the buns generously. Fill the buns with the mixture. Seal each securely in foil. Place on baking sheet.
3. Bake at 400° for 15 to 18 minutes. Or set them on a rack 6 inches above an open fire, and cook 20 minutes, turning often.

Makes 8 sandwiches.

Take-It-Along Tips: Follow the recipe through step 2, and take the franks to the party on their baking sheet. Complete once you get there.

Frankfurter Bake-In

A tasty supper dish for a hungry crowd on a cold day.

32 frankfurters	1 teaspoon caraway seeds
12 red-skinned apples	2 cups canned tomato sauce
4 tablespoons butter	6 thin lemon slices, unpeeled
1 teaspoon salt	1 tablespoon chopped parsley
¼ teaspoon pepper	
4 pounds sauerkraut	

1. Place the frankfurters in boiling water, cover, reduce heat and simmer 5 minutes.
2. Core and slice the apples; cut into thick rings, but do not peel.
3. In a big skillet over medium heat, sauté the apple rings in butter until soft but unbroken; season with salt and pepper.
4. Heat the sauerkraut with the caraway seeds and turn into a large serving casserole. Half-bury the frankfurters in the sauerkraut, and lay the apple slices in decorative rows over them. Cover and wrap the dish in foil.
5. Just before serving, bake in a 350° oven for ½ hour. Heat the tomato sauce and pour over the sauerkraut and frankfurters. Garnish with lemon slices and chopped parsley.

Makes 16 generous servings.

Take-It-Along Tips: Complete the recipe through step 5, but don't garnish until ready to serve. Wrapped in foil, and overwrapped in several layers of newspaper, the dish will stay warm more than an hour.

PART 5

When You Are Bringing the Main Dish

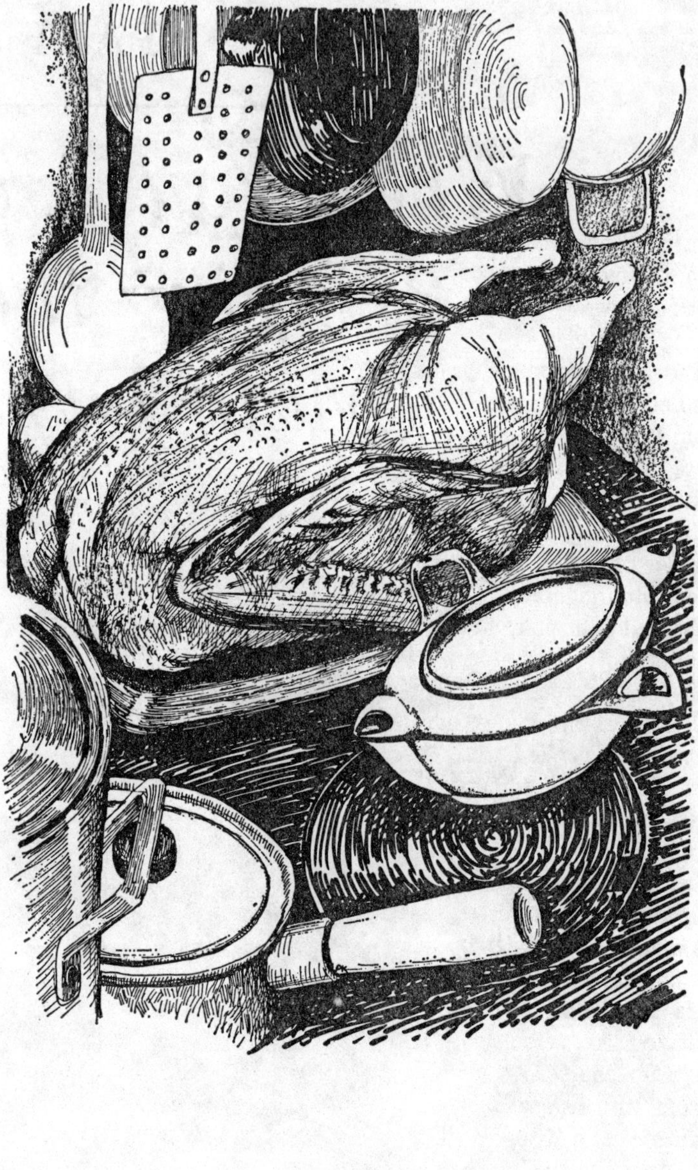

12. French Specialties

You can cook and take almost any roast, as long as you remove it from the oven twenty minutes to half an hour before it is done, wrap it in foil, overwrap in thick wads of newspaper: it will finish cooking during its travels.

But a roast for a take-it-along meal is most easily and logically handled by the hostess. The easiest dishes to bring are those you bring and cook before the guests, as Sukiyaki, in Chapter 15, or those that can be made ahead and finished, or rewarmed at the host's house.

In this chapter on specialties of French cuisine, are included a number of dishes that don't require vegetable side dishes—Cassoulet, Boeuf Bourgignonne, Blanquette de Veau among them. These can be served with plain buttered rice, crusty French bread, or just with a salad.

If you are creating a French gourmet meal, consider serving apéritifs, such as sweet or dry Vermouth, or Lilet, instead of cocktails. Serve these cooked wines over ice, and with a thin twist of lemon peel. The French don't usually serve an appetizer, but they do usually serve an hors d'oeuvre, or first course. A complete gourmet meal should include hors d'oeuvres, soup, entrée, a salad served before or with a cheese course of one to three soft (dessert) cheeses. To do it up really brown, serve a fish course after the soup course and before the meat course. Dessert can be any sweet—Crême Caramel, Chapter 20, is a favorite—or just fruit, which may be served with the cheese. Café filtre is served after the dessert, and brandy and liqueurs last.

If you like, serve sherry, dry, with the first course, wine only after the soup course. As a rule of thumb, white wine, dry and cold, is served with fish or seafood, rosé with light meats, red with strong dark meats, a light red with cheese, and a sweet cold white such as Sauternes, or else champagne, iced, with dessert.

Most recipes in this section cannot be doubled without losing their quality; that's sad to relate, but the difference between restaurant cooking and home cooking often lies in the fact that home foods are cooked in small batches.

Blanquette de Veau

A very delicate veal stew that tastes best the second day. Serve it with rice or noodles, green beans, a green salad, and a cold white wine. Peel the onions under running water—then they won't make you cry.

2 pounds boned veal shoulder, cut in 2-inch pieces	¼ cup butter
1 quart boiling water	1 pound (15) small white onions, peeled
1 small onion, peeled, stuck with 4 whole cloves	½ pound small mushrooms, wiped, stemmed
5 scraped carrots, quartered	2 tablespoons butter
1 bay leaf	¼ cup all-purpose flour
⅛ teaspoon dried thyme	2 egg yolks
½ cup diced celery	2 tablespoons lemon juice, strained
4 peppercorns	1 tablespoon minced parsley
1 teaspoon salt	

1. In a large, covered kettle, simmer the veal in the water with the onion stuck with cloves, the carrots, bay leaf, thyme, celery, peppercorns, and salt for one hour. Drain off the stock and reserve it; there should be 3½ cups. Discard the onion, bay leaf, and peppercorns. Place the veal in a large casserole.
2. While the veal cooks, melt ¼ cup butter in a medium skillet. Add the onions and simmer, tightly covered, over low heat for 25 minutes or until tender. Add to the cooked veal. In same skillet, sauté the mushrooms, uncovered, for 15 minutes, and add with liquid to the veal casserole.
3. Melt 2 tablespoons of butter in a skillet over very low heat, stir in flour slowly, stir in the reserved stock, and simmer until the mixture thickens.
4. Beat the yolks slightly with the lemon juice. Stir in ¼ cup of

the sauce. Stir this back into the rest of the sauce. Pour over the veal. Garnish with parsley. When you reheat, do not boil.

Makes 6 to 8 portions.

Take-It-Along Tips: Complete the day before the party, and reheat at the host home in a 350° oven for 20 minutes. Don't let it boil.

Navarin Printanier

Navarin, a lamb stew, is best made in spring when the lamb is young and the vegetables are *small,* fresh, and sweet. Make the Navarin the day before and reheat briefly. Offer a rosé wine with it.

- 4 tablespoons butter
- 4 small onions, peeled, sliced
- 4 pounds boned lamb shoulder or breast, cut in 2-inch cubes
- 3 tablespoons flour
- 2 cups beef bouillon
- 1 teaspoon salt
- ¼ teaspoon black pepper
- 2 sprigs fresh, or ⅛ teaspoon dried rosemary
- 1 large clove garlic, peeled, crushed
- 1 bay leaf
- 2 pounds small new potatoes, scraped
- 8 new carrots, scraped
- 8 baby turnips, peeled
- 1½ pounds fresh shelled peas, or 1 10-ounce package frozen

1. Over medium heat in a large, heavy enameled skillet, melt the butter, sauté the onions until translucent, add the lamb, and sauté until golden on all sides. Remove the lamb to a bowl. To the pan, add the flour and stir until it turns light brown. To this add the beef bouillon and stir quickly until the sauce becomes smooth.

2. Return the meat to the skillet, season with salt, pepper, rosemary, garlic, and bay leaf. Simmer with the lid on until the meat is nearly cooked, about one hour.

3. Add the potatoes, carrots, and turnips; cook slowly for another 35 to 40 minutes; then add the green peas. As soon as they are cooked, the Navarin is ready.

4. If the sauce cooks down drastically during the cooking, add more bouillon or water; it should be neither very thick nor very thin, about the consistency of a cream soup.

Makes 10 to 12 portions.

Take-It-Along Tips: This is another dish that is wonderful the second day, so make it ahead, take to the party in its serving casserole and reheat briefly—20 to 30 minutes at 350° just before serving.

Coq au Vin

Coq au vin is one of the most famous French chicken recipes. It is best made with a fresh capon and a good red Burgundy wine. Because the flavor is rich, offer plain vegetables with it, followed by a light dessert.

- 1 4-pound capon or roasting chicken, cut up
- ½ teaspoon salt
- ⅛ teaspoon black pepper
- ¼ cup cognac
- 3 cups red wine
- 2 garlic cloves, crushed
- ¼ teaspoon thyme
- 1 bay leaf
- 4 heaping tablespoons flour
- 2 cups chicken broth
- 12 small white onions, peeled
- ¾ pound mushrooms, wiped, stemmed
- 1 tablespoon butter
- 1 tablespoon chopped parsley

1. Remove the fat from the vent of the capon and dice it.
2. In a large heavy skillet over medium heat, place the diced fat and simmer until all the fat is rendered. With a slotted spoon remove the rendered bits. Sauté the capon pieces until browned all over; salt and pepper them, cover, and continue cooking slowly for 10 minutes, turning the pieces occasionally.
3. Warm the cognac, pour it over the capon, light it, and shake the pan back and forth until the flames subside. Remove the pieces to an ovenproof casserole. Pour the wine into the pan. Add the garlic and herbs. Stir up the pan juices and bring to a boil. Dissolve the flour into ½ cup of the chicken broth. Add to the pan, stirring briskly to avoid lumps. Pour in the rest of the bouillon. Pour over the chicken. Add the onions.
4. Place the casserole, covered, in an oven at 300° and bake until the meat is tender, about ¾ hour.
5. Sauté the mushrooms in butter 5 to 10 minutes. At the end, mix in the parsley. About 15 minutes before you serve, mix the mushrooms and parsley into the casserole.

Makes 8 to 10 portions.

French Specialties

Take-It-Along Tips: Follow the recipe through step 4, but don't mix the mushrooms and parsley into the casserole. Take the chicken, wrapped in foil to the party, add in the mushrooms and parsley, reheat 15 to 20 minutes in a 350° oven, then serve.

Chicken Breasts Chaud-Froid

Set in a big silver dish on a bed of watercress, these chicken breasts in a jellied cream sauce make an elegant entrée for a hot-weather party. Prepare them the day before the party and store the whole platter, sealed in Saran Wrap, in the refrigerator. Serve with a dry white wine or a dry Rosé.

- 3 large chicken breasts, split
- 4 cups cold water
- 1 teaspoon salt
- 1 stalk celery with leaves, cut into 2-inch pieces
- 1 carrot, peeled, cut into 2-inch pieces
- 1 sprig parsley
- 4 whole peppercorns
- 2 tablespoons butter
- 2 tablespoons flour
- 2 envelopes unflavored gelatin
- 1 egg yolk
- ¼ cup cream
- Truffles or ripe olives, slivered

1. Place the chicken breasts in a large saucepan. Add the water, salt, celery, carrot, parsley, and peppercorns. Cover and simmer 45 minutes, or until the chicken breasts are tender. Remove them and refrigerate until thoroughly chilled. Strain the stock into a medium kettle and boil, uncovered, until the stock is reduced to 2 cups.

2. Over low heat melt the butter in a skillet, blend in the flour. Gradually stir in the 2 cups of chicken broth. Cook, stirring constantly, until the mixture thickens and comes to a boil. Simmer 5 minutes over very low heat.

3. Soften the gelatin in cold water and stir it into the hot mixture until dissolved. Remove from the heat.

4. Beat the egg yolk with the cream. Blend a little of the hot sauce into the egg. Return the mixture to the hot sauce. Cook over low heat, stirring constantly, for 2 minutes. Do not boil. Remove from the heat and chill until slightly thickened.

5. Remove the skin from the cold chicken breasts and place them on a cake rack set over a shallow pan.

6. Spoon the thickened sauce over the chicken. If all the sauce runs off the chicken, it is not thick enough and should be chilled a few more minutes. If the sauce forms thick patches on the chicken, it is too thick. Heat it slightly to thin, then chill again. The sauce will become firm quickly on the cold chicken.

7. Press slivers of truffles or olive into the glaze before it sets to make a flowered design in the center of each breast. Refrigerate until ready to serve.

Makes 6 servings.

Take-It-Along Tips: These travel beautifully in Saran Wrap. If the dish is to travel on a very hot day, place it in an insulated bag for the trip—heat can melt the gelatin, or at least detach the breasts from the serving platter, and that makes a mess.

Boeuf Bourguignonne Marcel's Way

This is my father's method of making this great French casserole. Serve it with riced potatoes and a watercress salad with a strong garlic dressing. It deserves a really good red Bordeaux or Burgundy wine.

½-pound strip fatty pork
4 pounds beef, chuck or round, cut into 2- to 2½-inch pieces
3 tablespoons flour
4 cups dry red wine
2½ cups beef bouillon, warmed
2 teaspoons salt
½ teaspoon pepper
1 bay leaf
¼ teaspoon thyme
¼ teaspoon savory
3 tablespoons butter
1 small onion, peeled, minced
1 pound mushrooms, wiped
3 garlic cloves, finely minced
4 sprigs parsley, chopped

1. Cut the pork into ½-inch squares. In a heavy skillet over medium heat, sauté the pork to render the fat. Remove and reserve the pork.

2. Raise the heat and thoroughly brown the pieces of beef, a few at a time. Place the meat in a large heavy casserole. Lower the heat and stir the flour into the drippings, working rapidly. Stirring

constantly, mix in the wine and the bouillon. The sauce should be as thick as light cream. Add the salt and pepper, bay leaf, thyme, savory, and pork, and pour over the meat. Check the seasonings and add salt and pepper to taste.

3. Set the casserole in a preheated oven at 400°. Bring to a boil, then reduce the temperature to 300° and cook for 2½ hours, or until the meat is tender.

4. One hour before the end of the cooking period, melt the butter in a skillet and sauté the onion until golden. With a slotted spoon, remove the onion to the casserole. Separate the mushroom stems from the caps; cut both on a slant; sauté rapidly 2 minutes in the butter. Add the garlic and parsley. Skim the excess fat from the casserole and add the mushroom mixture to it. Finish the cooking and serve hot.

Makes 10 to 12 portions.

Take-It-Along Tips: Allow the dish to cool, if you like, before the trip, take to the party in its serving casserole, sealed in foil, and reheat when there for 15 to 20 minutes in a 350° oven.

Beef a L'Estouffade

This peasant recipe should be served from the casserole with big chunks of hot crusty French bread. You will be able to cut the meat with the back of a spoon. A full-bodied red wine is best with this. As a substitute for truffle, use ½ cup minced fresh mushrooms mixed with one teaspoon grated lemon rind.

- 1 canned truffle
- 1 large clove garlic, peeled
- 4 pounds top round of beef in a square piece
- 2 pork hocks
- 6 small carrots, scraped, sliced
- ¼ pound mushrooms, wiped, sliced
- 1 green pepper, thinly sliced
- 4 ounces pitted green olives
- 1 Bouquet Garni
- 1 bottle dry red wine
- 2 teaspoons salt
- ½ teaspoon black pepper

1. Heat the oven to 300°.
2. Chop the truffle and garlic together, then mash in a mortar with a pestle to make a paste.
3. In the bottom of a 3-quart Dutch oven, place the beef; spread the truffle paste on top, add the pork hocks, carrots, mushrooms, green pepper, olives, and Bouquet Garni. Pour the wine over the meat, add the salt and pepper. Cover the casserole tightly.
4. In an oven at 300°, bake the meat for 2 hours; reduce the temperature to 250° and continue baking for another 4 hours.

Serves 10 to 12.

Take-It-Along Tips: This is best when it has just finished cooking, so time it to be ready when you are ready to leave. Take the beef to the party in its cooking casserole, sealed in foil, and wrapped in newspapers. If the trip is long, deduct the time the trip will take from the cooking time: It will finish cooking in its own heat.

Elegant Stew by Nona Remos

This is the finest stew recipe I know. The trick to its very special flavor is the combination of beef and lamb, and the fact that the vegetables are cooked separately. This dish can be made a day or two ahead and reheated for a party. It will taste even better then. It can also be frozen and reheated, though the flavor won't be quite as fine. Serve it with a rich white wine, if you like, a Burgundy, or a light, dry red wine, a green salad with cheese and fruit for dessert.

- 1½ pounds stewing lamb
- 1½ pounds stewing beef
- 2 tablespoons all-purpose flour, mixed with 1 teaspoon salt and ⅛ teaspoon black pepper
- 1 tablespoon vegetable oil
- 2 tablespoons butter
- ⅛ pound salt pork
- 6 carrots, peeled
- 2 leeks
- 4 shallots
- 2 bay leaves
- 1 to 2 cups white Burgundy wine
- 1 to 2 cups beef bouillon
- 16 new white potatoes
- 16 small white onions
- 1 teaspoon sugar
- 1 pound mushrooms
- 2 tablespoons butter
- 1 teaspoon lemon juice, strained
- ¼ teaspoon salt
- ¼ cup brandy
- ¼ cup Madeira wine
- 1 tablespoon minced parsley

1. Cut away the fat and gristle from the meats and cut into 2-inch cubes. Dust the meats lightly with flour, salt, and pepper. Smear the bottom of a large, heavy skillet with oil, and over medium heat melt the butter. Brown the meats well, turning frequently. Place meats in a large casserole and scrape the pan juices over them.

2. Slice the salt pork into strips ⅛ inch thick. In the same skillet, render the fat from the salt pork.

3. Cut the carrots in half, then into 3-inch diagonals. Halve the leeks; peel the shallots, and mince. Brown the vegetables lightly in the salt pork fat. Scrape them into the casserole. Add the bay leaves, Burgundy wine, and beef bouillon. Turn the heat to medium high

until mixture boils, then simmer the meat covered, about 1½ hours, or until it is tender. As the liquid evaporates, add more Burgundy and bouillon.

4. Wash and scrape the potatoes. Peel the onions. Cover the potatoes with cold water. Add sugar. Cook until *barely* tender. Cover the onions with cold water and cook until *barely* tender. Keep warm. Wipe the mushrooms clean, slice lengthwise into ½-inch pieces. Sauté in butter until tender, sprinkle with lemon juice and salt.

5. When the meat is done, add the onions, potatoes, mushrooms, brandy, and Madeira wine to the casserole. Heat thoroughly. Garnish with parsley before serving.

Makes 8 to 10 servings.

Take-It-Along Tips: Make a day ahead or take this to the party as soon as it is done, sealed in foil, and overwrapped with newspapers. Add parsley garnish just before serving. If necessary, reheat briefly, 15 to 20 minutes in a 350° oven, before serving.

Paupiettes of Beef

Paupiettes, often called "birds," are thin slices of meat rolled up around a stuffing. This is one of my favorite dishes. It takes time but is well worth the effort. Serve the *paupiettes* with boiled rice, potatoes, or with rice and a green salad. Beaujolais wine is nice with it.

2 tablespoons butter	16 thin 4 by 4-inch slices bottom round of beef, no fat (1 ounce each)
2 medium onions, peeled, minced	Salt
½ pound fresh mushrooms, wiped, minced	Pepper
2 tablespoons grated lemon rind	Ground thyme
	All-purpose flour
2 tablespoons bread crumbs	4 tablespoons butter
½ cup minced fresh parsley	1 cup warm water
1 teaspoon salt	2 cloves garlic, peeled, crushed
¼ teaspoon black pepper	
2 eggs, slightly beaten	2 tablespoons French mustard

1. Over medium low heat in a heavy skillet, melt the butter and sauté the onions and mushrooms in it until the onions are golden. Stir in the lemon rind, bread crumbs, parsley, salt, and pepper. When the parsley is wilted, quickly stir in the beaten eggs to bind the mixture, and remove the skillet from the heat at once.

2. With a wooden mallet (or a rolling pin), flatten the beef slices until they are very thin and about twice their original size. As you finish *each* piece, season it with salt, pepper, and a pinch of thyme.

3. At the widest end of each piece of beef, place a little heap of the stuffing; roll up the beef (it will look like a lumpy sausage), and secure it with a wooden toothpick through the center. Roll each piece in flour. When all the pieces are ready, over medium-high heat in a large enameled skillet (or a plain iron one), brown the *paupiettes* in the butter and place them in a casserole or a Dutch oven. Pour warm water into the skillet, scrape up the pan juices, and pour them over the *paupiettes.* Add enough water to cover the

paupiettes, cover the casserole, bring contents to a boil, lower the heat, and simmer for 30 minutes. Mix in the garlic, add the French mustard, and cook for another 30 minutes. Taste and add salt if needed.

4. Before serving, reheat, and garnish with minced parsley.

Makes 6 to 8 portions as a main course; as an appetizer this serves 10 to 12.

Take-It-Along Tips: Follow through step 3 and take to the party in the cooking casserole. Reheat briefly, 15 to 20 minutes at 350°, before serving. If you are serving the *paupiettes* as appetizers, reheat them in a chafing dish over a very low flame. Or make the day before and reheat at the party.

Épaule De Porc à la Normande

This dish of roasted boned stuffed pork tastes best when it is cooked *with* the bones—so make sure the butcher gives them to you.

- ½ pound salt pork, diced
- 2 stalks celery, chopped
- 1 large onion, peeled, chopped
- ¼ cup chopped parsley
- Salt
- Pepper
- 5 apples, cored, peeled, cubed
- ⅓ cup brown sugar
- 2 cups croutons
- 2 pounds pork shoulder, boned
- ½ teaspoon sage
- ½ cup white wine

1. Preheat oven to 350°.
2. In a large heavy skillet over medium heat, heat the diced salt pork until the fat is rendered; remove from the pan and reserve. These pork pieces are called *lardons*.
3. To the rendered fat, add the celery, onion, parsley, salt, and pepper, and sauté 3 minutes. Remove and reserve with the *lardons*. Add the apples and brown sugar to the skillet, cover and simmer slowly until the apples are softened, 4 to 6 minutes. Remove to the bowl with the *lardons*. Mix the croutons with the *lardons* and check for seasoning. Add more salt and pepper if needed.
4. Place the boned meat on a cutting board and dust with the sage. Place the stuffing in the center; roll the meat and tie it securely with string so that it will retain its shape while cooking.

5. Place the meat in a roasting pan, bones around it, and roast at 350°. Baste the meat with the wine, turning the roast occasionally. When the pork is done, discard the bones and serve the meat.

Makes 4 to 6 portions.

For larger quantities, allow ½ pound of boned pork per person, and increase the other ingredients proportionally.

Take-It-Along Tips: Follow the recipe through step 5 and keep warm until ready to travel. Wrap in foil, overwrap in newspapers for the trip. If necessary, reheat at 350° for 20 minutes when you get to the host home.

Chou Farci Catalan

This Spanish-French stuffed cabbage is made with leftover chicken or ham and white wine or champagne. Though there is very little meat in it, it is so hearty it is served as a main course. It is nice with tiny sausages and boiled new potatoes.

1 medium leafy, green cabbage	2 slices bread, crusts removed, soaked in ½ cup milk
½ pound fresh-ground pork	1 medium onion, peeled, sliced
½ cup cooked, minced chicken or ham	4 carrots, scraped, sliced
1 medium onion, peeled, minced	1 Bouquet Garni
Salt	½ cup dry white wine or champagne
Pepper	1 cup chicken bouillon
⅛ teaspoon allspice	1 dozen chipolatas or small frankfurters or sausages

1. Place the cabbage head in boiling water for 5 minutes. Drain and let cool.
2. In a bowl, mix together pork, chicken, or ham, onion, salt, pepper, allspice, and bread.
3. Place the cabbage on a cutting board, part the leaves gently until you reach the center. Working from the center outward, spread a little of the stuffing on each leaf, pressing each back into place until the cabbage regains its original shape. Then tie it firmly with a string toward the top.

4. In a small Dutch oven, make a bed of sliced onions and carrots, add the Bouquet Garni and the cabbage. Pour the wine, mixed with the chicken broth, over the cabbage, and cover tightly. Cook for 30 minutes in a 350° oven, then lower the temperature to 250°; bake 3 hours. Then lower it again, to 200°, and bake 1½ hours more, or until a knife slides easily into the center of the cabbage. About 20 minutes before the end, set the chipolatas around the cabbage to bake.

Makes 6 to 8 portions.

Take-It-Along Tips: Take this to the party in its casserole, wrapped in foil, and overwrapped in newspaper. If necessary, reheat 15 minutes in an oven at 325° before serving.

Cassoulet

This is the French version of baked beans. Seasoned with herbs, roast meats, and garlic sausage, it is hearty and delicious. Wonderful reheated, it's a great dish to take to a party. Serve it with a green salad, French bread, and a strong white or dry rosé wine. Use Great Northern beans.

- 4 ounces salt pork
- 4 cups dried white beans, soaked overnight
- 1 bay leaf
- 3 sprigs parsley
- 1 teaspoon thyme
- 4 peppercorns
- 2 carrots, scraped, halved
- 1 whole onion, peeled, stuck with 8 cloves
- 2 teaspoons salt
- 2 pounds boned pork loin, cubed (keep the bones)
- 2 pounds boned shoulder lamb, cubed (keep the bones)
- 2 onions, peeled, chopped
- 2 cloves garlic, peeled, minced
- 1 cup tomato purée
- 1 cup beef bouillon
- 1 big garlic sausage, French or hot Italian
- 1 cup bread crumbs
- Freshly ground black pepper

1. Cover the salt pork with water, bring to a boil, and simmer 5 minutes. Drain and dice.

French Specialties

2. Put the soaked beans into a large Dutch oven or a heavy casserole. Add water to cover. Add the salt pork. Tie up the bay leaf, parsley, thyme, and peppercorns in a small piece of cheesecloth, and add to the pot with the carrots, onion stuck with cloves, and salt.

3. Over high heat, bring to a boil. Reduce the heat, cover and simmer gently for one to 1½ hours, or until beans are just tender. Do not overcook. Remove the herb bag, carrots, and onion.

4. While the beans are cooking, prepare the meats. Brown the pork and lamb cubes and bones in a heavy skillet. Stir in the chopped onions and garlic, and cook 2 minutes. Stir in the tomato purée. Cover and simmer one hour, or until the meat is tender. During cooking time, add beef bouillon to replenish the liquid in the skillet.

5. Prick the sausage all over with a fork. Place in a kettle and cover with water. Bring to a boil and simmer one hour. Drain, and cut in slices ½ inch thick.

6. When the pork and lamb cubes are done, remove the bones. Combine the meat cubes with the cooked beans. Taste and add salt and pepper if necessary. Add more beef bouillon if mixture is dry.

7. Preheat oven to 375°.

8. In a deep casserole, alternate layers of beans and meat mixture with sausage slices, ending with a layer of sausage slices. Combine bread crumbs with a good grinding of pepper. Sprinkle over the top layer.

9. Bake one to 1½ hours. As bread crumbs bake and dry out on top of the casserole, push gently down into the casserole. Serve bubbling hot.

Makes 12 to 16 portions.

Take-It-Along Tips: This is fine the next day, so make it ahead, take it to the party in its casserole, and reheat there in a 350° oven for 20 to 30 minutes. Moisten with a little beef bouillon before reheating.

Carbonnade de Boeuf à la Flamande

This Belgian beef stew is made with beer and served with a ring of boiled, buttered noodles. Offer beer or California Mountain Red wine with this.

4 tablespoons butter	1 cup beer
4 large onions, thinly sliced	½ cup beef bouillon
3 pounds chuck or round steak, cubed	1 teaspoon prepared mustard
1 cup all-purpose flour	2 teaspoons sugar
1 teaspoon salt	1 package (8 ounce) egg noodles, cooked, buttered
¼ teaspoon black pepper	Sprig of parsley

1. Preheat the oven to 325°.
2. In a heavy frying pan over low heat, melt the butter and sauté the onions until golden brown.
3. Coat the meat with flour and sauté with the onions for 4 minutes. Add the rest of the ingredients, except the noodles, bring to a boil, stirring constantly, and simmer until the sauce is smooth. Add salt and pepper if needed. Transfer to a covered casserole and place in preheated oven for 2 hours, or until the meat is tender.
4. Serve with a ring of buttered noodles around the outer edge of the casserole and a sprig of parsley across the center.

Makes 6 to 8 portions.

Take-It-Along Tips: Make this ahead but undercook the noodles. Reheat at the party in a 325° oven for 15 to 20 minutes.

Ratatouille Niçoise

This is one of the best vegetable casseroles; a good choice in August and early September when tomatoes and the other ingredients are plentiful. It is excellent cold, and tastes just as good reheated as it does when first made.

- ½ pound eggplant
- ½ pound zucchini
- 1 tablespoon salt
- ½ cup olive oil
- 1½ cups sliced onions
- 2 green peppers, seeded sliced
- 2 cloves garlic, peeled, mashed
- 1 teaspoon salt
- ⅛ teaspoon pepper
- 1 pound tomatoes, peeled, seeded, or
- 1 cup drained canned tomatoes
- ½ teaspoon oregano
- ½ teaspoon thyme
- 3 tablespoons minced parsley

1. Peel the eggplant and cut into long slices ⅜ inch thick. Cut off and discard the zucchini ends and slice into long pieces ⅜ inch thick. Toss these vegetables in a large mixing bowl with the salt; let stand 30 minutes. Drain, wipe dry. In a large enameled skillet over medium heat, heat the olive oil and sauté the eggplant and zucchini until browned lightly. Remove to a bowl.

2. In the same skillet, cook the onions and peppers slowly until soft. Stir in the garlic, salt, and pepper. Slice the tomatoes into strips, and place over the onions and peppers. Cover the pan and cook for 5 minutes, then uncover, raise the heat, and boil until the juice has almost completely evaporated. Correct the seasonings; fold in the oregano, thyme, and parsley.

3. Spoon a third of the tomato mixture into a medium casserole. Arrange half the eggplant and zucchini over the mixture, cover with half the remaining tomatoes, then with the remaining eggplant and zucchini, and top with the last of the tomato mixture. Cover, and simmer over low heat for 10 minutes. Uncover, tip the casserole, and baste with the juices. Correct the seasoning if necessary.

4. Raise the heat and simmer until the juices have almost entirely evaporated.

Makes 8 to 10 portions.

Take-It-Along Tips: Make this ahead, take to the party in an ovenproof serving dish and reheat at 325° for 20 minutes before serving. Or take in a serving bowl and serve chilled.

Veal Fondue

This is more Swiss than French. It makes an elegant picnic or patio meal, and you can cook it right at the table. You need a fondue dish and Sterno and forks for serving. Offer with crusty French bread, a green salad, and a cold white wine.

4 cups shredded leaf lettuce or escarole	1 cup light dry white wine
3 pounds veal shoulder, sliced very thin	½ teaspoon thyme
	⅓ cup vegetable oil
Salt	⅓ cup olive oil
2 tablespoons lemon juice	⅓ cup butter
	Hollandaise Sauce

1. Crisp the lettuce, turn into a salad bowl, and chill.
2. Cut the veal into narrow strips, about 2 inches long, and sprinkle with salt. Combine the lemon juice, wine, and thyme, and marinate the veal in the mixture for 2 hours or more.
3. Heat the oils and butter in a small saucepan and stir in ¼ cup of the marinade.
4. To serve, pour the oil, butter, and wine mixture into a fondue dish, light the burner under it, place it on the picnic table. Turn the veal strips onto the lettuce. Place the fondue forks and a dish of Hollandaise Sauce by the salad. On fondue forks, hold the meat strips in the simmering broth 1 to 2 minutes, then dip in the Hollandaise and enjoy it.

Serves 10 to 12.

Take-It-Along Tips: Prepare all the ingredients and take to the party ready for the guests to cook for themselves.

13. *Mediterranean Cooking*

Meals in Italy and Spain are put together much as they are in France, with an hors d'oeuvre course, a soup, an entrée, cheese, and a sweet or fruit for dessert. Wines are served in both those countries much as they are in France. In Spain there are touches of saffron in the cooking, a rice is often served, whereas in much of Italy, oregano and basil are the most common flavorings, and a pasta course—a course with spaghetti, ravioli, or some other form of pasta—is offered with most full course meals. Tomato and garlic appear in so many dishes you could almost say they were the rule.

The rules for the types of wine to serve with each food are similar in France, Italy, and Spain, but each country has its own vineyards and brand names.

Green Noodles Baked With Two Cheeses

A tasty pasta to serve with strongly flavored meat and meat casseroles. Prepare this one ahead and bake at the party, or bake at home and reheat at the party.

1 8-ounce package green (spinach) noodles	¼ cup grated Parmesan cheese
4 tablespoons melted butter	2 eggs, well beaten
½ cup grated Swiss cheese	1 teaspoon salt
	¼ teaspoon black pepper

1. Heat oven to 350°.
2. Cook the noodles as directed on the package. Do not overcook. Turn into a colander, rinse under rapidly running cold water, and drain.

3. Toss the noodles with 3 tablespoons of the melted butter, 6 tablespoons of the Swiss cheese, and 2 tablespoons of the Parmesan. Stir in the beaten eggs and mix well. Add salt and pepper to taste, and correct seasoning. Turn into a well-buttered 8-inch square pan. Top with the remaining cheese and dribble on the remaining melted butter.

4. Bake 30 minutes in a 350° oven. Serve cut into 6 or 8 slices. *Makes 6 to 8 portions.*

Take-It-Along Tips: Follow the recipe through step 2 and take to the party in the cooking pan and finish there.

Spinach Ravioli with Salsa Bianca

Ravioli are made from noodle dough cut into squares, stuffed and boiled. Making these takes time, but they rate lots of applause. Take the cooked ravioli to the party, reheat briefly. Make the *Salsa Bianca* (see below) in a fondue dish while the guests watch. Frozen ravioli keeps well. Chilled white Chianti is nice with this.

RAVIOLI

- 3 cups all-purpose flour
- ½ teaspoon salt
- 2 eggs, slightly beaten
- ¾ to 1 cup water, warmed
- Spinach Filling (see recipe below)
- 3 quarts water
- 2 tablespoons salt
- 1 tablespoon olive oil
- *Salsa Bianca*

1. Sift the flour and salt into a large bowl. Make a well in the center, pour the eggs into the well, and add ¼ cup of the warm water. Stir in the water with your fingers until it disappears. Repeat, working the dough with your fingers until it has picked up all the flour in the bowl. Add more water if necessary to get all the flour up. On a floured board, knead the dough until it doesn't stick anymore—for 5 to 10 minutes. Cover with a damp cloth and let rest for 15 minutes.

2. Make the Spinach Filling (directions below).

3. Flour the board and a rolling pin. Roll the dough very thin, then with a glass or cookie cutter, stamp out 3-inch circles. Spoon a

dab of Spinach Filling in each center. Fold over into half-circles, and with a wet fork, crimp around the edges on both sides to seal. Place each finished ravioli on a floured sheet of waxed paper.

4. In a large kettle, combine water, salt, and oil and bring to a rapid boil. Drop in the ravioli one at a time. Stir with a slotted spoon to keep them from sticking. Cook uncovered 10 to 15 minutes. Taste one to make sure the dough is cooked. Then drain.

Makes 8 servings.

SPINACH FILLING

- 4 cups fresh spinach, cooked
- 1 egg, slightly beaten
- 1/3 cup grated Parmesan cheese
- 1/4 cup diced mozzarella cheese
- 1/4 cup ricotta or cottage cheese
- 1 small clove garlic, crushed
- 1 teaspoon minced parsley
- 1/2 teaspoon minced fresh basil
- 1/4 teaspoon dry basil
- 1/8 teaspoon oregano
- Salt
- Pepper

1. Toss the cooked spinach over the heat to make sure all the water is gone. Then beat all the other ingredients into the spinach. Refrigerate to stiffen.

SALSA BIANCA

- 1 tablespoon olive oil
- 1/2 cup butter
- 1/4 cup grated Parmesan cheese
- 1/8 teaspoon minced fresh or dried basil
- 1 tablespoon minced parsley

1. Heat the oil over a fondue burner. Stir in the butter. Add the cheese, basil, and parsley, one at a time. Remove from the heat almost at once. Serve hot over the ravioli.

Take-It-Along Tips: This is better done at home, because the ravioli in sauce doesn't travel too well—they tend to get soft. However, if travel it must, complete the recipe, pour the sauce over the ravioli, turn into a deep serving dish, wrap in foil, and take to the party. If necessary, reheat briefly at the host home in a 325° oven for 10 to 15 minutes—just long enough to warm the ravioli through.

Gnocchi

An Italian specialty, these gnocchi are made from mashed potatoes flavored with cheese and baked with lots of melted butter—unlike any other potato dish.

- 3 pounds potatoes, peeled
- 1¼ cups grated Parmesan cheese
- 1½ cups flour
- 3 egg yolks, slightly beaten
- 2 teaspoons salt
- ¼ teaspoon pepper
- 1½ tablespoons melted butter
- ½ cup melted butter

1. Boil the potatoes until tender, drain thoroughly. Mash, or put them through a ricer. Stir in ¾ cup of the Parmesan cheese, the flour, egg yolks, salt, pepper, and 1½ tablespoons of the melted butter. The dough should be firm but not hard. Add a little butter to soften, or flour to stiffen, as needed.
2. Working on a lightly floured board, with the palms of your hands, roll the potato dough to form a rope ½ inch in diameter. Cut into one-inch lengths and place on waxed paper.
3. Add water in a large saucepan to a depth of 2 inches. Bring to a boil and then reduce to a simmer. Cook the pieces in small batches until they rise to the surface, about 5 minutes. Remove with a slotted spoon, drain well, and stack 2 or 3 deep in a shallow buttered baking dish. Sprinkle the gnocchi with the remaining half cup of cheese and pour melted butter over all.
4. Bake uncovered for 30 minutes in an oven at 325°. Brown quickly under the broiler.

Makes 6 to 8 servings.

Take-It-Along Tips: Bake, wrap in foil, take to the party, and brown briefly under the broiler before serving.

Osso Buco

An Italian favorite, this dish, native to Milan, Italy, is literally translated "hollow bone," wrongly however, since the part you eat is the marrow in the bone. Supply an oyster fork with it or a lobster pick to help guests get to the heart of the matter. The veal shanks should be young, weighing about 1½ pounds apiece. Whatever the age, the meat must be cooked until it begins to fall off the bone. Offer a dry white wine with this. A recipe for *Gremolata* to serve with the *Osso Buco* follows. Read it through before you decide to serve it.

- 6 pounds veal shanks, cut into 2-inch pieces
- ¼ cup flour
- ½ teaspoon salt
- ¼ teaspoon pepper
- ½ cup oil
- 1 medium onion, peeled, minced
- 1 medium carrot, scraped, minced
- 1 rib celery, minced
- 2 garlic cloves, peeled, minced
- 1 cup dry white wine
- 1 cup beef bouillon
- 1 12-ounce can whole tomatoes, drained and chopped
- ½ teaspoon basil
- ½ teaspoon rosemary
- *Gremolata*

1. Preheat the oven to 325°.
2. Coat the veal with the flour seasoned with salt and pepper.
3. Heat half the oil in a heavy skillet. Add a few pieces of veal at a time and brown them on all sides; they should be dark and crusty. In a large casserole or Dutch oven, sauté the onion, carrot, celery, and garlic in the remaining oil. Cook, stirring occasionally, until the vegetables are tender.
4. When all the veal is browned, arrange it on top of the vegetables. Stand the pieces up to keep the marrow inside the bones.
5. Put the wine, beef bouillon, tomatoes, basil, and rosemary in the skillet used for browning the veal. Cook, scraping up the pan juices until the mixture boils. Pour over the veal and vegetables. Cover the casserole and bake for 1½ hours or until the veal is tender. Test the sauce for seasoning and add salt and pepper if needed. Serve as soon as it is cooked—or reheat well before serving. Pass *Gremolata* to each guest.

Makes 6 to 8 portions.

GREMOLATA

This garnish is not quite as lethal as it sounds. Parsley is the traditional Italian antidote for garlic. Passing the sauce separately allows the sissies to skip it.

- 6 garlic cloves, peeled, minced
- 2 tablespoons grated lemon peel
- ½ cup chopped parsley

1. Combine ingredients and mix well.

Take-It-Along Tips: Take the *Osso Buco* to the party in its cooking casserole, sealed in foil, and reheat there at 325° for 15 to 20 minutes. Take the *Gremolata* in a sauce boat and offer with the *Osso Buco*.

Mrs. Bruzzese's Lasagna

A baked pasta-meat-and-cheese dish everyone loves. Substitute cottage cheese for ricotta if you are watching the budget. A good choice when the budget is low and the party large.

2 tablespoons olive oil	2 tablespoons vegetable oil
6 Italian sausages (hot or sweet)	2 tablespoons salt
1 small onion, peeled, minced	1 1-pound package lasagna noodles
1 clove garlic, peeled, minced	2 pounds ricotta cheese
1 28-ounce can whole tomatoes	2 tablespoons grated Parmesan cheese
1 16-ounce can tomato purée	1 teaspoon salt
2 teaspoons fresh basil	1/8 teaspoon pepper
1 teaspoon dried basil	2 eggs, beaten
1 teaspoon salt	1/2 pound mozzarella cheese, thinly sliced
1/8 teaspoon pepper	Parmesan cheese
2 pounds ground beef	Parsley
4 quarts water	

1. In a large skillet over medium heat, spread the oil and brown the sausages. Add the onion and garlic, and brown lightly. Meanwhile, at low speed, process the whole tomatoes, their juices, and the tomato purée in a blender. Pour the mixture over the onions and meat. Add the basil, salt, and pepper, and simmer 2 hours. Add salt and pepper to taste. After 2 hours, remove the sausages and reserve.

2. Just before the sauce is finished, in another skillet, heat one tablespoon oil and brown the ground beef over medium-high heat. Turn the ground beef into the simmering tomato sauce. Pour a little tomato sauce into the ground beef skillet, scrape up the pan juices, and return to the sauce.

3. While the tomato sauce is cooking, bring water to a full boil. Add the oil and salt. Put the lasagna into the water, one piece at a time. When tender, but not completely cooked (about 12 minutes), drain and then run cold water into the kettle. Leave the lasagna in the water until ready to use.

4. Turn the ricotta into a bowl with the Parmesan cheese, salt, pepper, and eggs. Mix until smooth.

5. Grease a 15- by 8- by 3-inch baking dish. Pour in a layer of tomato sauce, then place a layer of lasagna with the pieces overlapping ¼ inch. Next smooth a layer of the ricotta mixture over the lasagna. Over this, spoon a thin layer of sauce and top with a layer of mozzarella slices. Place slices of the reserved sausage over the mozzarella. Repeat these layers and top with lasagna covered with tomato sauce and sprinkled with Parmesan cheese. Place in preheated oven set at 350° for 20 minutes or until brown.

Makes 8 to 10 portions.

Take-It-Along Tips: Follow the recipe through step 5, but don't bake until you get to the party. Wrap the lasagna pan well in heavy-duty foil for the trip so the juices won't drip.

Francesca Bosetti Morris's Risotto alla Milanese

Fran's parents were natives of Como, Italy, and this is her favorite Italian recipe. She uses Italian rice when she can get it; otherwise, the long-grain type. Dried mushrooms are sold in Italian specialty shops. She serves this with sautéed chicken livers and sautéed mushrooms and a nice Beaujolais wine.

¾ stick of butter	Pinch of saffron strands
1 small onion, peeled, minced	2 to 4 tablespoons grated Parmesan or Gruyère cheese
1½ cups rice, washed, drained	Salt
⅔ cup dry white wine	Pepper
6 cups hot Chicken Bouillon	
4 pieces dried mushrooms soaked 5 minutes in hot water, drained	

1. Melt half a stick of butter in a heavy saucepan over medium heat and sauté the onion until golden. Add the rice, stir until butter-coated. Stir in the wine. Let simmer until the wine is almost absorbed.

2. Add the bouillon, a cupful at a time. Do not cover. After the

first cupful, add the mushrooms. As each cupful of bouillon is absorbed, add another, stirring the rice occasionally to keep it from sticking. After 20 minutes of cooking, test the rice for doneness. When almost done, stir in the saffron, previously steeped in a few spoonfuls of the broth. Adjust seasonings to taste. All the broth should now be in and the rice a little soupy.

3. When you are ready to serve, over low heat, warm the risotto and stir in the remaining ¼ of the butter and 2 to 4 tablespoons of cheese. (The amount depends on how much you like cheese.) Serve immediately.

Makes 6 portions. For larger quantities, the rule of thumb is ¼ cup of rice per person, and 4 times as much broth as rice. But the amount of broth will vary, depending on the rice and also on the humidity of the day.

Take-It-Along Tips: Follow the recipe through step 3, wrap in foil, and take to the party along with remaining ingredients. Complete the recipe there.

Casserole Poulet Marengo

Chicken in a rich tomato sauce flavored with wine. Since a good white cooking wine is hard to find and expensive, we often use a very dry white vermouth. Make this ahead and reheat in a 325° oven.

- ½ cup diced salt pork
- ½ cup chopped onion
- 2 garlic cloves, peeled, minced
- 2 sprigs parsley
- 1 4-pound chicken, cut up
- 1 teaspoon salt
- ⅛ teaspoon pepper
- ¼ cup all-purpose flour
- 1 cup dry white wine
- 1 cup boiling water
- 4 ounces tomato purée
- ⅛ teaspoon thyme
- 1½ cups quartered mushrooms
- Pinch cayenne

1. In a heavy skillet over medium heat, render the fat from the diced pork. Remove the pork bits and reserve in a casserole. Drain half the fat from the skillet and reserve.

2. Over high heat, sauté the onions, garlic, and parsley 3 minutes and place in the casserole.

3. Return the reserved fat to the skillet, turn the heat to medium, sauté the chicken pieces until golden on all sides; salt and pepper them, and place in the casserole.

4. Lower the heat, sprinkle the flour over the remaining fat and brown it slightly; stir in the wine and boiling water, the tomato purée, thyme, and mushrooms, and simmer 5 minutes. Then scrape the mixture into the casserole. Place in the oven at 300°, cover, and bake ¾ hour. Sprinkle with cayenne just before serving.

Makes 8 to 10 servings.

Take-It-Along Tips: Follow the recipe through step 4, but undercook the dish by 20 minutes. Take to the party sealed in foil, and reheat in a 300° oven for 10 minutes.

Casserole Veal Marengo

To add a touch of luxury, slice ½ pound of mushrooms, sauté in butter with 2 minced garlic cloves, and 2 chopped sprigs of parsley, and mix in the casserole 10 minutes before serving. The Sauce Marengo can be served with any leftover meats or poultry. Cube the meat and simmer in the sauce for 30 to 40 minutes. Offer with a strong rosé or a light red wine.

- 2 tablespoons butter
- 3 pounds of boned breast or shoulder of veal, cut into 2-inch pieces
- 1 teaspoon salt
- ⅛ teaspoon pepper
- ½ cup very dry white wine, or white dry vermouth
- 2 cups chicken bouillon
- ¼ cup butter
- 2 tablespoons chopped onion
- ½ cup diced carrots
- 1¼ teaspoon salt
- ½ teaspoon savory
- ⅛ teaspoon pepper
- Pinch cayenne pepper
- 2 tablespoons all-purpose flour
- 4 ounces tomato purée

1. In a heavy skillet, slightly brown the butter, then add the veal and sauté rapidly until golden on all sides. Salt and pepper the meat, then place it in a medium casserole. Pour the wine into the skillet and scrape the bottom of the skillet with a spatula to get up all the pan juices. Stir in the chicken bouillon.

2. Melt the ¼ cup butter in another skillet; add the onion, carrots, salt, savory, pepper, and cayenne. Simmer for 3 minutes. Stir in the flour; mix till smooth. When the mixture begins to brown, add the hot consommé and wine mixture, stirring gently, then the tomato purée. Check and correct the seasonings. Pour over the veal in the casserole, cover, bake in an oven at 300° for 3 hours.
Makes 8 to 10 servings.

Take-It-Along Tips: Undercook the veal by about 20 minutes, seal in foil in the casserole, take to the party, and reheat there, if necessary, for 15 to 20 minutes in an oven at 350°.

Paella Valenciana

Chicken, shellfish, and Spanish sausage are combined in this delicious, saffron-flavored Spanish dish with which Sangria is served as cocktail and wine. The fruits, marinated in the Sangria, are offered as dessert. Cook paella in a paella dish—a wide shallow metal pan for the top of the stove—or, if you have a Chinese wok, use that. An electric frying pan will work almost as well and so will a large, heavy skillet.

6 chorizos (Spanish sausage), or fresh Italian sausages
4 tablespoons olive oil
2 tablespoons butter
2 pounds cut-up chicken
1 tablespoon lemon juice, strained
Salt
Pepper
½ cup minced onion
¼ cup minced shallot (or double the onion)
2 medium cloves garlic, peeled, minced
1 medium green pepper, seeded, minced
1 cup uncooked rice
2 medium tomatoes, chopped, or 1 can (8¼ ounces) whole tomatoes
1½ cups chicken broth, boiling
¼ teaspoon powdered saffron
2 teaspoons salt
¼ teaspoon black pepper
12 large raw shrimp, shelled, deveined
24 large raw mussels or littleneck clams
1 tablespoon finely minced parsley

1. Prick the sausages all over, then drop them into boiling water, and simmer, uncovered, 20 minutes to get rid of excess fat. Remove from the kettle, and drain the sausages.

2. In a wok or a very large heavy skillet, over medium heat, warm the oil, and melt the butter in it. Fry the chicken pieces until golden brown all over. Sprinkle with lemon juice, and salt and pepper each piece well. Remove and place in a large bowl.

3. In the same skillet, fry the sausages until almost done, about 10 minutes; then add to the chicken. Lower the heat a little, drop the onion and shallots into the skillet, and stir until they begin to turn golden brown.

4. Add the garlic and the pepper, and stir and fry until the pepper begins to lose its bright green color. Remove to the chicken bowl with a slotted spoon. Stir the rice into the fat, and cook, stirring, until it begins to look chalky, about 5 minutes. Do not let it begin to brown.

5. Stir the tomatoes into the rice with one cup of the chicken bouillon, the saffron, salt, and pepper. Scrape up the pan juices until the bottom of the pan feels smooth. Bring to a simmer and cover tightly.

6. Let the rice cook, covered, until it is almost, but not quite, soft. Add the remaining ½ cup of stock if the dish dries out. Remove from the heat. Fluff the rice. Poke the chicken and sausage down into the bottom of the cooking dish, and pour their drippings onto the rice. Push the shrimp and the mussels down into the upper layer of the rice, pour on any remaining chicken stock, cover the dish, and cook until the shrimp turns pink and all the mussels have opened. Serve at once.

Makes 12 portions.

Take-It-Along Tips: If this dish is to travel, allow the rice to cook only 8 minutes, then cool rapidly, and take to the party with the remaining ingredients, cooked and uncooked. Complete the recipe at the host home.

14. Rhineland Fare

When you're taking a dish to a party whose theme originates in the Rhineland, consider pork—no one does pork quite as well as Deutschlanders.

Side dishes to serve with German pork dishes can be plain boiled potatoes or noodles or dumplings. Of course, potato pancakes would be great, but that is one of those dishes that just doesn't travel well.

Any of the Rhine wines is excellent with pork, but more often served is a hearty German beer.

Bavarian Potato Dumplings

Wonderful with the Rhineland dishes, including Sauerbraten and Hasenpfeffer.

- 2 pounds old potatoes
- ¾ cup all-purpose flour
- ⅓ cup plus 2 tablespoons butter or margarine
- ½ teaspoon salt
- 1 egg yolk
- 1 slice white bread, crustless
- 3 quarts boiling water
- 3 cubes chicken bouillon

1. Peel and boil the potatoes until breaking apart. With the electric beater, or by hand, whip the potatoes and ⅓ cup butter or margarine until smooth. Beat in the egg yolk. Beat in enough flour to make a dough that won't stick. Let the dough rest 15 minutes.

2. Cut the bread into ½ inch cubes and fry these in butter or margarine over medium heat until golden brown.

3. Break the potato dough into balls about 2 inches around. Press a cube of bread into the center of each ball and reform the ball around it.

4. Dissolve the chicken bouillon in the boiling water. With the heat at medium, drop the potato balls, one at a time, into the water, and when the water returns to a boil, simmer the dumplings for 20 minutes. Dumplings will float and be slightly puffed when done. Drain on paper towels and serve immediately.
Serves 8 portions.

Take-It-Along Tips: Follow the recipe through step 3. Take the dumplings ready to cook, along with the other ingredients, to the party, and finish the recipe there.

White Cabbage

A Westphalian dish to serve with German meat platters or casseroles.

- 6 tablespoons butter or margarine
- 4 medium apples, peeled, chopped
- 1 medium head cabbage, peeled, chopped
- 2 green apples, cored, peeled, chopped
- 1½ tablespoons white vinegar
- 2 tablespoons granulated sugar
- 2 teaspoons salt
- ½ teaspoon black pepper
- 4 cups hot water
- ½ cup mashed potatoes

1. In a heavy skillet, over medium heat, melt the butter or margarine and simmer the onions until golden brown, about 5 to 10 minutes.
2. In a Dutch oven, or an ovenproof medium casserole that has a lid, make alternate layers of cabbage and apple. Add the vinegar, sugar, salt, and pepper. Pour 3 cups of hot water over the cabbage mixture, cover tightly, bring to a boil, and simmer 30 minutes. Mix the remaining 1 cup of water into the mashed potatoes with the onions and stir into the hot cabbage.
3. Bake at 350°, covered, for ½ hour.

Serves 8 portions.

Take-It-Along Tips: If the dish is to travel, undercook by about 10 minutes, wrap in foil, overwrap in newspapers, and let it finish cooking in its own heat as you travel to the party.

Hasenpfeffer

This classic German dish is made with hare—a big, wild rabbit—but you can make a less tangy version of it with the domestic rabbits available fresh in the South, frozen in specialty markets in the North.

- 3 pounds cut-up hare or rabbit
- 2 cups red wine
- 1 cup cold water
- ⅓ cup wine vinegar
- 1 onion, peeled, sliced
- 1 tablespoon granulated sugar
- 2 tablespoons salt
- 6 whole cloves
- ½ teaspoon black pepper
- 3 bay leaves
- ½ cup all-purpose flour
- ¼ cup melted butter or margarine

1. Marinate the hare or rabbit in the wine mixed with water, vinegar, onion, sugar, salt, cloves, pepper, and bay leaves, for 12 hours in a cool place. Turn the meat pieces often in the marinade.

2. Drain and dry the meat, and reserve the marinade. Dredge the meat in flour. Melt the butter or margarine in a Dutch oven or a medium casserole over medium high heat, browning the pieces well on all sides. Strain the marinade and pour it over the meat. Scrape up the pan juices. Cover and simmer over a low heat for one hour.

3. Remove the meat to a serving platter and keep warm. Simmer the sauce stirring often, until it has thickened, then pour over the meat and serve.

Serves 6 portions.

Take-It-Along Tips: Take this to the party in the Dutch oven it cooked in, wrapped in foil, and overwrapped in newspaper to keep warm. Or take it along and reheat before serving.

Meatballs with Lemon Sauce

A traditional East Prussian dish. Serve with it noodles or small new potatoes flavored with fresh dill snips.

1 pound ground bottom round	1 cup hot water
½ cup seasoned bread crumbs	1 tablespoon lemon juice, strained
1 teaspoon grated lemon rind	
2 teaspoons salt	1 teaspoon cornstarch
½ teaspoon black pepper	2 tablespoons cold water
½ cup half and half, or cream	1 egg yolk, slightly beaten
2 beef bouillon cubes	

1. In a large mixing bowl, combine ground meat, bread crumbs, and lemon rind, with salt and pepper. Mix thoroughly. Make a well in the center of the meat, pour in the half and half or cream, and with a fork mix the meat into the cream, lightly. Shape into 12 meatballs.
2. In a large, shallow saucepan, over medium heat, dissolve the beef bouillon cubes in the water. Place the meatballs in the simmering bouillon and cook 8 to 10 minutes. Drain the meatballs on paper towel and keep warm in a slow oven. Reserve the bouillon.
3. Stir the lemon juice into the bouillon. Dissolve the cornstarch in the cold water, and stir into the bouillon. Cook until slightly thickened and clear. Add 2 tablespoons of the bouillon to the egg yolk, stir, then return the yolk to the sauce. Over very low heat—don't let it boil—simmer the sauce 3 or 4 minutes.
4. Pour the sauce over the hot meatballs and serve.

Serves 4. Double the recipe to serve more.

Take-It-Along Tips: Place the cooked meatballs and the sauce in a serving dish that is ovenproof. Take to the party and reheat briefly in a 325° oven—about 15 to 20 minutes. Don't let the sauce boil.

Beef Platter

Round, rump, or boneless chuck roast served Rhineland style. Offer with it chilled German beer or a Riesling wine.

- 4 pounds boneless beef
- 1 cup water
- ¼ cup chili sauce
- 2 large onions, peeled, slivered
- 1 tablespoon caraway seeds
- 1 tablespoon paprika
- 1 27-ounce can sauerkraut
- ½ cup light brown sugar, firmly packed
- 8 ounces sour cream

1. Trim excess fat from roast. Melt the trimmings in a big Dutch oven, or a large casserole with a lid, over medium high heat, then brown the roast in it on all sides. Add the water, chili sauce, onions, caraway, and paprika, scraping up the pan juices. Cover and simmer with the heat at low, for 2 hours, turning the meat once or twice.
2. Drain the sauerkraut and mix with the brown sugar. Combine with the juices around the roast, cover, and simmer one hour more.
3. Remove the meat to a serving platter. Over low heat, mix the meat sauce and the sauerkraut with the sour cream, return the mixture to the Dutch oven, and heat gently but do not boil.
4. Spoon the sauerkraut into a deep serving bowl. Slice the meat ¼ inch thick and place over the sauerkraut.

Serves 8 to 10 portions generously.

Take-It-Along Tips: Follow the recipe through step 3. Return the meat to the Dutch oven, cover, seal in foil, overwrap in newspaper, and take to the party. Reheat 10 minutes, if necessary, in an oven at 350° before serving.

Bavarian Pork

You'll need pork hocks to make this; it's a Pennsylvania specialty.

- 8 fresh pork hocks (3 pounds)
- 2 large onions, peeled
- 1 bay leaf
- Tops from 1 bunch celery
- 4 cups cold water
- 2½ teaspoons salt
- ¼ teaspoon pepper
- 2 2- to 3-pound cans sauerkraut
- 2 green apples, cored, peeled
- ½ cup light brown sugar, packed firmly

1. Over high heat, bring to a boil the pork hocks, onions, bay leaf, celery tops, and enough cold water to cover, about 4 cups. Simmer over low heat for 3 hours. Remove the hocks and place in a small casserole. Open the sauerkraut.
2. Heat the oven to 325°.
3. Cut the apples into wedges and place the apples over the hocks. Cover both with the sauerkraut, undrained, and sprinkle with brown sugar. Cover and bake the hocks ¾ of an hour.

Serves 8 to 10.

Take-It-Along Tips: If this dish is to travel, underbake the hocks by about 10 minutes, seal in foil, overwrap in newspaper, and take to the party. They'll be just right by the time you are ready to serve. You can reheat in an oven at 350° for 20 minutes if necessary.

Bratwurst in Sour Cream

The best dishes with sausages are made by the German cooks. This sweet and sour style goes well with dumplings.

- 2 12-ounce packages cooked bratwurst or knockwurst
- 1 tablespoon butter or margarine
- 2 medium onions, peeled, sliced thin
- 3 tablespoons all-purpose flour
- ½ teaspoon salt
- 1½ cups apple cider
- 8 ounces sour cream

1. In a large, heavy skillet over medium heat, brown the sausages in the butter or margarine until colored all over. Prick them to let out steam as they cook. Remove the sausages.

2. In the same skillet, sauté the onion slices until golden and translucent. Stir in the flour, cider, and salt and keep stirring as the sauce thickens. Return the sausages to the skillet and simmer 10 minutes.

3. Spoon the sour cream into a bowl and blend into it one cup of the hot sauce. Stir the mixture, then return to the skillet.
Serves 4.

Take-It-Along Tips: Turn the finished recipe into a serving casserole and take to the party sealed in foil and overwrapped in newspaper. If necessary, reheat the dish over a medium low burner before serving. Or reheat over Sterno in a chafing dish at the table: unorthodox, but attractive.

Sauerkraut Dinner

A boiled dinner from the Rhine country, serve this with a Riesling, a dry California wine, or with German beer.

- 5 cups sauerkraut
- 2 to 3 pound piece corned beef
- 2 carrots, scraped, cut in rounds
- 1 stalk celery
- ½ teaspoon marjoram
- ½ teaspoon thyme
- 1 onion stuck with 3 cloves
- ½ teaspoon chervil or parsley
- 1 crumbled bay leaf
- 2 Polish sausages
- 8 large potatoes, peeled, halved
- 2 tablespoons butter
- 2 tablespoons flour
- 1 cup stock from the cooked meats
- 1 cup dry white wine
- Salt
- Pepper
- 1 cup heavy cream
- 1 teaspoon caraway seeds, optional
- 1 tablespoon minced parsley

1. Drain the sauerkraut, soak in cold water for ½ hour, changing the water 3 times.

2. Put the corned beef into a large soup kettle and cover with cold water. Add the carrots, celery, marjoram, thyme, onion with

cloves, chervil, and bay leaf. Cover and simmer for 3 hours. Add the sausages and enough water to cover the meats. Simmer one hour more. Add the potatoes to the stock, cover, return to a boil and turn off the heat.

3. Over very low heat, melt the butter in a large heavy skillet. Stir in the flour and mix until smooth. Stir in one cup of stock and the wine, working rapidly. Simmer 5 minutes, stirring. Add salt and pepper to taste, and stir in cream.

4. Drain the sauerkraut thoroughly and stir it into the cream sauce. Add partially cooked potatoes to the sauerkraut and simmer until the potatoes are tender, 20 to 30 minutes. Add caraway seeds, if desired.

5. Arrange the corned beef and sausages on a large platter; surround with potatoes and sauerkraut. Garnish with carrot rounds and minced parsley.

Makes 12 to 16 portions.

Take-It-Along Tips: Undercook this by about 10 minutes, wrap in foil and newspapers, and take to the party. The potatoes will be done by the time you are ready to serve. Or you can reheat in a 350° oven for 15 minutes if necessary.

Beef-and-Pork Casserole

A fine meat-and-vegetable dinner. A light Riesling wine is suitable. Nice with rice or noodles and a green salad.

- 3½ pounds boned beef shoulder
- 1½ pounds boned pork shoulder
- 1 medium onion, peeled, chopped
- 2 cloves garlic, peeled, minced
- 4 tablespoons all-purpose flour
- 3½ cups chicken bouillon, very hot
- 1 teaspoon Worcestershire sauce
- 2 teaspoons salt
- ¼ teaspoon pepper
- ¼ teaspoon savory
- ¼ teaspoon thyme
- 1 bay leaf
- 2 cups red cabbage, shredded
- 2 cups potatoes, peeled, diced

1. Cut the meats into 2-inch cubes, removing all fat. Cut the fat into very small cubes. In a heavy skillet over medium heat, melt down the fat and remove the rendered bits. Discard. Add the meat to the fat in the skillet and stir constantly until the meat is browned on all sides. Add the onions and garlic. Sprinkle the meat with the flour, stir rapidly, then stir in the chicken bouillon, the Worcestershire sauce, salt, pepper, savory, thyme, and bay leaf.

2. Scrape into a covered casserole, cover with red cabbage, and cook in a 400° oven for 30 minutes. Then lower the heat to 250° and cook for 2 hours more.

3. About ¾ of an hour before the end of the cooking, add the potatoes. Check the seasonings. Cook ¾ hour more, or until the potatoes are tender.

Makes 10 to 12 servings.

Take-It-Along Tips: If the dish is to travel, undercook by about 10 minutes, wrap in foil and newspapers, and it will be done by the time you are ready to serve. Or reheat in a 325° oven for 15 to 20 minutes.

15. From the East and Far East

Dishes typical of the Near and the Far East include broiled kabobs, rice dishes like Moussaka and pilafs, curries, and flash-cooked foods made familiar here by Chinese restaurants. Though seasonings vary from country to country, and each country has its own specialties, they mix and match well—kabobs go as well with curries as they do with Chinese or Japanese dishes.

The collection of Eastern recipes in this chapter was put together because the recipes all work well with each other. The country in which each recipe is a specialty is noted. A further selection of dishes that mix well with an Eastern meal is to be found in the chapter on Hawaiian Luaus, Chapter 10.

Shrimp toast is a good appetizer for an Eastern meal, and boiled rice—unless you are serving another rice dish, such as a pilaf—is the proper starch. In Chapter 19 you'll find recipes for Raita and Sambal, Indian side dishes of onion and cucumber. Saffron Fruit Cream, or chilled, canned mandarin oranges, make good desserts for Eastern meals.

Try a warmed rice wine for Chinese or Japanese banquets; or serve cold beer or Chinese or Indian tea, plain.

Holubste

Make these tasty Ukrainian Stuffed Cabbage Rolls as a side dish for pork or grilled meats. (Use a leafy, green cabbage for this.)

2½ cups boiling water	Salt
2 teaspoons salt	Oil
2 cups uncooked rice	1½ cups tomato juice
¼ cup butter	2 tablespoons butter, melted
1 medium onion, peeled, minced	1 teaspoon salt
1 teaspoon salt	Pinch black pepper
¼ teaspoon pepper	1 pint sour cream, optional
1 medium-large cabbage	

1. In a saucepan combine boiling water, salt, and rice; bring to a boil, cover, simmer until the water is absorbed, about 14 minutes. Turn off the heat and let stand.

2. In a large skillet, melt the butter, add the onion, and sauté until light golden. Combine with the rice and season with salt and pepper; let cool.

3. Turn the cabbage upside down and cut out the core; place in a deep kettle and pour boiling water into the hollow until the cabbage is covered. Let stand until the leaves are pliable. Drain and carefully pick off the leaves. Reserve 2 large whole leaves. Cut the hard center rib from each of the remaining leaves. The leaves are now halved.

4. Oil a large skillet or casserole. Place a spoonful of rice filling on each leaf half. Tuck in the ends and roll up tight. Place any extra leaves (except the large reserved leaves) in the bottom of the casserole. Arrange the stuffed leaves in layers and lightly salt each layer.

5. Combine the tomato juice with the melted butter, salt, and pepper and pour over the cabbage rolls. The liquid should barely show between the rolls. Place the large reserved leaves over the top, then cover tight.

6. Bake in a preheated 350° oven for 1½ to 2 hours, or until both cabbage and filling have cooked. Serve hot with sour cream at room temperature, if desired.

Makes about 30 rolls, and serves 10 to 14.

Take-It-Along Tips: Undercook by about 10 minutes and take to the party with the sour cream. Wrap the casserole in foil and overwrap in newspaper to keep it warm.

Lamb Kabobs

Wonderful patio fare, lamb kabobs are popular with everyone. The secret of success with kabobs is to brush them well, and often, with the marinade, and to keep them at the right distance from the coals, otherwise they'll be black outside and raw inside.

1 cup rosé wine	¼ teaspoon pepper
½ cup orange juice	2 pounds boned lamb, cut into 2-inch cubes
½ cup finely chopped onions	
½ cup chili sauce	12 mushrooms, wiped clean
¼ cup vegetable oil	2 green peppers, seeded, cut into 1½-inch squares
1 clove garlic, peeled, minced	
1 tablespoon brown sugar	4 tomatoes, cut into wedges
1 teaspoon oregano	

1. Combine in a mixing bowl wine, orange juice, onions, chili sauce, vegetable oil, garlic, brown sugar, oregano, and pepper. Pour over the lamb and marinate for 2 hours, covered, or overnight in the refrigerator. Drain the meat and reserve the marinade.

2. Thread lamb cubes, mushrooms, green pepper squares, and tomato wedges alternately on skewers. Broil 4 to 6 inches from the heat for 20 minutes, turning skewers frequently and brushing with reserved marinade.

Makes 6 to 8 servings.

Take-It-Along Tips: Wrap threaded skewers in foil and take to the party to finish there. Don't forget to bring the marinade and a brush with which to apply the marinade to the broiling kabobs.

Moussaka

This is a Greek specialty—baked in a mold of eggplant skins—and good hot or cold. This is often served as a main course.

5 pounds small eggplants	½ teaspoon ground rosemary
1 tablespoon salt	
3 tablespoons olive oil	1 small clove garlic, mashed
2½ cups ground cooked lamb	
⅔ cup minced onions, cooked in butter	¼ teaspoon corn starch
	⅔ cup beef bouillon
⅛ teaspoon pepper	3 tablespoons tomato paste
½ teaspoon thyme	3 large eggs, well beaten

1. Remove the tops and cut the eggplants in half, lengthwise; cut deep gashes in the flesh of each half. Sprinkle with salt and let stand 30 minutes. Squeeze out the water, dry the cut sides, and brush with olive oil. Pour ½ inch of water into a roasting pan, place the eggplants cut-side up, and bake 30 to 40 minutes, or until tender. Scoop out the pulp, leaving the eggplant skins intact.

2. Chop the pulp and sauté over medium heat for a minute or 2 in the olive oil. Turn into a mixing bowl.

3. Line a lightly oiled medium casserole with the eggplant skins, pointed ends meeting at center-bottom of the mold and purple sides against mold.

4. Beat the remaining ingredients into the chopped eggplant. Turn into the lined mold, and fold eggplant skins over the surface. Cover with aluminum foil and a lid. Bake in a pan of boiling water in a 375° oven for 1½ hours. Let cool 20 minutes; just before serving, unmold onto a serving plate.

Makes 8 to 10 servings.

Take-It-Along Tips: If you are going to serve this hot, take it to the party in its baking dish, wrapped in foil and overwrapped in newspapers to keep it hot. Unmold at the host home.

Pilaf Bokhari

This Persian pilaf, which combines rice and chicken livers, makes a delightful one-dish dinner. Offer rosé wine with this.

3 ounces chicken fat	3 cups chicken bouillon
10 to 12 chicken livers	1½ teaspoons turmeric or curry powder
4 carrots, peeled, grated	
2 medium onions, peeled, chopped	1 clove garlic, peeled, crushed
Small bunch parsley, minced	2 large tomatoes, peeled, chopped
10 ounces converted rice	

1. In a large, heavy skillet, a wok, or an electric frying pan, heat the chicken fat over low heat, then add the chicken livers and sauté until slightly browned. Remove, drain, cut into small pieces.

2. Still over low heat; sauté the carrots, onions, and parsley in

the chicken fat for 5 minutes, taking care the onions do not brown. Add the rice, bouillon, turmeric, and garlic, and return the liver to the pan. Stir until well mixed. Cover tightly and cook without stirring, over low heat, for approximately 20 minutes until the rice has absorbed the liquid. Don't overcook it.

3. Bury the raw tomatoes in the rice mixture, and allow 5 minutes for them to warm before serving.

Makes 6 servings.

Take-It-Along Tips: If this is to travel, you can prepare it ahead and reheat at the party in a 325° oven for 15 to 20 minutes. Or prepare just before leaving, seal in foil, and overwrap in newspapers for the trip. Undercook by 10 minutes if the dish is to travel hot.

Chinese Mushrooms, Snow Peas, and Bamboo Shoots

This is a meaty vegetable dish to serve with Oriental dishes. If Chinese mushrooms and oyster sauce are unavailable, use fresh mushrooms and omit the oyster sauce. Do not precook mushrooms. Make this just before serving in a wok or in an electric skillet.

2 cups dried Chinese mushrooms	4 tablespoons oyster sauce
1 teaspoon soy sauce	1 teaspoon cornstarch mixed in 2 tablespoons water
½ teaspoon salt	
1 teaspoon sugar	1 tablespoon vegetable oil
1 teaspoon cornstarch	4 ounces snow peas, parboiled, or 1 package frozen, or flat Italian beans
2 tablespoons vegetable oil	
2 scallions, in 1-inch shreds	
1 slice fresh ginger, ½-inch thick, minced very fine	
	1 can bamboo shoots, rinsed, drained
½ cup chicken broth	
½ cup mushroom water	1 teaspoon salt

1. Cover the mushrooms with boiling water, soak 20 minutes. Drain, reserving ½ cup liquid. Sprinkle with soy sauce, salt, sugar, cornstarch, and mix well. Set by the stove with the remaining ingredients, measured. Place a serving platter in an oven at 250°.

2. Set the wok over high heat for 30 seconds, swirl in the oil, count to 30, add the mushrooms, stir and toss 2 minutes. Lower the heat to medium, add the scallions and ginger; stir and toss for 5 minutes. Add the chicken broth and mushroom water; cover, simmer 15 minutes. Add the oyster sauce; stir well. Stir in the cornstarch mixed with water, and simmer until the sauce thickens and clears. Scrape into the serving dish and keep warm.

3. Turn the heat to medium high; add one tablespoon oil, count to 20, add snow peas and bamboo shoots. Sprinkle with salt, stir and toss 3 minutes. Mix with the mushrooms and serve at once.

Makes 6 to 8 portions for an Oriental meal of several dishes.

Take-It-Along Tips: Measure all the ingredients and prepare the Chinese mushrooms as described in step one. Wrap solid ingredients in twists of foil, and seal liquids and liquid mixtures into small jars. Take to the party ready to flash cook, and follow step 2 at the host home, starting about 25 minutes before the dish is due to be served.

Indian Chicken Pulao with Shrimps

This Indian specialty combines rice with chicken and shrimps cooked with exotic spices. Serve it with hot rolls, and a green salad. Make it in a Chinese wok, a big enameled skillet that has a heavy lid or in a large electric skillet. Offer a rosé wine or beer with it.

- 1 teaspoon oil
- 2 sticks butter or margarine
- 2 large onions, peeled, sliced
- 1½ pounds cut-up chicken
- 1 teaspoon salt
- 3 cloves garlic, peeled, minced
- 3 tablespoons dark, seedless raisins
- ¼ teaspoon cinnamon
- ⅛ teaspoon ground cardamom
- ⅛ teaspoon ground mace
- 1 teaspoon ground cloves
- ⅛ teaspoon pepper
- 2 cups converted rice
- 1 pound raw shrimps, shelled, deveined
- 2 cups chicken bouillon
- 2 cups beef bouillon
- ½ teaspoon ground saffron
- 1 tablespoon water
- 2 tablespoons whole almonds, skinned

1. Warm the oil over medium heat, melt the butter, and sauté the onions until crisp. Remove and reserve. Add the chicken pieces,

salt them, and sauté one minute. Add the garlic, raisins, cinnamon, cardamom, mace, cloves, and pepper, and sauté until the chicken is browning, about 5 minutes. Add the rice and sauté 5 minutes, or until it becomes opaque. Add the shrimps, mix well; add the chicken and the beef bouillon, stir until boiling, cover, reduce heat to a minimum, simmer until liquid is absorbed, about 20 minutes. Mix the saffron in the water, and stir into the mixture.

2. Add the almonds 5 minutes before rice is tender. Serve hot, sprinkled with the crisped onions.

Makes 6 to 8 servings.

Take-It-Along Tips: Undercook by 5 to 8 minutes, wrap in foil, overwrap in newspapers, and let it finish cooking while it travels. Or complete cooking, allow to cool rapidly so the rice won't overcook, and reheat with a little chicken bouillon, ¼ cup, at the host home.

Lamb Korma

This is a dish from India, a curry made with yogurt. It is creamy, aromatic, and delicious. Serve with boiled rice, chutney, and the Raita and Onion Sambal. Offer beer or a rosé wine.

1 pound lamb, from leg, cut into 1-inch cubes	6 whole cloves
½ teaspoon salt	¼ teaspoon red-pepper flakes
1 pint plain yogurt	1 8-ounce can tomato sauce
1 tablespoon ground coriander	1 tablespoon oil
1 tablespoon ground cumin	3 tablespoons butter
2 cardamom seeds, peeled	1 large onion, peeled, sliced
½ teaspoon ground ginger	1 clove garlic, peeled, minced

1. Marinate the lamb with the salt and yogurt for 15 minutes. Mix the coriander, cumin, cardamom seeds, ginger, cloves, and red-pepper flakes in the tomato sauce.

2. Set a large heavy skillet over medium heat for 30 seconds, swirl in the oil, melt the butter, add the onion and garlic and sauté, tossing, until the onion is golden, 3 to 5 minutes. Add the lamb and yogurt, and the tomato sauce with spices. Stir well, cover, simmer

until the meat is tender, about 20 to 30 minutes. Remove the cover the last few minutes of cooking so that the sauce reduces.

Serves 4 to 6. Double the ingredients to serve 8 to 12, or better yet, offer other Oriental dishes along with it. (See Index.)

Take-It-Along Tips: Reheat at the host home over a slow fire. Do not boil.

Malaysian Chicken Curry

Just the smells that come from the kitchen as this cooks makes it worth the effort. Increase the chili if you like hot curries. Serve with rice and with a good chutney. Get all the ingredients ready and carry them to the party—do the cooking there, in a wok or a big skillet.

- 2 cups milk
- 1 cup grated fresh or packaged unsweetened coconut
- 1 teaspoon oil
- 3 tablespoons butter or margarine
- 3 medium onions, peeled
- 1 tablespoon ground coriander
- 1 teaspoon ground anise
- ½ teaspoon saffron
- 1 teaspoon ground ginger
- 1 teaspoon chili powder
- 2 cloves garlic, peeled, minced
- 2 tablespoons grated lemon rind
- 3 tablespoons lemon juice
- 2 tablespoons damson preserves or other plum jam
- 1 teaspoon sugar
- 1 teaspoon salt
- 1 3-pound chicken, skinned, boned
- 1 cup peeled whole almonds
- 6 cups *cooked* rice
- Chutney

1. Bring the milk to a boil, add the coconut, turn off the heat, and let the coconut soak 30 minutes. Drain, reserving the liquid. Squeeze the coconut dry, and reserve.

2. Measure the oil and the butter. Slice the onions into rings, place in a medium bowl, and toss with the coriander, anise, saffron, ginger, chili, garlic, grated lemon rind, lemon juice, preserves, sugar, and salt. Cut the chicken into one-inch cubes.

3. Set the wok over medium heat for 30 seconds, swirl in the oil, melt the butter, add the coconut shreds, sauté stirring constantly, until lightly browned. Remove and toss with the onion and spice

mixture. Add the chicken to the wok, toss to coat with butter. Add the onion mixture and toss. Add the coconut milk and almonds. Bring to a rapid boil, lower the heat, and simmer 10 minutes or until the chicken is tender and sauce is thickened. Serve at once with warmed rice and chutney.

Makes 6 to 8 portions.

Take-It-Along Tips: Prepare all the ingredients and do the cooking at the host home. Carry the rice in a serving dish that is ovenproof. You'll need a wok or a large electric skillet in which to cook the chicken, so bring your own.

Sukiyaki

This Japanese favorite makes a delicious one-course party meal. The raw meat and vegetables are cooked in a wok over the flame in a small hibachi, or they can be cooked in an electric skillet set right on the dinner table. (Use a hot pad if necessary.) Serve with boiled rice. At a Japanese dinner, 2 or 3 flowers decorate the platter of raw foods, and the cooking is done at the dinner table.

1¼ pounds beef fillet or good chuck steak	6 celery stalks
10 green onions	1 large green pepper
½ pound large mushrooms, wiped	¼ cup beef bouillon
1 can bamboo shoots, drained	¼ cup soy sauce
	2 tablespoons sugar
	2 tablespoons butter

1. Have the butcher cut the meat across the grain into thin, flat pieces; cut these into 2- by 4-inch strips. Cut the onions, mushrooms, bamboo shoots, celery, and green pepper into strips of the same size. Heap the meat in the center of a large serving platter and pile the vegetables around it.
2. Mix the bouillon, soy sauce, and sugar in a small decorative bowl. Take meat, vegetables, and sauce to the party.
3. Melt the butter in an electric skillet set at medium high. Sauté the beef, tossing it constantly for about 2 minutes. Add the blended bouillon and cook for 2 minutes.

4. Now add the vegetables, one at a time. Stir and toss until all are well moistened, keeping the vegetables in separate piles. Cover and simmer for 15 minutes.

Serves 4 to 6.

Take-It-Along Tips: Carry all the ingredients, ready to cook, to the party and do the cooking there.

16. New Orleans and New England Dishes

The New Orleans cooking tradition is mostly French, and the New England tradition is mostly English. What they have in common is that they appeal to most everyone.

Gumbo, seafood, and the elegance of a cuisine that at its best rivals that of its French originators characterizes New Orleans dishes. The few here are typical. With them, if you are doing dessert, serve Cherries Jubilee or another southern specialty, such as New Orleans Pecan Pie. Offer later Café Brûlot Diabolique.

The New England school of cooking reflects the fact that for a long time winter foods couldn't depend on fresh garden produce and that hard work in cold weather required sugar for energy and the filling properties of thick hearty stews and pies.

Baked Beans the New England Way is a typical cold weather specialty, and so are any number of hearty meat pies. Pies are excellent bake-and-take dishes when you haven't time or money to waste and want a rave review. Some of the recipes in the group here are descended from recipes French-Canadian immigrants to Vermont and Maine brought with them.

At cocktail time, many New Englanders offer crackers with relishes of cucumbers and tomatoes—sour cream dips, too.

Most recipes here cannot be doubled. You'll have to cook two if you have a crowd to feed. Baked Beans can, of course, be done in huge quantities.

Louisiana Ham Pot

A tangy specialty of the South: It takes a lot of baking, so start early in the morning or prepare the day before.

- ¼ cup all-purpose flour
- 2 teaspoons salt
- 1 teaspoon curry powder
- 2 pounds uncooked ham, in 1-inch cubes
- 6 medium yams or sweet potatoes, peeled, cut into slices ¼ inch thick
- 6 leeks, washed, sliced in lengths
- 1 10-ounce package frozen green peas
- ¼ cup stuffed olives, sliced
- 2 cups boiling water
- 2 tablespoons butter

1. Turn the oven to 350°.
2. Mix flour, salt, curry powder, in a large bowl, and toss the ham cubes in the mixture.
3. In a medium casserole that is ovenproof, place ⅓ of the meat cubes; cover with a layer made of half the yam or sweet potato slices, the leeks and the peas and olives; cover with another third of the ham cubes; repeat the vegetable layer, and finish with a layer of ham cubes. Pour the boiling water over the casserole and dot the top with butter. Cover and bake 3 hours or until the ham is tender.

Serves 6.

Take-It-Along Tips: You can take this to the party in its cooking casserole, hot, sealed in foil, and overwrapped in newspapers, or you can take it cold and reheat once there in a 350° oven for 20 to 30 minutes.

New Orleans Fresh Crab Gumbo

You need fresh crabs for this one. Serve with boiled rice, crisp salad, and chilled white wine.

12 small or 3 medium crabs	1 bay leaf
3 tablespoons butter	1 pound okra
6 tomatoes, peeled	2 quarts boiling water
1 onion, chopped	Salt
⅛ teaspoon thyme	Pepper
1 teaspoon parsley, minced	

1. Wash, scald, and clean crabs. Cut off the claws; crack, and remove the body of the crab from the shell and cut into quarters.
2. Heat butter in a large skillet and sauté crab quickly till slightly colored. Add tomatoes, chopped onion, thyme, parsley, and bay leaf. When the onion begins to brown slightly, add okra, sliced into rounds, and cover with 2 quarts of boiling water. Season with salt and pepper. Simmer for one hour.
3. When you serve the gumbo, give each person a portion of the crab claws as well as the crab meat. If you are using large crabs, remove meat from claws just before serving as it is hard to do it gracefully in a soup plate!

Serves 6 portions.

Take-It-Along Tips: Time this so that it finishes cooking as you are ready to leave for the party. Undercook by about 10 minutes. Seal in foil, wrap in newspapers to keep warm, and serve as soon as possible. You don't want the crab meat overdone.

Poached Salmon with Sauce Verte

A specialty in one of the French Quarter's best restaurants, this is poached salmon covered with a savory green mayonnaise. Prepare sauce, recipe below, before the salmon. For a party, garnish the salmon platter with watercress and peeled, hollowed, and well-drained tomatoes, stuffed with diced cucumbers, seasoned with French dressing and minced parsley. Blanc de Blanc, well chilled, is a lovely wine to serve with this. Offer crusty French bread and butter with it, too.

THE SALMON
- 2 quarts water
- 1½ cups dry white wine, or 1 tablespoon white wine vinegar
- 1 carrot, scraped, chopped
- 1 onion, peeled, quartered
- 2 sprigs parsley
- 1 bay leaf
- ½ teaspoon thyme
- 6 peppercorns
- 1 tablespoon salt
- 3 pounds fresh salmon, tail end or center piece

Pour water into a kettle large enough to allow the salmon to lie flat. Simmer all the ingredients except the salmon for 30 minutes. Lower the heat, lay the salmon wrapped in washed cheesecloth in the bottom of the kettle. When the liquid returns to a simmer, cover the kettle, reduce the heat, and poach the salmon for 30 minutes. Let it cool in the liquid, uncovered; then drain and unwrap it, chill it, and skin the top and sides. Set on a serving platter.

Makes 8 to 10 servings.

SAUCE VERTE
- 1 cup spinach
- ½ cup watercress
- ½ cup parsley
- ¼ cup fresh tarragon or 2 teaspoons dried tarragon
- ¼ cup sour cream
- 2 cups Fresh Mayonnaise, or commercial mayonnaise

1. Trim the stems from the spinach, watercress, parsley, and tarragon. Drop into boiling water and boil for 3 minutes, uncovered. Drain, cool under running water, and squeeze dry in a paper towel. Turn the sour cream into the blender, add the greens, and blend. Mix the green purée with the mayonnaise.

2. Coat the salmon with Sauce Verte, reserving a portion to offer in a sauceboat.

Take-It-Along Tips: Take the salmon on its serving platter to the party, and take the Sauce Verte in a sealed jar. At the host home, coat the salmon with the sauce, reserving some sauce to offer in a sauceboat.

Brandied Chicken with Mushroom Sauce

Grilled tomatoes and a green salad are nice with this. Offer with a red Burgundy or Mateus or Rosé d'Anjou wine.

4 pounds chicken, cut up	2 tablespoons butter
2 teaspoons salt	½ teaspoon salt
¼ teaspoon white pepper	1½ tablespoons onion, peeled, minced
⅛ teaspoon curry powder	
2 tablespoons oil	2 tablespoons brandy
½ pound mushrooms, wiped, quartered	¾ cup heavy cream
	¼ cup chicken broth

1. Wipe the chicken pieces dry, season with salt, pepper, and curry powder.
2. Over medium heat, warm the oil in a large heavy skillet, and sauté the chicken until it is golden on all sides, about 10 minutes. Lower the heat.
3. In another skillet over medium-high heat, sauté the mushrooms in butter for 5 minutes and salt them. Add to the chicken with the minced onion. Reduce the heat a little and continue cooking the chicken slowly, without letting the onion burn, for 15 minutes or until the smaller pieces are tender. Remove these to a serving dish and let the larger pieces cook another 5 minutes. Remove the excess fat. Return the smaller pieces to the pan.
4. Heat the brandy in a ladle, set it on fire, and spoon over the chicken. Then add the heavy cream, and the chicken broth. Scrape up the pan juices and coat the chicken pieces well. Simmer another 5 minutes, basting the chicken with the sauce, and serve.

Makes 8 to 12 servings.

Take-It-Along Tips: Prepare the recipe through step 3, then take to the party along with the brandy, cream, and broth. Flambé the chicken over a sterno fire at the dinner table and finish the cooking before the guests. Very effective.

New Orleans Marinated Venison

What to do when you are invited to cook a portion of the day's hunt? If it's venison, I ask for a roast or a rack and cook it this way. I serve a red Burgundy with it.

- 1 4-pound venison roast or rack
- 1 teaspoon cracked pepper
- 3 bay leaves
- ½ teaspoon ground allspice
- 6 whole cloves
- ½ cup Burgundy wine
- ½ cup brandy
- ½ cup olive or vegetable oil
- 6 carrots, peeled, cut into 2-inch pieces
- 12 small white onions, peeled
- ¼ cup butter
- ¼ cup flour
- 1 cup strong beef bouillon
- Salt

1. Place the venison in an earthenware or glass bowl. Add pepper, bay leaves, allspice, cloves, wine, brandy, and oil. Cover and refrigerate overnight. Lift the roast out of the bowl and place in a shallow roasting pan; pour the marinade into the *bottom* of the pan.
2. Roast in a preheated 350° oven for 2 to 2½ hours or until the venison is tender. Spoon the marinade over the meat every 15 minutes as it cooks. Forty minutes before the roast is ready, add the carrots and onions to the pan.
3. Remove the cooked meat and vegetables to a platter and keep them warm.
4. Measure one cup of the pan drippings. In a small skillet over medium-low heat melt the butter and stir in the flour. Gradually stir in the pan drippings and the beef bouillon. Simmer, stirring constantly, until the sauce bubbles and thickens. Season to taste with salt.

Serve the meat in thin slices, cut across the grain, and offer vegetables and sauce with each portion.

Makes 8 to 10 portions.

Take-It-Along Tips: Remove the finished meat to a casserole and keep warm. Finish the recipe and place the vegetables with the roast

Baked Beans the New England Way

Here is my favorite recipe for home-baked beans, New England style. Cooked in an old-fashioned crock, this always makes a big hit at a casual party. The beans take 8 hours to cook—so start early. A real treat with roasted franks and very inexpensive.

- 2 cups navy or pea beans
- 12 cups water
- 1 small onion, peeled
- ⅓ cup dark brown sugar, lightly packed
- 1 teaspoon salt
- 1½ teaspoons dry mustard
- ½ teaspoon pepper
- ¼ cup dark molasses
- 3 tablespoons catsup
- ¼ cup maple syrup
- ¼ pound fat salt pork, sliced
- Boiling water

1. Wash the beans and soak them overnight in cold water to cover.
2. Drain, then turn the beans into a heavy kettle. Cover them with fresh water. Bring to a boil, then simmer, uncovered, until the skins split when blown upon, about 30 to 40 minutes.
3. Drain, and place the beans in a bean crock or a small, heavy casserole. In the center, bury the onion. Mix all the other ingredients, except the pork, and pour over the beans. Insert the slices of salt pork just below the surface. Add sufficient boiling water to cover the beans.
4. Bake, covered, in a 250° oven for 8 hours, adding a small amount of boiling water from time to time so the beans do not become dry. Uncover during last 30 minutes of baking.

Makes 6 servings.

Take-It-Along Tips: Take to the party in its cooking dish and reheat there on the stove top, stirring often. You can take these to a cold picnic party in a wide-mouthed thermos.

Chicken Breasts, Vermont Style

The maple syrup in this recipe gives the chicken a sweet, nutty flavor that goes particularly well with such vegetables as yams and parsnips. Serve with a well-chilled, semidry rosé wine.

4 boned chicken breasts	½ cup finely diced ham
½ cup flour	½ teaspoon dried chives
1 teaspoon salt	¼ cup butter
¼ teaspoon pepper	1 cup thinly sliced onion
2 tablespoons butter	⅛ teaspoon savory
3 large mushrooms, wiped, sliced	4 tablespoons maple syrup
	½ cup water

1. Preheat oven to 350°.
2. Roll the chicken breasts in flour, season with the salt and pepper. In a large heavy skillet, melt the 2 tablespoons of butter and sauté together the mushrooms, ham, and chives. Cook 3 minutes or until the mushrooms are tender.
3. Slit the thick portion of each chicken breast lengthwise to make a long pocket and insert one spoonful of the mushroom mixture. Pinch the edges together to seal. Brown the breasts in the skillet in ¼ cup of butter and remove to a casserole.
4. To the frying pan, add the sliced onion and sauté until slightly browned. Top the chicken with the onion and sprinkle with the savory. Spoon over each chicken breast one tablespoon of the maple syrup. Add the water to the frying pan. Scrape up the juices and pour them into the casserole. Bake, uncovered, in a 350° oven for 30 minutes.

Makes 4 to 8 servings.

Take-It-Along Tips: Underbake by about 5 minutes. Cool, and take to the party wrapped in Saran Wrap. Reheat there 10 minutes in an oven at 350°.

Hamburger Wellington

A take-off on Beef Wellington—a fillet of beef cooked in a crust—this makes an elegant, but economical, party dish. Great hot or cold for a picnic.

- 1½ pounds bottom round ground beef
- ¾ cup rolled oats
- ⅓ cup celery, peeled, chopped
- ⅓ cup onion, peeled, chopped
- ¼ cup peeled, shredded carrots
- 2 tablespoons parsley, minced
- ½ teaspoon oregano
- 1 teaspoon curry powder
- 1½ teaspoons salt
- ⅛ teaspoon pepper
- 1 egg, beaten
- ¼ teaspoon chili sauce
- ½ cup tomato juice
- 1 package pie-crust mix, prepared according to directions
- 1 bunch watercress

1. Heat the oven to 450°.
2. In a large bowl, mix together the meat, oats, celery, onion, carrot, parsley, oregano, curry powder, salt, and pepper. In a smaller bowl, mix the egg, chili sauce, and tomato juice. Combine the mixtures.
3. Shape the meat into a roll about 9 inches long.
4. Roll the pastry for the crust into a rectangle, 12 by 14 inches. Place the meat loaf in the center and seal the pastry on top. Place the loaf in a baking dish, seam-side down.
5. Bake in a preheated oven at 450° for 10 minutes; reduce the temperature to 300°, continue baking 50 minutes more. With 2 spatulas, lift the loaf onto a bed of watercress and serve.

Makes 6 to 8 portions. Make 2 loaves to serve 12 to 16.

Take-It-Along Tips: Prepare the recipe through step 3 and finish it at the host home if you wish to serve this hot. To serve cold, chill in the pan, turn onto a watercress-lined serving platter, overwrap in Saran Wrap, and take to the party.

Pork Casserole New York Style

You need a large, heavy skillet and a Dutch oven to get this just right. The other essentials are not to overcook the onions, and not to underbrown the pork chops. Spinach or watercress salad with a tart dressing is excellent with this dish. Serve with a cold rosé wine.

- 12 to 16 small pork chops
- 6 large Bermuda onions
- Salt
- Black pepper
- 1½ cups chicken broth
- ¼ cup dry white wine
- ⅛ teaspoon sage, optional
- Green garnish of parsley, spinach, or watercress

1. Trim the excess fat from the chops and melt the fat down over medium heat in a large, heavy skillet. Discard the bits of fat.
2. While the fat is rendering, peel the onions and slice into rounds ¼ inch thick. Keep the rounds intact. With the heat turned to medium-low, sauté the onions in the fat until golden. Remove to a bowl.
3. Turn the heat to medium-high, brown the pork chops, and salt and pepper them generously. As each skilletful of chops is browned, transfer them to an ovenproof casserole and cover with a layer of the cooked onions. Continue making layers of chops and onions, ending with a layer of onions. Mix one cup of chicken broth with the wine, pour over the chops. Add enough broth so the chops are covered. Sprinkle sage, if desired, over the top.
4. Bake at 325° for 2 hours, moistening the top layer occasionally as the broth level lowers. Serve in the casserole with a ring of parsley around the edge and a sprig of parsley across the center.

Makes 8 to 12 generous servings.

Take-It-Along Tips: Take to the party cooled and reheat for 10 minutes in an oven at 375°.

Lamb Pie

Meat pies are rare at parties and yet they are very popular, judging by how quickly they disappear.

- ¼ cup flour
- ½ teaspoon salt
- ¼ teaspoon pepper
- ⅛ teaspoon nutmeg
- 2 pounds boned shoulder of lamb, cut in 2-inch cubes
- 2 tablespoons butter
- 2 tablespoons vegetable oil
- 1 large onion, peeled, thinly sliced
- 1¾ cups dry red table wine
- 1 small bay leaf, crushed
- 1 cup fresh sliced mushrooms
- 2 large tomatoes, peeled, seeded, cubed
- 1 12-ounce package frozen lima beans
- 1½ teaspoons salt
- ¼ teaspoon pepper
- ¼ teaspoon thyme
- 2 tablespoons chopped parsley
- 1 tablespoon finely chopped chives
- ¼ pound peperoni, thinly sliced
- 1 package pie-crust mix
- 1 egg yolk
- 1 tablespoon water

1. Preheat the oven to 375°.
2. In shallow dish, mix the flour, salt, pepper, and nutmeg. Remove excess fat from the lamb cubes; roll in the seasoned flour.
3. Heat the butter and the oil in a heavy shallow skillet and simmer the onion in it for about 2 minutes. Remove the onion with a slotted spoon and place in the bottom of a large shallow casserole. Sauté the lamb in the fat remaining in the skillet until browned on all sides, then transfer to the casserole.
4. Pour the wine into the skillet and scrape up the pan juices. Add the bay leaf. Pour the mixture over the lamb, cover tightly, and bake in the oven one hour or until the meat is partly tender. Add mushrooms, tomatoes, lima beans, salt, pepper, thyme, and parsley. Cover and continue cooking 30 minutes or until all ingredients are tender. Remove from the oven. Raise the temperature to 450°.
5. Sprinkle chives over the meat and cover the surface with the sliced peperoni.

6. Make a thick pie crust the size of the skillet and fit over the meat and vegetables, sealing the edges; slash the crust to let out the steam. With a fork, beat the egg yolk and one tablespoon of water and brush over the surface of the crust. Bake 10 minutes at 450°, then reduce the temperature to 375° and continue baking for 20 minutes or until the crust is golden brown.

Makes 8 to 10 portions. Make 2 pies to serve 16 to 20.

Take-It-Along Tips: Prepare ahead and cool. Take to the party and reheat at 350° for 10 to 15 minutes.

Beef-and-Kidney Pie

One of the tastiest dishes to originate in England, this makes elegant, economical party fare. Caution—the kidneys must be fresh. They taste best if they can be soaked overnight in water in the refrigerator.

- 1¼ pounds chuck steak
- 1¼ pounds fresh lamb kidney
- 1 large onion, peeled, sliced
- 2½ tablespoons butter, or margarine
- 2 tablespoons flour
- 1⅓ cups chicken bouillon
- 1¼ tablespoons Worcestershire sauce
- ½ teaspoon salt
- ⅛ teaspoon pepper
- 1 package pie-crust mix
- 1 egg yolk
- 1 tablespoon water

1. Wipe the steak, remove and reserve the fat, cut the lean meat into ¾-inch cubes. Unless already soaked, soak the kidneys for at least an hour in cold water; split in half and remove the white membrane; cut away the fat lobes and tubes; cut into ¼- and ½-inch slices.

2. Melt the beef fat in a heavy skillet over medium heat; add the onion and sauté until well browned, stirring constantly. Add the butter, chuck, and kidneys and sauté until all the meat is browned. With a slotted spoon, remove the meat and onion from the skillet and set aside. Turn the heat to very low.

3. Stir the flour into the fat remaining in the skillet. Stir in the chicken bouillon, working rapidly to keep the sauce from becoming lumpy. Strain the sauce.

4. Return the strained sauce to the skillet; add the meat, Worcestershire sauce, salt, and pepper. Cover tightly and simmer gently about 2 hours or until the meat is tender.

5. Place meat in a greased 2-quart casserole. Prepare a thick pie crust and fit it over the casserole. Slash the crust and brush with the beaten egg mixed with water. Bake in a preheated oven at 425° for 35 minutes or until the pastry is golden brown.

Makes 8 to 10 portions. Make 2 pies to serve 16 to 20.

Take-It-Along Tips: Prepare through step 5, but do the baking at the host home. Or, bake and reheat in a 425° oven before serving.

Creamy Chicken Pie

This is a creamy, delicately flavored chicken pie. Cook the fowl the day ahead, remove the meat, and store it in the refrigerator in the cooking liquid—then the chicken pie will take very little time to prepare. It can also be made with leftover turkey breast.

- 1 4-pound fowl
- 1 tablespoon salt
- 2 stalks celery
- 1 bay leaf
- Boiling water
- 14 small white onions, peeled
- 3 tablespoons chicken fat
- 3 tablespoons flour
- 1 cup light cream
- 2 cups chicken broth
- Salt to taste
- 1/8 teaspoon pepper
- 1/8 teaspoon mace
- 1/2 teaspoon Worcestershire sauce
- 2 tablespoons sherry (optional)
- 1/8 teaspoon tarragon
- 1 13¾-ounce package biscuit mix

1. Place chicken in large soup kettle, add salt, celery, bay leaf, and enough boiling water to cover the chicken halfway. Simmer, covered 1½ hours; add the onions for the last 20 minutes of cooking. Replenish the boiling water if level falls.

2. Remove the chicken and onions from the broth. Cool the broth, skim, and reserve the fat; strain the broth and reserve it. Remove the skin and bones from the chicken and discard. Cut the meat into large pieces.

3. Heat the fat in the top of a double boiler over boiling water, stir in the flour, then slowly add the cream and 2 cups of the reserved broth. Cook, stirring frequently until thickened. Add salt to taste, pepper, mace, Worcestershire sauce, sherry, and tarragon.

4. Preheat the oven to 450°. Arrange the chicken chunks with onions in a greased 2-quart casserole. Pour the sauce over the meat.

5. Prepare biscuit mix according to package directions.

6. Top casserole with biscuit dough spread evenly over the surface. Bake in a 450° oven for 20 to 25 minutes or until the biscuit is golden brown.

Serves 8 to 10. Double the ingredients and bake in 2 casseroles to serve 16 to 20.

Take-It-Along Tips: You can serve this fresh from the oven by preparing the chicken and sauce ahead, adding the pie crust once you get to the host home, and baking it there. Or complete the recipe and reheat at 350° for 10 to 15 minutes.

Pâté Chinois

This is an imported French-Canadian version of shepherd's pie. Make it from leftover beef and gravy. The flavor depends on the gravy. You can stretch the gravy if you haven't enough by adding a prepared gravy mix to drippings you have saved.

- 6 medium potatoes, peeled
- 2 cups roast beef gravy
- 1 teaspoon Worcestershire sauce
- ¼ teaspoon thyme
- $\frac{1}{16}$ teaspoon ground nutmeg
- 1½ teaspoons salt
- 1 medium onion, thinly sliced
- 4 cups of cooked roast beef, chopped fine
- 3 tablespoons butter
- 1 teaspoon salt
- ½ cup light cream, heated
- 2 eggs, well beaten
- Paprika

1. Set the potatoes to boil in water while preparing the meat mixture.

2. Bring to a boil in medium saucepan, the roast beef gravy, the Worcestershire sauce, thyme, nutmeg, salt, and onion. Cover, re-

duce the heat, and simmer 10 minutes. Add the meat. Check the seasonings. Pour into a greased 2-quart casserole.

3. Drain the potatoes as soon as they are tender, hold the potful of potatoes over low heat for a minute to dry them. Mash, beat in the butter, salt, and the hot cream. Work the potatoes into a light purée, then whip in the eggs with an electric beater.

4. Cover the casserole with the puréed potatoes, sprinkle with paprika. Bake in a 350° oven 30 minutes or until potatoes are slightly browned.

Makes 8 portions. Double the ingredients and bake in a large shallow casserole to serve 16.

Take-It-Along Tips: Prepare through step 4, wrap in foil for the trip to the host home, and serve lukewarm. Or, you can reheat once you get there for 10 minutes in a 350° oven.

Tourtière Canadienne

Originally, French-Canadians prepared this specialty with passenger pigeons or *tourtes* as they were called. Since the disappearance of these game birds, fresh pork or a mixture of ground meats is used. Traditionally tourtières are served Christmas Eve. I like this pie cold as well as hot, and sometimes prepare it in the form of small turnovers with a tablespoon or 2 of the meat mixture set onto 3-inch squares of thin pie pastry.

3 medium potatoes, peeled	¼ teaspoon celery salt
1½ pounds ground lean pork	¼ teaspoon pepper
1 small onion, peeled, minced	¼ teaspoon sage
	⅛ teaspoon ground cloves
½ cup boiling water	Package pie-crust mix
1 clove garlic, peeled, minced	Milk
1½ teaspoons salt	

1. Boil the potatoes until well done.
2. In a heavy saucepan, combine all other ingredients except the pie-crust mix and milk and cook over low heat, stirring constantly, until the meat loses its red color and half the liquid has evaporated. Cover and simmer 45 minutes.

3. Drain and mash potatoes and mix into cooked meat mixture. Cool.

4. Preheat oven to 450°, if you are going to bake immediately.

5. Prepare sufficient pastry for a 2-crust, 9-inch pie. Roll out half the pastry and line a deep 9-inch pie plate with it. Fill with the cooled meat mixture. Roll out the remainder of the dough and top the pie. Flute and seal edges and slash top crust. Brush with milk.

6. Bake in a preheated 450° oven for 10 minutes. Reduce heat to 350°; bake for 30 to 40 minutes longer or until the crust is golden.

Makes 6 generous portions. Prepared as turnovers, this recipe will serve as a snack for 12.

Take-It-Along Tips: Follow through step 6, wrap in foil, and reheat in a 350° oven at the host home.

17. Holiday Birds

A few special ways with birds for Christmas—duck, partridge, goose. If none of these is the bird of your choice, choose a large capon or a small turkey and follow the recipe for Christmas Goose; a regular roasting chicken can be done following the recipe for Christmas Duck with Cherries; and small Cornish game hens are wonderful as pretend–Partridge in a Pear Tree.

Christmas Duck with Cherries

Two roasted birds, sauced with a tangy cherry-brandy sauce, garnished with bright red cherries on a bed of curly dark green chicory, make a wonderful Christmas dish. If wild duck is available, hang it for several days, then marinate it before cooking.

THE BIRDS
- 2 3-pound birds
- ½ teaspoon salt
- ⅛ teaspoon black pepper
- 1 small sliced onion, crushed
- 1½ cups beef bouillon

1. Heat the oven to 425°.
2. Salt and pepper the duck cavities, and rub with onion. Prick the skin around the neck, back, and lower breast. Sear in an uncovered pan, breast side up, in heated oven 15 minutes. Lower the heat to 350° and roast for 60 minutes, removing the fat frequently. When the juices from the ducks run pale yellow, they are done. Turn

off the oven and keep the birds warm on a serving platter while you finish the sauce.

3. Pour the bouillon into the roasting pan, scrape up the pan juices, simmer until reduced to two-thirds.

THE SAUCE
3 dozen red cherries, fresh, frozen, or canned
1 tablespoon lemon juice, strained
1 tablespoon brandy
2 tablespoons brown sugar

1. While the birds cook, drain stemmed, pitted cherries and toss in a bowl with the lemon juice, brandy, and sugar. Set aside. When the ducks are done, pour the cherries into the reduced pan juices, simmer on low heat for 3 to 4 minutes. Remove the cherries and sprinkle them over the birds.

2. Boil the sauce rapidly to reduce and thicken. Add more lemon juice if sauce isn't tart enough. Serve in a sauceboat with the birds.
Makes 8 servings.

Take-It-Along Tips: Finish cooking the birds, but undercook by 10 minutes and place them in a serving dish. Overwrap with foil and cover with newspapers to keep warm. Finish the sauce and take this in a sealed jar to the party. Reheat the sauce at the party and serve over the lukewarm duck.

Partridge in a Pear Tree

Partridge is a small game bird, about 1½ pounds. A similar bird is the commercially raised "chukker" sold in specialty markets. Wild partridge should be hung 3 to 5 days to develop flavor before plucking. Marinate wild birds overnight. Allow one bird per person, half a bird if there is more than one course. You can also use Cornish game hens for this recipe. Offer a Burgundy or a full-bodied red wine with this dish.

THE PEARS
3 tablespoons butter
3 tablespoons honey
6 canned pear halves, drained
Juice of 1 lemon, strained
6 teaspoons red currant or cranberry jelly

1. Melt the butter over low heat in a small, heavy saucepan. Stir in the honey. Add the pears and lemon juice. Simmer, spooning syrup over the pears until the syrup glazes the fruit. Just before serving, fill the centers with the currant jelly, and place the pears around the birds.

THE BIRDS

6 partridges	Pepper
Salt	½ stick butter

1. Split birds along the backbone without separating the halves; salt and pepper them; tuck in the wing tips. Place birds, skin-side down, in a pan in an unheated broiler. Turn the heat to medium high; broil 10 minutes, basting twice with the butter. Turn the birds and, with the heat low enough to avoid blackening the birds, broil 15 minutes. Baste with the remaining butter and pan drippings frequently.

2. Set the birds on a platter and keep them warm while you finish the sauce.

MUSHROOM SAUCE

Neck and giblets of 3 birds	1 teaspoon salt
2 cups water	Salt to taste
⅛ teaspoon each, thyme, cloves, marjoram	3 mushroom caps per bird, wiped, chopped
½ bay leaf	1 teaspoon grated lemon rind
1 large onion slice	

1. Before you start the birds, simmer until tender the neck and giblets (except the liver) in water, uncovered, with the herbs, onion, and 1 teaspoon salt, about 1½ hours. Add the liver, simmer 15 minutes. Discard everything but the giblets and ½ cup stock. Process these one minute at low speed in a blender.

2. When the birds are done, pour the stock into the drippings in the pan, scraping up the juices. Place over low heat, add the mushrooms, and simmer until gravy has been reduced and thickened, 5 to 10 minutes. Turn off the heat, stir in the lemon rind, mix well, and pour into a gravy boat. Ladle over birds before serving.

Makes 6 servings.

Take-It-Along Tips: Finish cooking the pears and birds, set them on a serving platter, cover with sealed foil, overwrap with newspapers. Finish the sauce. Take the sauce, enclosed in a jar, to the party along with the birds. Reheat the sauce at the host home and serve with lukewarm birds.

Christmas Goose with Chestnut Stuffing

Serve roast goose with a special side dish of horseradish mixed with whipped cream and decorated with slivers of fresh cranberries. Goose is traditional for Christmas and no more difficult to handle than a big chicken. Offer a rich red wine with it—Cold Duck, for instance.

THE STUFFING
- 4 cups peeled, cooked chestnuts or canned unsweetened chestnuts, drained
- 1 goose liver
- 1 tablespoon butter
- 1 cup minced onion
- 2 pounds fresh ground pork, preferably fatty
- 2 teaspoons salt
- ⅛ teaspoon black pepper
- ⅛ teaspoon ground allspice
- ½ teaspoon thyme
- Salt

1. Break chestnuts into large pieces.
2. Sauté the liver in butter for 3 minutes over medium heat; chop, mix with the onion into the ground pork. Sauté, stirring for 5 minutes, over medium-low heat. Stir in the salt, pepper, allspice, and thyme. Taste and adjust seasoning.

THE BIRD
- 1 9-pound goose, stuffed
- Salt
- ½ cup butter
- 1½ cups beef broth

1. Preheat oven to 350°.
2. Season goose inside and out with salt. Pack the cavity, alternating layers of chestnuts and pork/liver mixture. Skewer the vent and truss the bird.
3. Rub the goose with half the butter, prick the skin all over, place in an uncovered roasting pan. Pour one cup of the broth over

the goose and roast 2½ to 3 hours, basting often. The bird is done when a drumstick moves slightly when tugged.

4. Place the bird on a warm platter in the warming oven. Pour the remaining broth into the pan, set over a burner at medium heat; stir, scraping up the pan juices. When slightly thickened (about 2 minutes), pour juices into a gravy boat and serve with the bird.

Serves 8 to 10.

Take-It-Along Tips: Undercook the bird by about 10 minutes, seal in foil, overwrap in newspapers. Finish the sauce and take in a closed jar, with the bird, to the party. Reheat the sauce and serve it hot over the lukewarm bird.

PART 6

When You Are Bringing the Vegetable

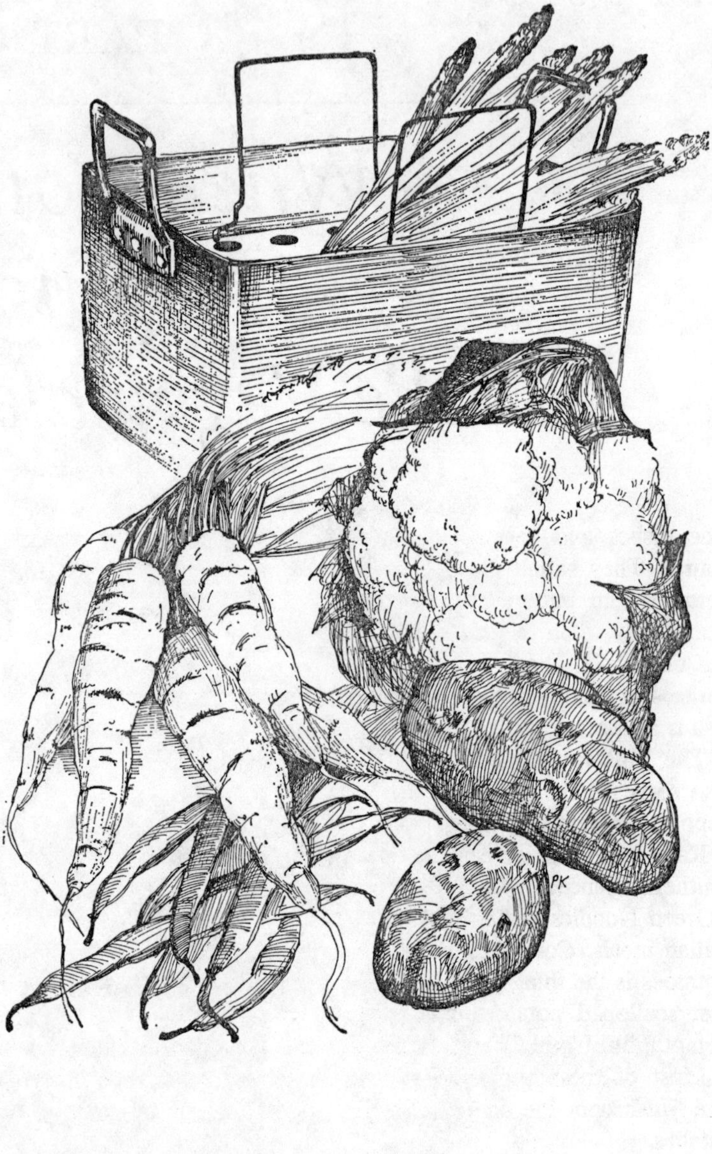
PK

18. Portable Side Dishes

Side dishes and vegetables for a party should enhance the main course. They should be light if the main dish is rich (plain baked potatoes and buttered green beans are light), and they should be heavy only when the main dish has to be stretched to serve a number of people. Diana Walton's Mushroom Pie is just about my favorite, but don't serve anything as filling and rich as this if the main dish is a casserole with a sauce and vegetables.

The Mushroom Pie and many of the vegetable recipes here can also serve as the main course—Stuffed Baked Tomatoes or Stuffed Peppers Provençale, for instance.

Ratatouille, hot or cold, goes with anything though it is native to southern France. In Chapter 13 you will find the Italian pasta dishes —Green Noodles and Spinach Ravioli—which can be side dishes for Italian meals. Corn Pudding is just great with ham, and In-the-Bag Potatoes is the thing to prepare if you are doing potatoes to go. The best scalloped potatoes I've ever tasted are given under Janson's Temptation. It's in Chapter 4 because it is a staple at a smorgasbord.

Most of these vegetable recipes can be doubled, but not those like Mushroom Pie and Corn Pudding, which must be made in two batches.

Diana Walton's Mushroom Pie

This is one of the best vegetable side dishes I know—it keeps well and is just as good when reheated.

1 pound mushrooms, wiped
¼ cup butter
5 green onions, minced, or 1 medium onion, peeled, chopped
1 clove garlic, peeled, minced
1 teaspoon salt
Grating of black pepper
¼ cup all-purpose flour
1 cup hot beef bouillon
1 cup heavy cream
¼ cup dry sherry
⅔ package pie-crust mix, mixed and chilled
1 tablespoon cold butter
Milk

1. Preheat the oven to 375°.
2. Cut the mushrooms into ¼-inch thick slices, lengthwise. In a large heavy skillet over medium-low heat, melt the butter and sauté the onions, garlic, and mushrooms 10 minutes. Salt and pepper, then add the flour. Stir it in to make a smooth paste, then stir in the hot bouillon and the cream, working quickly to keep the sauce from getting lumpy. Simmer, stirring for about 5 minutes. Stir in the sherry. The sauce should be as thick as thick heavy cream. Add a little bouillon if it seems too thick; cook a few more minutes if it seems too thin. Taste, and add salt and pepper if needed.
3. Select a medium casserole, and roll out all the pie-crust mix, making a *thick* crust of a size to fit the casserole. Turn the mushrooms and sauce into the casserole, fasten the crust over the top. Slash it to vent the steam. Trim away excess crust. With a pastry brush dipped in milk, moisten the crust surface.
4. Bake for 35 minutes or until the crust is a dark, golden brown. *Makes 8 to 10 portions.*

Take-It-Along Tips: Finish the pie, take to the party sealed in foil and overwrapped in newspapers. Reheat 10 minutes at 325° just before serving.

Baked Stuffed Tomatoes

These are good take-to-the-party subjects. If you do the cooking at home, bake only 25 minutes, seal the whole baking dish in foil, and keep warm. Or prepare the tomatoes, wrap each in foil for the trip, open the foil, and bake at the host's house. Also makes a good main course.

6 large firm tomatoes	¾ cup bread crumbs
2 tablespoons butter	3 tablespoons beef bouillon
1 medium onion, peeled, minced	3 tablespoons parsley, minced
1 clove garlic, peeled, minced	Bread crumbs
⅜ pound sausage meat	2 tablespoons butter

1. Preheat oven to 300°.
2. Slice off and reserve the smooth tops of the tomatoes; scoop out and chop the pulp and discard the seeds.
3. In a small skillet over medium heat, melt the butter and sauté the onion and garlic until the onion begins to brown.
4. In a bowl, combine the sausage meat and the bread crumbs. Moisten with bouillon. Add the onion and garlic, the tomato pulp, and minced parsley. Mix well.
5. Stuff the tomatoes, sprinkle them with fine bread crumbs, dot each one with small pieces of butter, and put the reserved caps on top.
6. Bake in a lightly oiled casserole or ovenproof dish at 300° for 35 minutes. Serve on a bed of parsley.

Makes 6 portions.

Take-It-Along Tips: Bake only 25 minutes, seal the whole baking dish in foil, overwrap in newspapers, and take to the party. Or prepare the tomatoes and take them in their baking dish to the party and cook there.

Stuffed Peppers Provençale

Makes a good main dish as well as a vegetable course.

- 8 large green peppers
- 2 tablespoons olive oil
- 2 onions, peeled, slivered
- ¾ pound ground veal or lamb
- 2 tomatoes, peeled and chopped
- 1 clove garlic, peeled, minced
- 1 teaspoon salt
- ⅛ teaspoon pepper
- 1 small bay leaf, crushed
- ¾ teaspoon thyme
- 2 cups *cooked* rice
- 1 cup tomato sauce
- 2 tablespoons butter
- ½ teaspoon minced fresh basil, or ¼ teaspoon dried

1. Cut off the tops of the peppers and reserve. Seed the peppers, remove excess white pulp, and drop the peppers into rapidly boiling water to cover. In 5 minutes, remove and drain well.

2. Preheat the oven to 350°.

3. Heat the oil in a large skillet and sauté the onions until golden brown. Mix the meat with the onions, and brown a little, stirring constantly. Stir in the tomatoes, garlic, salt, pepper, bay leaf, and thyme. Cook until the tomatoes are pulpy but not dry. Remove from the heat, add the cooked rice, and mix well.

4. Stuff the peppers with the rice-and-meat mixture, replace the caps loosely, and set the peppers in an oiled baking dish. Bake about 25 minutes, longer if the peppers are very thick. During the last few minutes of cooking, heat the tomato sauce and melt the butter into it, season with the basil, and pour the sauce over the peppers. Serve on a bed of fresh basil if it is available.

Makes 8 portions.

Take-It-Along Tips: Bake these and take them in the baking dish wrapped in foil to the party.

In-the-Bag Potatoes

New potatoes, herb flavored, cooked in individual foil envelopes. Prepare them ahead, pop them into the host's oven for 30 to 40 minutes, and serve still in their sealed containers.

36 small new potatoes	12 mint leaves, or dill sprigs
1½ tablespoons salt	4 tablespoons butter

1. Scrape the potatoes; arrange them in threes on small squares of aluminum foil. Salt the potatoes lightly, divide the herbs among them. Fold the squares and seal the edges.
2. Put the bags in an oven at 375° and cook for 30 to 40 minutes until tender.

Makes 12 portions. To increase the number of servings allow 2 potatoes, one herb sprig, and one teaspoon of butter for each guest.

Take-It-Along Tips: Prepare these through step one, take to the party, and bake at the host home.

Corn Pudding

Super with baked ham or a ham casserole.

2 cups whole corn kernels, fresh or canned	⅛ teaspoon paprika
	⅛ teaspoon nutmeg
4 egg yolks	2 tablespoons sifted flour
1 teaspoon salt	1 teaspoon baking powder
⅛ teaspoon pepper	2 tablespoons butter, melted
1 teaspoon sugar	
1 small green pepper, seeded, minced	2 cups milk, scalded
	4 egg whites

1. In the blender, process corn kernels at low speed, drain, and turn into a large bowl. Beat the egg yolks until thick and lemon colored; add to the corn, beating it in with salt and pepper, sugar, minced green pepper, paprika, and nutmeg. Mix with the flour, baking powder, and melted butter; then beat in the milk.

2. Preheat the oven to 325°.

3. Beat egg whites until stiff but not dry, and fold into the corn mixture. Turn into a 2-quart buttered baking dish; set this in a pan of hot water in the bottom third of the oven. Bake until a knife inserted in the middle comes out clean, about 45 minutes.

Makes 8 to 10 portions.

Take-It-Along Tips: You'll have to bake this at the host home. Follow step one and turn the mixture into the baking dish. Take the egg whites to the host home in a sealed glass jar, whip there until stiff, fold gently into the corn mixture, and bake as directed.

Gratinée of Cauliflower with Watercress

Here is a vegetable dish that always wins compliments.

1 medium cauliflower	⅛ teaspoon pepper
2 cups milk	⅛ teaspoon nutmeg
3 tablespoons butter	4 tablespoons bread crumbs
3 tablespoons flour	2 tablespoons melted butter
½ cup grated Parmesan and Swiss cheese, mixed	2 cups watercress, washed and dried
1 teaspoon salt	

1. Break the cauliflower into small flowerets of uniform size. Cut away thick stem parts.

2. Bring the milk to a boil in a heavy kettle; toss in the flowerets and simmer 5 minutes, or until almost cooked. Drain and reserve milk.

3. Melt the butter in an enameled skillet, stir in the flour; beat in the reserved milk, plus enough more milk to fill 2 cups. Simmer, stirring, for 5 minutes. Remove from the heat and beat in the grated cheese, salt, pepper, and nutmeg.

4. Butter a circular, oven-proof glass dish. Spread ⅓ of the sauce over the bottom of the dish, arrange the flowerets on this. Pour over them the rest of the cream sauce, sprinkle with the crumbs, and dribble on the melted butter. Bake in the lowest third of the oven long enough to brown the crumbs lightly, 15 to 20 minutes.

5. Before serving, brown the crumbs under the broiler, then poke the stem ends of the watercress around the outer edges of the dish to form a ring. Place 2 or 3 branches of watercress under each serving.
Makes 6 to 8 portions.

Take-It-Along Tips: Follow through step 4, then take the baking dish to the party, and finish the browning there.

Casserole of Root Vegetables

This is a delicately flavored potpourri of root vegetables excellent with pork, duck, venison, or any strongly flavored casserole.

- 2 cups peeled, diced white turnips
- 2 cups scraped, diced carrots
  Boiling water
- 2 cups peeled, diced white potatoes
- 4 tablespoons butter
  Salt to taste
- ½ teaspoon lemon juice
- 1 tablespoon minced chervil or parsley or dill

1. Cover turnips and carrots with the boiling water and cook 15 minutes. Add the potatoes and boil until just tender, about 15 minutes. Drain and shake over heat to remove moisture. Add butter and salt, sprinkle on the lemon juice, and turn off the heat. Sprinkle with the minced herbs before serving.
Makes 8 to 10 portions.

Take-It-Along Tips: Reheat briefly on the stove top at the host home, then add the herbs, and serve.

Green Beans Lyonnaise

A vegetable that goes with anything.

2 pounds green beans, washed	Salt
6 cups boiling water	Pepper
2 teaspoons salt	1 teaspoon wine vinegar
3 small onions, peeled, chopped	2 tablespoons butter
4 tablespoons butter	1 tablespoon parsley, chopped

1. Snap off ends of beans; if slender, leave whole; if large, slice through the center (French cut). Drop beans into boiling salted water and cook uncovered until tender, but firm. The color should still be a very bright green.

2. In a heavy skillet over medium heat, sauté the onions in the butter until soft and golden. Add the green beans and mix well. Salt and pepper to taste, add the wine vinegar, remove from the heat. Place in an ovenproof serving dish.

3. Warm the beans in an oven at 325° for 15 minutes. Just before serving, in a small skillet, heat the butter until it froths and begins to turn golden brown. Remove and sprinkle over the beans with the parsley. Serve at once.

Makes 8 to 10 portions.

Take-It-Along Tips: Follow through step 2, take the beans in their serving dish to the party, and finish the recipe there. It takes only a minute or two.

Baked Green Beans

Dill-flavored green beans with mushrooms in a creamy sauce.

1 pound green beans	½ teaspoon salt
3 slices bacon, diced	¼ teaspoon pepper
1 large onion, peeled, chopped	1 teaspoon minced dill
	2 tablespoons cornstarch
1 cup wiped, sliced, mushrooms	1½ cups chicken broth

1. Heat the oven to 350°.
2. Snip ends from green beans, wash and drain. Arrange in a big, shallow casserole.
3. In a medium skillet, sauté the bacon until crisp. Add the onions and mushrooms, and sauté until the onions are soft but not brown. Add salt, pepper, and dill. Dissolve the cornstarch in the broth in a small saucepan and simmer for 5 minutes. Pour over the beans.
4. Cover and bake in a preheated 350° oven for 30 to 40 minutes, or until the beans are almost cooked; they can finish cooking when reheated.

Makes 4 to 6 portions.

Take-It-Along Tips: Make this ahead and reheat, uncovered, at 350° once you get to the host home.

Sweet Potatoes, Vermont Style

A sweet-potato casserole flavored with apples and butter; good with pork and duck or turkey.

6 sweet potatoes	½ cup light brown sugar
4 cooking apples	1 teaspoon salt
2 tablespoons lemon juice, strained	5 tablespoons butter
	3 tablespoons heavy cream

1. Heat oven to 375°.
2. Boil the sweet potatoes in their skins 20 to 30 minutes, or until almost tender. Peel, slice into rounds, and place a third of them in a buttered baking dish.
3. Peel the apples, slice more thinly than the potatoes, toss well in the lemon juice, and spread half the slices over the potatoes. Sprinkle with half the sugar, a bit of salt, dot with half the butter; repeat the layers and top with potatoes. Moisten with heavy cream. Cover and bake 30 minutes.

Makes 6 to 8 portions.

Take-It-Along Tips: Cook and cool; reheat in a 325° oven once you get to the party. Or serve lukewarm.

Maple-Candied Butternut Squash

A delicious accompaniment to poultry or pork. Try this recipe on sweet potatoes and yams, too.

- 1 medium butternut squash, peeled, halved, seeded
- ½ cup maple syrup
- 2 tablespoons butter
- 1 teaspoon salt
- 1 cup apple cider or juice
- ½ cup water

1. Preheat oven to 300°.
2. Boil the squash until half tender. Slice into rounds and place in a buttered baking pan.
3. Heat the maple syrup, butter, salt, cider, and water in a small saucepan until mixture begins to boil. Pour this over the squash and bake for one hour or until the squash is glazed and the syrup almost gone. Baste 3 or 4 times.

Makes 6 to 8 portions.

Take-It-Along Tips: Take this cooked and cooled, to the party, and reheat for one or 2 minutes under a hot broiler.

PART 7
When You Are Bringing the Salad

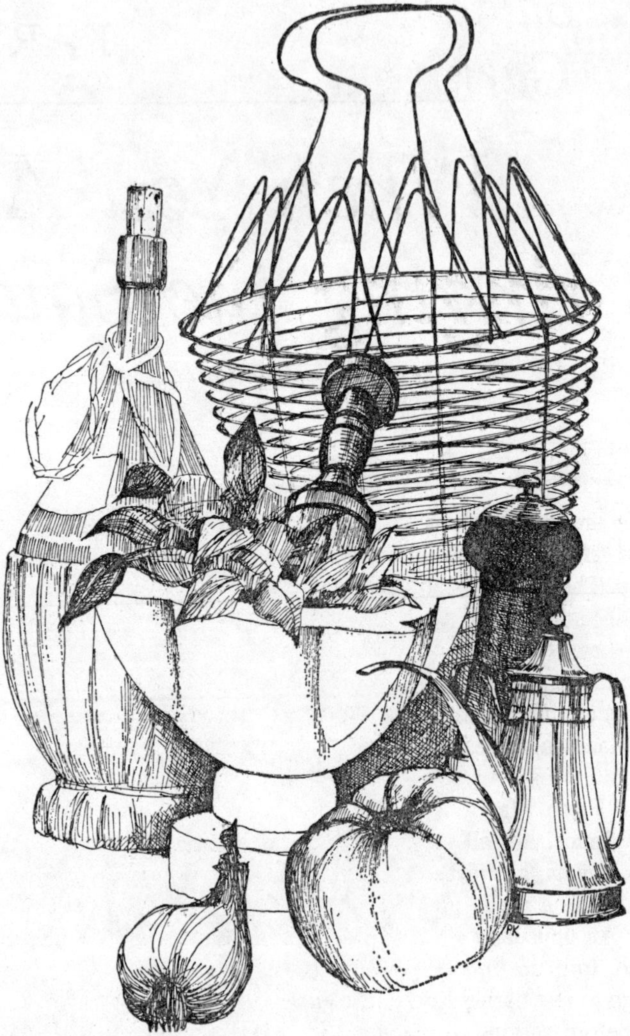
PK

19. Salads, Dressings, Garnishes

Salads are meant to refresh and, among serious eaters, are usually served after the main course—unless the salad itself is the main course. The Green Salad in this chapter will go with almost anything: the Oil-and-Vinegar Dressing is a classic French Dressing. Make it up in batches; it will keep, refrigerated, for weeks. After you have dressed your salad, taste it because you may find you want more salt or vinegar with the ingredients that make up a particular salad. Salads with bland ingredients, potatoes, for instance, require a heavier seasoning.

The Fresh Mayonnaise, the Marinade for Vegetables, the Vinaigrette Sauce, are all sauces that do wonders for leftover cold vegetables, meats, and fish.

To make a really good salad, you must crisp the greens, and chill them. An unusually good and different salad consists of plain iceberg lettuce, torn up into bite-sized bits and then put in the freezer long enough to just barely freeze the torn-up bits. Toss in Parsley Dressing. Just before serving you must also toss the salad well; I toss mine twenty-eight times. I actually count, that is, as I lift and toss.

When you are bringing the salad, prepare the ingredients and chill them, wrapped in Saran Wrap, in their serving bowl. Prepare, bottle, and chill the dressing. Dress and toss the salad just before serving.

French or Oil-and-Vinegar Dressing and Variations

A basic dressing.

6 tablespoons olive oil, or vegetable oil	¼ teaspoon sugar
1½ tablespoons vinegar	1 teaspoon salt
⅛ teaspoon dry mustard	⅛ teaspoon pepper

Put all ingredients in a blender and mix at low speed. *Makes about ¼ cup.*

VARIATIONS:

HERB DRESSING. Add one teaspoon fresh, or ½ teaspoon dried, tarragon, dill, mixed Italian herbs, or other herbs, to the dressing before blending.

PARSLEY DRESSING. Add ½ cup minced parsley to the salad *after* it has been tossed in the dressing.

GARLIC DRESSING. Slice one small, peeled clove of garlic, and blend with Oil-and-Vinegar Dressing.

LEMON DRESSING. Use lemon juice, strained, instead of the vinegar.

ROQUEFORT OR BLUE CHEESE DRESSING. In a blender, process 3 tablespoons cheese and one small clove garlic, peeled and sliced, with the basic Oil-and-Vinegar Dressing.

Thousand Island Dressing

1 cup Fresh Mayonnaise, or commercial mayonnaise	1 tablespoon chopped pimiento
⅓ cup chili sauce	½ cup whipped cream or sour cream
1 tablespoon chopped chives	
2 tablespoons chopped seeded green pepper	

Mix all ingredients except the cream. Fold in cream last. *Makes 2 cups.*

Calorie-Counter Dressing I

- ¼ cup wine vinegar
- 1 cup tomato soup
- 1 tablespoon Worcestershire sauce
- 1 teaspoon prepared mustard
- 1 teaspoon celery seed
- ⅛ teaspoon pepper
- 1 small garlic clove, peeled

Put all ingredients in a blender and blend at low speed for one minute.
Makes about 1¼ cups.

Calorie-Counter Dressing II

- 1 cup plain yogurt
- 1 tablespoon lemon juice, strained
- ½ teaspoon celery salt
- 1 small clove garlic, peeled, minced *or*
- 1 small thin slice onion

Mix all ingredients one minute in a blender at low speed.
Makes one cup.

Vinaigrette Sauce

A very sharp, green sauce to serve with cold meats or vegetables.

- 2 cloves garlic, peeled
- 1 teaspoon salt
- ⅛ teaspoon pepper
- 1 cup olive, or vegetable, oil
- ½ teaspoon dry mustard
- 2 tablespoons white wine vinegar
- 2 tablespoons tarragon vinegar
- 1 shallot, peeled, or 1 slice onion
- 2 tablespoons minced chives
- 3 tablespoons minced parsley
- 1 teaspoon salt
- ⅛ teaspoon pepper

Mix all the ingredients in a blender for 2 minutes at low speed. Store covered in the refrigerator until ready to serve.
Makes about 1⅓ cups.

Fresh Mayonnaise

Mayonnaise made with vinegar and lemon juice instead of lemon juice alone and stored in a tightly capped jar in the refrigerator will keep 2 weeks. This is the best mayonnaise I know—very different from a commercial preparation. Delicious as a sauce for any cold vegetable, meat, or fish.

2 egg yolks	1 to 2 cups vegetable oil
1 teaspoon salt	2 tablespoons lemon juice, strained, or vinegar
½ teaspoon dry mustard	
1 tablespoon vinegar	

1. Place a medium bowl, narrow at the bottom, inside a larger bowl lined with wet, crumpled paper towels, and set the bowl in a corner of the sink. This keeps the smaller bowl from turning as you whip. Drop the yolks into the bowl and with a fork beat the yolks until thick; beat in the salt, the mustard, the vinegar. A few drops at a time, beat in half the oil. Be sure the yolks have absorbed each dribble of oil before you add more. Then beat in the lemon juice. In larger dribbles, beat in the rest of the oil. To make a larger quantity of mayonnaise, work in up to another cupful of oil, with another tablespoon of lemon juice. Taste. It often needs more salt, depending on what it is to be served with.

Makes about one cup.

Note: If the mayonnaise starts to curdle (separates into oil and solids) *immediately* add a few drops of vinegar, and beat like crazy. If you end up with a curdled sauce anyway, break an egg yolk into a new bowl and beat in the curdled mayonnaise, a drop at a time, until it is all in. Then proceed with the recipe.

VARIATIONS:

HERB MAYONNAISE. Beat one teaspoon fresh, or ½ teaspoon dried, herb into the finished mayonnaise.

AÏOLI. Mash up to 4 cloves of peeled garlic in the bottom of the bowl in which you will make the mayonnaise, and proceed with the Fresh Mayonnaise recipe.

Salads, Dressings, Garnishes

MAYONNAISE CHANTILLY FOR FRUIT SALADS. Fold ½ cup of whipped cream into the finished mayonnaise.

HONEY MAYONNAISE FOR FRUIT SALADS. Flavor the finished mayonnaise with honey to taste and ½ teaspoon celery seed.

RUSSIAN DRESSING. Mix ½ cup of mayonnaise with ½ cup chili sauce, 2 tablespoons finely chopped onion, 2 tablespoons minced pimiento, one hard-boiled egg, diced, and 2 tablespoons lemon juice.

GREEN GODDESS DRESSING. Blend one cup mayonnaise with one peeled, minced clove garlic, 3 teaspoons minced chives, 4 teaspoons lemon or lime juice, ½ cup minced parsley, and ½ cup heavy cream.

Hollandaise the Fast Way

A delicious sauce for meats, fish, and any vegetable, as broccoli or asparagus. Make it at the home of your hostess this quick and easy way.

3 egg yolks or 2 whole eggs
2 tablespoons lemon juice, strained
¼ teaspoon salt or more
Freshly ground black pepper
¼ pound butter

1. Put egg yolks, lemon juice, salt, and pepper into the blender; turn on low.
2. Heat the butter to bubbling but don't brown it. Remove from the heat at once. Pour the hot butter into the blender in a steady stream. When all the butter has been added, turn off the blender.

Makes about one cup. To make a larger quantity, use ½-pound butter and 4 egg yolks.

Lemon-Butter Sauce the Fast Way

2 tablespoons lemon juice
⅛ teaspoon salt
¼ pound butter

1. In a tiny enameled saucepan, simmer the lemon juice and salt until the liquid is reduced to one tablespoon. Remove from the heat.
2. Stir in half the butter until it melts; then return the pan to the heat and beat in the rest of the butter, a lump at a time. During this process take care that the butter doesn't get so hot that it browns. (If you are in a hurry, you can simply melt together one stick of butter and 2 to 4 teaspoons of lemon juice, but the result isn't quite the same.)

Makes about ½ cup.

Marinade for Vegetables

Marinate any leftover cooked vegetables—beans, carrots, potatoes, broccoli—in this and serve it up as a salad or a first course.

½ cup olive oil
3 tablespoons lemon juice
3 tablespoons wine vinegar
⅛ teaspoon pepper
1 clove garlic, peeled, minced
1 teaspoon salt
2 teaspoons fresh, or 1 teaspoon dried tarragon

Combine all ingredients and beat for 2 minutes, or blend for one minute at low speed in an electric blender.

Makes ¾ cup.

Marinade for Game

1 cup oil
½ cup lemon juice or dry white wine
2 tablespoons chopped parsley
2 tablespoons chopped onion
1 teaspoon salt
Freshly ground pepper

Pack the game into the smallest glass dish it will fit, and douse with half the oil. Rub in remaining ingredients, add remaining oil. Store, covered, overnight in the refrigerator. Turn the game as often as you think of it.

Makes 1¾ cups.

Pineapple Chutney

To serve with Indian curries, or use bottled Major Grey's Chutney.

- 1 cup green pepper in ¾-inch pieces
- ½ cup chopped onion in ½-inch pieces
- 1 pound tomatoes in ¾-inch pieces
- 1 lemon, with skin, in ½-inch cubes
- ½ cup black seeded raisins
- 1 cup fresh pineapple in ½-inch cubes
- 1 cup white vinegar
- 1 cup dark brown sugar
- 4 tablespoons candied ginger
- 1 tablespoon salt

Simmer all the ingredients together, covered, 30 minutes. Pour into 9 8-ounce jelly jars, scalded; seal with a coat of wax; let cool, fill jars to the top with wax and cover.

Makes nine to ten 8-ounce jars.

Raita

A cool-tasting relish to serve with curried dishes.

- 2 medium cucumbers
- 1 medium onion, peeled
- ½ teaspoon salt
- ½ teaspoon ground cumin
- ½ pint plain yogurt

On the coarse side of a grater, shred the cucumbers, and set aside in the refrigerator for 6 hours. Pour off the cucumber juices; squeeze dry. Grate the onion over the cucumbers and sprinkle with salt and cumin. Mix in the yogurt, and chill for one hour or more before serving.

Makes 8 to 10 servings.

Onion Sambal

This delicious onion relish is served with East Indian dishes and curries.

2 large onions, peeled	1 bunch fresh mint, or 1 drop spearmint
½ teaspoon salt	
4 tablespoons lemon juice, strained	

Mince the onion and salt it. Set in a shallow bowl and sprinkle with lemon juice. Cover with mint leaves. (Or mix a drop of spearmint into the lemon juice before adding it.) Marinate 2 hours before serving.
Makes 8 to 10 portions.

Green Salad

A mixed, tossed, green salad to serve with everything. Nice with almost any dressing and very good with Roquefort Dressing.

1 medium head iceberg lettuce	1 sprig dill
1 small head Bibb or Boston lettuce	2 sprigs parsley
	1 green onion
1 heart of escarole or Chinese cabbage	½ to ¾ cup Oil-and-Vinegar Dressing, Garlic Dressing, or Roquefort Dressing
2 cups fresh spinach	
1 sprig basil	

1. Wash, drain, and dry well the lettuces and spinach; tear into bits and chill in a plastic bag until ready to serve.
2. Turn torn greens into a large salad bowl; mince basil, dill, parsley, onion, over them. Pour dressing over and mix 25 to 30 times. Taste, and add salt if needed.

Makes 8 to 10 portions.

Spinach-and-Mushroom Salad

Elegant salad to serve a gourmet.

1 pound raw spinach, stems cut off	¾ cup Oil and Vinegar Dressing, made with tarragon vinegar
1 pound mushrooms, wiped	1 hard-boiled egg

1. Wash, dry, and tear spinach into bits. Cut mushrooms into T-shaped slices ¼ inch thick.
2. Toss mushrooms with dressing in a salad bowl, and marinate in the refrigerator for 30 minutes, or until ready to serve.
3. Toss spinach with mushrooms, taste, and add more salt and more vinegar if desired. Over the salad, rub the egg through a sieve. Toss again just before serving.

Makes 8 to 10 portions.

Cold Vegetable Salad

Make this with leftover or with canned vegetables.

1 shallot, peeled, minced	1 large lettuce heart
1 cup Oil-and-Vinegar Dressing	1 tablespoon olive oil
4 to 6 cups cooked green or lima beans, peas, carrots, cauliflower, or other vegetables	2 tablespoons butter
	1 clove garlic, peeled, crushed
	2 slices stale French bread
	2 sprigs fresh dill or other herb

1. Blend the Oil-and-Vinegar Dressing with the shallot. Pour over the vegetables. Simmer, uncovered, 3 minutes; then chill, covered.
2. Break the lettuce into bits and chill. Heat the oil and butter in a skillet. Brown the garlic in it, then remove it. Fry the stale bread slices until golden, turning often so both sides absorb all the butter.
3. When you are ready to serve, toss lettuce bits with the chilled vegetables. Crumble the fried bread and add. Toss briefly and serve at once. Garnish with dill, or your favorite herb.

Serves 8 to 10.

Italian Rice Salad

A hearty salad to use as a substitute for a vegetable, especially with hamburgers and other cook-out foods.

2 green peppers, seeded	2 green onions, minced
3 tomatoes, peeled	2 cups converted rice, cooked
1 medium eggplant, stemmed	
2 tablespoons olive oil	½ to 1 cup Garlic Dressing

1. Shred the peppers, slice the tomatoes, cut the eggplant into thin slices. Over medium heat in oil, sauté onions, peppers, tomatoes, and eggplant until tender but not mushy. Add the cooked rice and toss over low heat for 3 minutes.
2. Turn into a large salad bowl; add ½ cup Garlic Dressing, and toss. Chill well.
3. Just before serving, toss again, taste, and add more dressing as needed.

Makes 8 to 10 portions.

VARIATIONS:

NOODLE SALAD. Replace rice with cooked, chopped noodles.

SPAGHETTI SALAD. Replace rice with cooked spaghetti, chopped into bits.

MACARONI SALAD. Replace rice with cooked macaroni.

Mediterranean Salad

Serve this with Italian or Spanish dishes.

4 ripe tomatoes
½ green pepper, seeded
½ Bermuda onion, peeled
1 head lettuce
1 cucumber

⅓ cup Garlic Dressing or Oil-and-Vinegar Dressing
2 tablespoons minced basil
10 ripe black olives, pitted

1. Peel the tomatoes and cut into wedges. Mince the green pepper and onion. Tear the lettuce into bits. Peel the cucumber and cut into small chunks. Chill everything but the tomatoes.
2. When ready to serve, toss the vegetables with the Garlic Dressing and basil. Garnish with olives.

Makes 6 to 8 portions.

Potato Salad

A truly delicious potato salad; serve it at picnics, cookouts, and cold buffets.

16 to 20 tiny new potatoes
½ cup Oil-and-Vinegar Dressing
½ teaspoon coarse salt (sea or kosher)
2 cloves garlic, peeled, minced

2 scallions or shallots, peeled, minced
½ cup Fresh Mayonnaise
Carrot shreds and parsley sprigs for garnish, optional

1. Wash the potatoes and drop, unpeeled, into a kettle of cold water to cover. Cook rapidly until potatoes are almost done; they should be just slightly underdone. Drain and let cool 5 minutes.
2. With 2 knives, slash the potatoes into halves and quarters. Pour Oil-and-Vinegar Dressing over them, sprinkle with salt, and toss with the garlic and scallions. Marinate at room temperature until cool, tossing occasionally.
3. When cool, toss well with the mayonnaise. Garnish with shreds of carrot and sprigs of parsley if desired. Cover and refrigerate until ready to serve.

Makes 6 to 8 servings.

Carrot-and-Raisin Slaw

This is on the sweet side, and even kids who hate salads love it.

⅔ cup seedless raisins, dark or light	¼ cup Fresh Mayonnaise or commercial mayonnaise
2 cups coarsely grated raw carrot	1 very small onion, peeled
	1 teaspoon lemon juice
	¼ teaspoon salt

1. Soak raisins in hot water for 5 minutes. Drain and dry.
2. Moisten carrots with Fresh Mayonnaise to taste. Using the fine side of a grater, grate the onion over the carrots. Stir in the raisins, lemon juice, and salt, and toss well. Add more salt if desired. Chill 2 hours before serving.

Makes 6 servings.

Cole Slaw

A simple but simply delicious version.

½ cup Fresh Mayonnaise or commercial mayonnaise	1 thin, small onion slice, minced
½ tablespoon wine vinegar	6 cups shredded green cabbage

Mix Fresh Mayonnaise with vinegar and onion. Toss cabbage with the dressing. Taste and add salt if needed. Chill before serving.

Makes 8 to 10 portions.

Salade de L'Île Barbe

A fish-and-meat salad to serve as a main course.

1 pound potatoes	2 ounces cooked ham or beef
2 red or green peppers, seeded	½ cup Lemon Dressing
1 lobster or crawfish tail, frozen or fresh	4 large mushrooms, wiped

1. Boil potatoes in their skins until done; peel and slice thin. Boil the peppers until tender; core, skin, and cut into strips. Boil lobster tail or crawfish, until done; shell and slice ¼ inch thick. Put in salad bowl and add ham or beef. Toss all with Lemon Dressing. Chill.
2. Just before serving, cut mushrooms into ¼-inch-thick slices, and toss with the salad. Taste, and add more dressing, or just more salt, if needed.

Makes 6 to 8 portions.

Cucumber Mousse

A gorgeous creamy molded salad ring to serve on a bed of tender lettuce.

1 large unpeeled cucumber, sliced	¼ cup lemon juice, strained
Salt	1 small onion, peeled, grated
1 3-ounce package lime gelatin	1 cup sour cream
⅔ cup boiling water	1 head of Boston or Bibb lettuce, crisped

1. Layer the cucumber slices in a bowl, sprinkling each layer lightly with salt. Leave overnight, then drain and squeeze out as much cucumber juice as possible. Dry with paper towels.
2. Dissolve the gelatin in boiling water and add the lemon juice. Let cool, then stir in the onion, sour cream, and cucumber.
3. Pour into a mold rinsed in cold water. Allow to set overnight.
4. Just before serving, unmold on a bed of lettuce.

Makes 6 to 8 portions.

PART 8

When You Are Bringing the Dessert

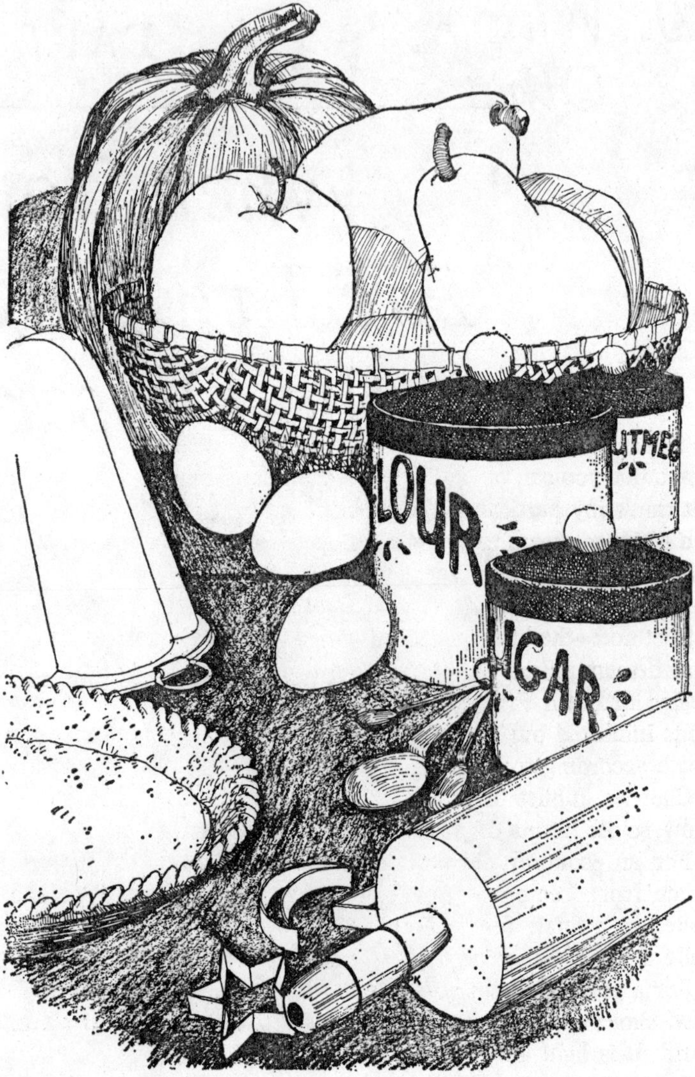
LOUR
UTMEG
UGAR.

20. Whipped Cream and Other Delights

I maintain you can put whipped cream on anything and call it dessert, but that's my particular weakness. Left to my own devices I would add whipped cream to every recipe here that doesn't have it. But you shouldn't.

Desserts are meant to top off a meal, complement it, end it on a perfect note—therefore, rich, heavy meals should be followed by light, cool desserts. Fruit in Champagne is a refreshing dessert, and the Basket of Fresh Fruit is especially festive. You needn't use just the fruits indicated but may substitute others you have or find easier to locate according to season.

Cherries Jubilee flambéed is the most effective show-stopper I know, so use it for a dramatic finish. It is light, too.

For an economy dessert, the Lime Pie qualifies, and is a pretty switch from Lemon Meringue Pie. The Saffron Fruit Cream is included as a finale for Oriental suppers; it is economical, too, especially if you make your own yogurt.

For a group that considers itself gourmet, the Crême Caramel is a good choice. In fact, many people think it is the best dessert in the world. It is light and, well, exquisite.

Only a few of these dessert recipes can be doubled. You'll have to make them in 2 batches if you want to serve more guests. The fruit salads, Stuffed Baked Apples, and the Saffron Fruit Cream are exceptions.

Crême Caramel

A luscious custard that has an extra measure of caramel sauce.

3½ cups half-and-half, milk and cream	1 teaspoon cognac
2½ cups sugar	1 teaspoon vanilla extract
4 large eggs	½ cup boiling water

1. In a saucepan, scald the milk with ½-cup sugar.
2. In a bowl, beat the eggs slightly, stir in the cognac and vanilla. Beat until eggs are lemon-colored.
3. Preheat the oven to 350°.
4. In a heavy frying pan, over low heat melt the 2 cups sugar, stirring it with a long-handled fork. When the sugar turns golden-brown and is caramelized, pour half onto a greased marble slab or a cookie sheet to cool. Return the skillet to the top of the stove, and stir into the caramel ½ cup boiling water. Cook and stir until the sauce has the consistency of light cream. Pour into a small serving pitcher.
5. With a wooden mallet or a rolling pin, crush the cooled, hard caramel, and with it line the bottom of a buttered 2-quart mold. Pour the custard mixture over the caramel.
6. Set the mold in a pan of boiling water in the middle of the oven. Custard is done in about 45 minutes, or when a knife plunged through the center comes out clean. Cool at room temperature, then chill overnight, covered.
7. To serve: Loosen edges of crême with a sharp knife, invert the serving plate over the mold, quickly flip over. Serve the extra caramel sauce on the side.

Makes 6 to 8 portions.

Take-It-Along Tips: Take the custard to the party in its mold and turn out onto a serving plate. Take the extra sauce in its serving pitcher, covered well with Saran Wrap or foil.

Mayonnaise au Chocolat des Sables

This is called a "Mayonnaise" because it is made in much the manner of Fresh Mayonnaise. It is the richest, thickest, chocolate pudding there is.

2 egg yolks	5 egg whites
4½ ounces French or Swiss dark sweet chocolate	1 tablespoon confectioners' sugar
4½ ounces butter	1 teaspoon rum, optional

1. Whip the egg yolks thoroughly.
2. In a small saucepan over very low heat, melt the chocolate and butter; beat the mixture into the yolks a little at a time.
3. Beat the egg whites until stiff; sift the sugar over the stiff whites and beat in.
4. Fold the egg whites into the chocolate cream, very gently, always turning in the same direction. Stir in the rum. Scrape into a deep serving bowl and chill slightly.

Makes 4 to 6 portions.

Take-It-Along Tips: Take this to the party in its serving dish, sealed in Saran Wrap or foil.

Chilled Fruit Mousse

A mousse that never falls and never fails to delight.

1 quart raspberries or strawberries	1 envelope gelatin
1 cup sugar	2 tablespoons cold water
	1 pint heavy cream

1. Hull the berries, reserving half a cup for garnish. Crush, strain, and bring the juiced berries to the boiling point.
2. Soak the gelatin in the cold water and dissolve in the hot juices. Mix into the fruit pulp. Refrigerate until the mixture thickens.
3. Whip the cream until stiff, and fold into the berry mixture. With the reserved whole berries, line the bottom of a mold rinsed in cold water. Pour the cream into the mold and let set for 12 hours. Unmold just before serving.

Makes 8 to 10 portions.

VARIATIONS:

Coffee Mousse: Omit fruit, sugar, and gelatin; heat one cup strong coffee with 14 marshmallows, refrigerate until thickened; fold into the whipped cream, pour into a mold.
Serves 4 to 6.

Mocha-Brandy Mousse: Melt ½ square unsweetened chocolate in one cup strong coffee and proceed as for coffee mousse. Add one tablespoon brandy to the whipped cream before combining with the mocha jelly.

Take-It-Along Tips: Take this to the party in its mold and turn out onto a serving dish at dessert time.

Saffron Fruit Cream

This is a good finale for a Far Eastern dinner.

1 pint vanilla yogurt	1 cup drained, canned
1 pint sour cream	Mandarin oranges or
½ cup granulated sugar	crushed pineapple
⅛ teaspoon saffron	

In a large bowl, mix the yogurt into the sour cream, and fold in the sugar and saffron. Fold in ¾ of the fruit. Scoop into a large serving dish and garnish with remaining fruit.
Makes 6 to 8 portions.

Take-It-Along Tips: Cover with Saran Wrap, or foil, and take to the party.

English Trifle

My father's recipe for a creamy custard-and-cake concoction.

4 egg yolks	½ cup sherry
2 cups light cream	2 cups heavy cream
¼ cup sugar	½ cup confectioners' sugar
½ tablespoon vanilla extract	1 teaspoon vanilla extract
2 8-inch layers of sponge cake	12 peeled, toasted almonds
1 10-ounce jar raspberry jam	

1. Beat the egg yolks until thick. Heat the cream with the sugar and vanilla until the sugar dissolves. Beat into the eggs. In the top of a double boiler over simmering water, cook the mixture, stirring continuously, until the custard coats the spoon. Turn into a bowl. Cover and refrigerate until well chilled.
2. Spread one side of each sponge cake with the jam, and cut the cake into finger-length pieces. Dip each piece quickly in sherry.
3. Spread half the fingers over the bottom of a deep glass serving bowl. Cover with half the custard.
4. Whip the cream with the sugar and vanilla. Spread half the cream over the custard.
5. Repeat the layers, ending with the whipped cream, and garnish with the toasted almonds.
6. Refrigerate, covered, overnight.
Serves 10 to 12.

Take-It-Along Tips: Take this to the party in its serving dish, covered with Saran Wrap or foil.

Berry Ice Cream

You'll need an ice cream churner to make this—either a hand-operated churner or an electric one.

- 5 egg yolks
- 1 cup granulated sugar
- ½ pint light cream
- ½ pint heavy cream
- 2 teaspoons vanilla extract
- 1 quart fresh strawberries or raspberries

1. Beat together the yolks and sugar until thick and lemon-colored. Stir in the light cream, and pour the mixture into the top of a double-boiler. Over simmering water, with a wooden spoon, stir the custard constantly until thickened enough to coat the spoon. Remove the double-boiler top from the heat and stir the contents until cool.
2. Beat the heavy cream with the vanilla until thickened to the consistency of custard. Fold into custard.
3. Crush the berries coarsely, enough to extract some, but not all the juice. Fold this into the cream custard.
4. Place the custard in the churner and churn until thickened.
5. Pack into a mold rinsed in cold water and place in the freezer. Allow to freeze an hour or 2 before serving.

Serves 8 portions.

Take-It-Along Tips: Take the makings to the party and let everyone help with—or at least admire—the making. Or, freeze the ice cream in a fluted mold, take it to the party frozen, bedded in an insulated soft drink carrier on a layer of ice. Unmold at the party just before serving.

Indian Pudding

Popular in New England, this is a spicy confection to make in the winter months when puddings taste so good.

2 cups whole milk	½ teaspoon salt
2 cups light cream	½ teaspoon ground ginger
¼ cup corn meal	1 teaspoon ground cinnamon
2 eggs	
2 tablespoons dark molasses	4 tablespoons butter or margarine
½ cup light brown sugar, firmly packed	¾ cup dark raisins
	½ pint heavy cream

1. Heat the oven to 325°.
2. In a heavy saucepan, heat the milk and half the cream. Combine the remaining cream with the corn meal and add to the saucepan. Stir constantly until the mixture begins to simmer. Cook over lowest heat, stirring constantly, for 20 minutes.
3. Beat the eggs to a froth in a small bowl, and stir in the molasses, sugar, salt, ginger, and cinnamon.
4. When the cream mixture is finished, remove from the heat. Cut the butter into the mixture, and stir in the raisins. Add the egg mixture, whipping quickly, and pour into a 2-quart mold. Bake one hour and 15 minutes in a preheated oven at 325°; test by inserting silver knife in the center—if it comes out clean, the custard is done.
5. Cool and unmold, and serve with cream. Or serve lukewarm from the baking dish.

Serves 8 portions.

Take-It-Along Tips: If you like this lukewarm, make shortly before it is time to go to the party, wrap in foil, overwrap in newspapers. Take the cream in a closed jar.

Cheesecake with Strawberry Sauce

This is a very rich, moist cheesecake, marvelously good.

- 14 double graham crackers
- ⅓ cup sugar
- ¼ teaspoon vanilla extract
- ¾ stick butter, melted
- 2 16-ounce packages cream cheese
- 2 tablespoons cream or milk
- 3 eggs, well beaten
- ½ cup sugar
- ¼ teaspoon vanilla extract
- 1 pint sour cream
- ⅓ cup sugar
- ¼ teaspoon vanilla extract
- 1 pint fresh strawberries, hulled
- ¼ cup sugar

1. Heat the oven to 325°.
2. In a large bowl, crush the crackers, add the next 3 ingredients. Spread over the bottom of a 9-inch cake pan and press an 8-inch pie plate over it to create a firm crust.
3. In an electric mixer, combine the cream cheese with the milk. Beat in the eggs, the ½ cup of sugar, and ¼ teaspoon vanilla extract.
4. Scrape the mixture over the pie crust and bake 15 minutes in a 325° oven; then increase the temperature to 450° and bake 15 minutes more. Remove and cool for 20 minutes. Reduce the oven heat to 400°.
5. Mix the sour cream with the remaining ⅓ cup sugar and ¼ teaspoon vanilla, and pour over the cooled cheesecake. Bake 5 minutes at 400°.
6. Let stand overnight. Just before serving, invert onto a cake dish. Crush the berries, marinate 2 hours with the sugar, and offer with the cheesecake.

Makes 8 to 10 portions.

Take-It-Along Tips: Take to the party in its baking dish. Take the crushed berries in a sealed glass container. You can turn the cake out of its baking pan onto a serving dish if you want to make an impression, and serve it with the berries poured over the cake. Or serve it from the baking dish with berries on the side.

Lime Meringue Pie

Meringue-topped pies, homemade, are always a hit at a party. Use the juice from fresh, ripe limes.

1 9-inch unbaked pie shell	3 egg whites
5 egg yolks	¼ teaspoon cream-of-tartar
Pinch of salt	6 tablespoons confection-
½ cup sugar	ers' sugar
½ cup lime juice, strained	½ teaspoon vanilla
½ teaspoon grated lime rind	

1. Bake the pie shell until light gold.
2. Beat egg yolks until thick; add the salt, and the ½ cup of sugar. Beat well. Place in a double boiler over simmering water and stir constantly until thick. Remove from the heat, beat in the lime juice and rind, and cool. Pour into the cooled pie shell.
3. Heat the oven to 425°.
4. Beat the egg whites with the cream-of-tartar until stiff, then beat in the 6 tablespoons of sugar, one tablespoon at a time. Beat in the vanilla. Spoon the meringue over the pie and cover the edges of the crust. Swirl into peaks. Bake 10 minutes, or until peaks are golden.

Makes 6 to 8 servings.

Take-It-Along Tips: Tear off a big sheet of heavy-duty foil, set the pie dish on it, and pull the sides of the foil up high over the meringue top, and seal them in a tight fold. Take to the party.

New Orleans Pecan Pie

One of the great desserts of the South. Try it with soft vanilla ice cream.

1½ tablespoons butter	¼ teaspoon salt
1 cup light brown sugar, firmly packed	1 cup pecan meats, chopped
3 eggs, *well* beaten	1 teaspoon vanilla extract
1 cup light corn syrup	1 9-inch unbaked pie shell
	1 cup whole pecan meats

1. Preheat the oven to 450°.
2. Cream the butter and sugar; add the eggs, syrup, salt, coarsely chopped pecans, and vanilla. Turn into the pie shell. Arrange whole pecans over the surface.
3. Bake in the oven for 10 minutes at 450°. Reduce the heat to 350° and continue baking 30 minutes, or until firm. Serve cold.

Makes 6 to 8 portions.

Take-It-Along Tips: Wrap in Saran Wrap or foil, and take to the party.

Pumpkin Pie

This is our favorite for taking to Thanksgiving dinners and Halloween parties. Make this recipe sometime with leftover, mashed butternut squash—it's great.

- 3 eggs
- ¾ cup light brown sugar, firmly packed
- 1 cup heavy cream
- 1½ cups canned pumpkin
- 1 teaspoon cinnamon
- ¼ teaspoon nutmeg
- ½ teaspoon ground ginger
- ½ teaspoon salt
- 1 8-inch unbaked pastry shell
- ½ cup heavy cream, sweetened and flavored with brandy, or
- 1 pint vanilla ice cream

1. Preheat the oven to 450°.
2. Beat the eggs with the sugar until lemon-colored. With a whip, beat in the cream, pumpkin, cinnamon, nutmeg, ginger, and salt. Pour into the pastry shell, and bake at 450° for 15 minutes. Reduce the heat to 300° and bake 45 minutes longer, or until a knife inserted in the center comes out clean.
3. Serve warm with sweetened brandy-flavored whipped cream or with ice cream.

Makes 8 to 10 portions.

Take-It-Along Tips: Wrap in foil and take to the party. Whip the cream when you get there, just before serving.

Sour-Cherry Ribbon

2 packages pie-crust mix	4 cups stemmed pitted sour cherries
2 cups sugar	
½ teaspoon cinnamon	2 eggs
½ teaspoon nutmeg	1 teaspoon vanilla extract
	¼ stick butter

1. Preheat the oven to 425°.
2. Roll half the pastry into a rectangle 15 by 8 inches. Place it on a greased cookie sheet and turn up the edges to make a ridge one-inch high.
3. Combine sugar, cinnamon, and nutmeg. Toss the cherries in the sugar mixture. Beat the eggs until thick; add the vanilla. Then combine with the cherries. Turn into the pie shell and dot with butter.
4. Roll out the rest of the pastry and cut into ½-inch ribbons. Lay them across the pie in a lattice-work pattern. Bake 30 to 40 minutes. Cool thoroughly and slide whole onto a serving platter.

Makes 14 to 18 portions.

Take-It-Along Tips: Take to the party in its baking dish, wrapped in foil, and set on a serving platter at the host home.

Angel Food Shortcake

A quick-and-easy variation on the usual shortcake; this travels well.

1 package angel food cake mix	1 pint heavy cream
2 tablespoons sweet butter	1 tablespoon confectioners' sugar
1 pint strawberries, raspberries, or peaches, hulled, crushed, sweetened	1 teaspoon vanilla extract

1. Mix and bake the angel food cake and cool. Spread lightly with the sweet butter.
2. Turn the fruit into a serving bowl. Chill.
3. Whip the cream with the sugar and vanilla. Just before serving, spread the cake with the whipped cream.
4. To serve, break cake apart with 2 forks into wedges, and cover with the crushed fruit.

Makes 8 to 10 portions.

Take-It-Along Tips: Take this to the party in its baking dish, turn onto a serving platter at the host home. Take the fruit, cream, sugar, and vanilla to the party in their containers, and whip the cream and ice the cake there.

A Charlotte from the Isles

This is usually greeted with groans of pleasure. If you can stand the extra calories, serve with more sweetened cream.

- 12 lady fingers
- 2 envelopes gelatin
- 1 cup milk
- 4 egg yolks
- ½ cup superfine sugar
- Pinch salt
- 1 teaspoon vanilla extract
- 2 tablespoons light rum
- 1 cup heavy cream, whipped
- 4 slices canned pineapple, drained, diced
- 2 bananas, peeled, cubed

1. Split the lady fingers. Cut a sliver from one end of each to square it and stand the fingers upright around the sides of an 8-inch spring-form pan.
2. In a medium kettle over low heat, dissolve the gelatin in ½ cup of the milk and let set for 10 minutes with the heat off.
3. Beat the egg yolks with the sugar, salt, vanilla, and remaining milk, and add to the gelatin mixture. Return to low heat, stirring constantly, until the cream thickens enough to coat a spoon. Do not boil. Cool.
4. To the cooled cream, add the rum and whipped cream. Fold in the fruits and pour into the pan. Refrigerate overnight, or until firm.
5. To unmold, release spring and remove the sides of the mold carefully. Place on a serving plate.

Makes 10 to 12 portions.

Take-It-Along Tips: Take this to the party in its mold, wrapped in Saran Wrap, and unmold at the party.

Dick Engelbretsen's Carrot Cake

Great texture, great flavor, and a favorite in New England.

2 cups all-purpose flour
2 cups sugar
2 teaspoons baking powder
1 teaspoon salt
2 teaspoons ground cinnamon
4 eggs
1 cup vegetable oil
4 cups grated raw carrot (about 8 carrots)
½ cup chopped pecans
Frosting (See below)

1. Preheat the oven to 350°.
2. Measure flour, sugar, baking powder, salt, and cinnamon into a flour sifter and sift together 3 times.
3. In a large bowl, beat the eggs until thick and, still beating, dribble in the oil. With electric beater on low, dribble in the flour mixture. Fold in the carrots and the nuts, and mix well. Pour into 2 well-greased and floured 8-inch cake pans.
4. Bake 25 to 30 minutes. Cool in the pans for 10 minutes, then turn out onto racks and cool completely. Spread the frosting between the layers and over the top of the cake.

Makes 10 to 12 portions.

DICK'S CREAM-CHEESE FROSTING
6 tablespoons sweet butter, softened
10 ounces cream cheese, softened
2 cups confectioners' sugar
1 teaspoon vanilla extract
1 teaspoon maple flavoring

In a medium bowl, beat the butter, beat in the cheese, then beat in the sugar. Blend in the vanilla extract and the flavoring.
Makes enough filling and icing for one two-layer cake.

Take-It-Along Tips: Finish the cake, wrap in Saran Wrap, and take to the party. Unwrap and smooth the icing with a spatula. Or, reserve the icing meant for the top of the cake, and ice the cake top at the host home.

Joe Bednerz' Christmas Cake

This is the most outrageously rich nut-and-fruit cake ever invented, but remarkably easy to make. Sealed in its brandy-soaked wrapping, it will keep months in the refrigerator. A great cake for Christmas giving and for tree-trimming parties.

1½ cups whole Brazil nuts	¾ cup sugar
1 cup pecan halves	½ teaspoon baking powder
1 pound pitted dates	½ teaspoon salt
1½ cups maraschino cherries, drained	3 eggs
	1 teaspoon vanilla extract
¾ cup plus 1 tablespoon all-purpose flour	2 teaspoons brandy
	Brandy

1. Heat the oven to 300°.
2. In a large bowl, mix nuts, dates, cherries.
3. Measure into the sifter the flour, sugar, baking powder, and salt, and sift 3 times.
4. Beat the eggs with the vanilla and the brandy until thick. Stir the flour into the eggs, and pour this over the nut-and-fruit mixture. Combine thoroughly. Turn into a greased and paper-lined 9- by 5- by 3-inch loaf pan.
5. Bake one hour and 30 to 40 minutes, or until a toothpick inserted into the center comes out clean. Let cake rest in the pan for 10 minutes; then turn out onto a rack to cool. Wrap in a double layer of cheesecloth soaked in brandy; then wrap completely in foil and refrigerate for at least one week. Resoak the cheesecloth with brandy weekly for as long as the cake is being stored.

Makes 20 portions.

Take-It-Along Tips: Remove the cheesecloth, wrap closely in foil, and take to the party.

Golden Layer Cake

This cake stays fresh for days, and freezes beautifully. Try it with the quick-and-easy Maple-Nut Frosting. A good recipe for a layered birthday cake.

Whipped Cream and Other Delights

3 cups sifted cake flour
3 teaspoons baking powder
⅛ teaspoon salt
1 cup shortening
2 cups sugar
4 eggs
1 cup milk
1 teaspoon vanilla, almond, or other extract

1. Preheat the oven to 375°.
2. Measure the flour, baking powder, and salt into a sifter set in a large bowl, and sift 3 times.
3. In a large bowl with an electric beater, cream the shortening with the sugar until fluffy. One at a time, add the eggs, beating well after each. Then add the flour mixture, alternately with the milk in small amounts, beating smooth after each addition. Add the extract and blend.
4. Butter two 8- by 8- by 2-inch square or round cake pans. Pour the batter into the pans and bake 25 minutes, or until a straw comes out clean.
5. Cool on a rack. Fill and frost with Maple-Nut Frosting or frosting of your choice.

Makes 10 to 12 portions.

MAPLE NUT FROSTING

½ cup butter or margarine, softened
½ cup maple syrup
½ teaspoon salt
1 egg unbeaten
2 teaspoons vanilla extract
2¾ cups confectioners' sugar sifted
½ cup chopped walnuts or pecans
12 whole nuts

1. In an electric mixer, cream the butter and beat in the maple syrup, salt, egg, and vanilla. Beat in the sugar, a little at a time, until the mixture reaches a good spreading consistency.
2. Use ¾ of the topping mixed with the chopped nuts as filling. Spread the remaining frosting on the top and sides of the top layer and garnish with the whole nuts.

Take-It-Along Tips: Ice several hours before the party, then wrap the cake loosely in Saran Wrap, and take it along.

Cherries Jubilee

There is no dessert I know more dramatic than this one—and it's easy to take to a party. You'll need a can of Sterno or a candle end to set the brandy on fire.

4 cups ripe black cherries, or 2 16-ounce cans Bing cherries	½ cup Marsala wine
	1 cup sugar
	¼ cup cherry brandy or cognac
1 whole clove	
2 cups dry red wine	

1. Pit the cherries. Stick the clove into one cherry. Crack the pits with a mallet and place with the clove-stuck cherry in a small cheesecloth bag. Put the bag in a kettle and add the red wine, the Marsala, and the sugar. Simmer 5 minutes. (If using canned cherries, drain the cherries and proceed as above but simmer only 3 minutes.)
2. Add the cherries to the kettle, and simmer, covered, 10 minutes more. Remove the cherries to the serving dish. Remove the bag of pits, and boil the syrup until it has reduced to about 1½ cups. Return the cherries to the syrup.
3. When you are ready to serve, reheat the cherries, and bring to the table with the brandy, a can of Sterno, and a silver ladle. Pour the brandy into the ladle, heat till simmering over the Sterno flame, tilt the ladle so the brandy catches fire, and ladle the flaming brandy onto the warm cherries. Ladle from the flaming bowl into dessert dishes.

Makes 8 to 10 portions.

Take-It-Along Tips: Take the cherries to the party in their cooking kettle, or in a silver serving dish that has a close fitting lid. Wrap carefully in foil so the juice doesn't spill out. Take along a can of Sterno and a silver ladle. Finish step 3 there, at the table, in front of the guests.

Stuffed Baked Apples

Serve hot or cold, with or without plain or whipped cream, *unsweetened.*

8 medium apples
1¼ cups brown sugar
½ cup white raisins
2 tablespoons orange rind
¼ cup butter
½ cup boiling water
3 tablespoons orange juice
½ pint heavy cream, optional

1. Heat oven to 375°.
2. Wash, core, stem the apples; do not peel. Stand in buttered glass baking dish and stuff ¾ cup sugar, the raisins, and the orange rind down into the centers. Fill the cavities with butter, and sprinkle the apples with remaining brown sugar.
3. Pour boiling water into the bottom of the dish, and set it in the oven. In 20 minutes, baste the apples and sprinkle the orange juice over them. If liquid is disappearing, add a little more juice. Bake 15 minutes longer, or until the apples are tender, throughout.
Makes 8 portions.

Take-It-Along Tips: Take these to the party in their cooking dish, and reheat to lukewarm in a 325° oven before serving—or serve cold.

Fruit in Champagne

Easy to prepare, and a treat after a heavy meal.

4 pints hulled fresh berries
  or 8 cups melon balls,
  or peeled sweet grapes,
  or peeled, sliced, peaches
  or oranges
⅔ cup sugar
½ cup cognac
1 bottle chilled semisweet champagne

1. Place fruit in a serving dish, sprinkle with the sugar and cognac. Cover and chill several hours.
2. Just before serving, pour champagne over the fruit.
Makes 8 to 10 portions.

Take-It-Along Tips: Take these to the party in their serving dish, carefully sealed in foil, so juices won't spill.

Fruit Mix for a Luau

Sometimes a sauce made of coconut milk is served with this in Hawaii, but I prefer it plain or with whipped cream.

1 ripe medium pineapple, peeled, cubed, or 1 can (20-ounce) pineapple cubes	1 stick cinnamon
	2 strips lemon peel
	1 teaspoon whole cloves
1 medium cantaloupe, cut in balls	1 piece candied ginger, minced
2 cups water	8 fresh pears, peeled, cored, halved
1 cup sugar	

1. Combine pineapple and juice and melon balls in a large serving bowl and chill, covered.
2. In a medium kettle, combine the other ingredients, except the pears. Bring to a boil; simmer 5 minutes. Add the pears; simmer gently until fruit is transparent and just tender, about 20 minutes.
3. Combine pineapple, cantaloupe, pears, and cooking syrup. Chill and serve.

Makes 10 to 12 portions.

Take-It-Along Tips: Take to the party in the serving dish, carefully wrapped in heavy duty foil. Watch that the juice doesn't spill while you travel.

Basket of Fresh Fruit

1 large ripe pineapple
6 cups mixed fresh fruit: pineapple, grapes, strawberries, grapefruit, pears, oranges, peaches, bananas

2 tablespoons sugar
1 tablespoon lime juice, strained
¼ cup kirsch or Cointreau
Bunch fresh mint

1. Slice the pineapple in half lengthwise. Remove the flesh and dice it. Grapes should be seeded; pears, peeled, diced, or sliced and dipped in lemon juice to keep them white; grapefruit should be divided into small segments, all pits and seeds removed; halve large strawberries; remove pith and seeds from orange slices. Peel and core other fruits, then cube.
2. Mix fruits with sugar, lime juice, kirsch, and chill. Just before serving, pile back into the pineapple cases. Garnish with mint leaves.

Makes 8 to 10 portions.

Take-It-Along Tips: Finish the recipe, then wrap the pineapple halves carefully in heavy-duty foil, doubled. Pineapple cases will rip Saran Wrap or thin foil. Make sure they travel upright so juices don't spill. I place mine on a shallow glass baking dish for the trip, so that juice that does spill can be poured back into the cases.

PART 9

When You Are Bringing the Drinks

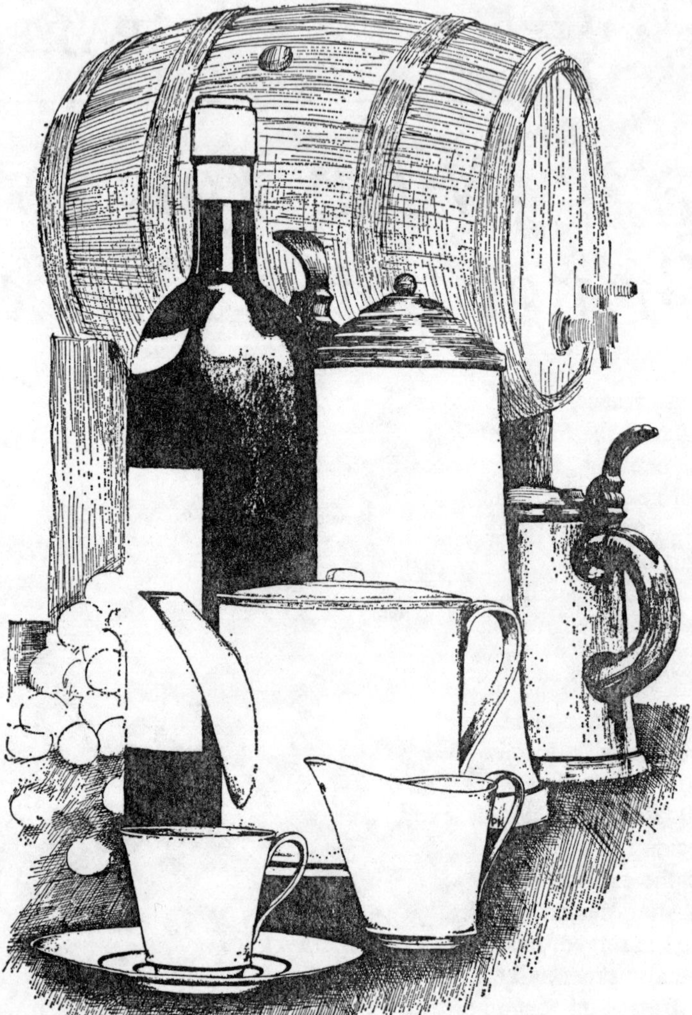

21. From Café Brûlot to Peach Champagne

What you serve with dinner is a personal matter. However, wines do enhance the flavor of foods, especially of French, Italian, and Spanish cooking. Beer usually goes very well with German and other Nordic cuisines, and so do the Rhine wines. With Oriental food, rice wine is a proper choice, or a light dry sherry or white wine, or a light beer.

As a generalization, white wines taste best with white meats (chicken, veal), rosé is good with pork, red wines with dark meats, such as beef. However, in France, we often serve a rosé or red wine with chicken and, while it is traditional, to serve a light Bordeaux with an after-salad cheese course. One of the finickiest gourmets I ever knew (a former chef to one of the French Rothschilds) offered me a fruity white wine with a plate of cheeses, and it was wonderful. All of which is to say, try various wines with your favorite dishes, decide for yourself what suits your palate, and don't be intimidated by the experts.

After dessert, in Europe, a rich, thick espresso coffee, or *café filtre* is served; this is made from dark-roasted coffee beans, available in most supermarkets. Usually, it is well sweetened before drinking. A dressed-up version of this is Café Brûlot Diabolique.

The other drinks here are hot and cold wine punches, and punches without liquor. Take your choice. Garnish the cold ones with small fruits or fruits frozen in ice cubes.

All these drink recipes can be doubled, but, when doubling, add only half again as much of the spices and taste before adding more.

Café Brûlot Diabolique

This strong, dark coffee concoction is served in demitasse cups or in big balloon glasses that are then filled up with whipped cream. Use espresso coffee for this. The original was made with dark roast drip coffee.

8 cubes sugar
8 whole cloves
1 stick cinnamon

1 orange peel, cut into strips
4 ounces cognac
4 cups espresso-type coffee

1. Place all ingredients, except the coffee, in a chafing dish over heat. Do not stir. Ignite the cognac in a flameproof ladle with a match and stir carefully until ingredients are well blended. Slowly pour in hot coffee and continue to stir.
2. To serve, ladle into demitasse cups.

Serves 6 to 8.

Take-It-Along Tips: Take the chafing dish, and the ingredients in individual containers to the party and make the Café Brûlot there.

Champagne Punch

A New Year's Eve special at our house. Make it with a nice California champagne. (I use Lejon but there are less costly brands that are good.) Serve this in a large glass bowl set in a punch bowl filled with crushed ice. Chill the champagne well before mixing.

8 cubes sugar
16 ounces cognac
3 bottles dry champagne

8 to 10 drops Angostura bitters

Soak sugar cubes in the cognac in the bottom of the serving bowl. Pour in the champagne and add the bitters. Stir with a silver ladle and serve.

Serves 10 to 16.

VARIATION:

MAY WINE PUNCH. Substitute May Wine for champagne, omit the bitters, and float one pint of small ripe whole strawberries in the punch; serve one berry in each cup of punch.

Take-It-Along Tips: Take the punch bowl, and all the ingredients in their individual containers, to the party and make the punch there.

Peach Champagne

A delicious wine punch. To make it less alcoholic and less expensive, substitute ginger ale for champagne.

12 very ripe peaches	1 bottle medium-dry white wine
½ cup superfine sugar	
1 bottle rosé wine	1 bottle brut champagne

1. Wash, peel, and pit the peaches; slice very thin and sprinkle with the sugar. Let stand until sugar has dissolved in the peach juice, about 2 hours.
2. Turn fruit into a large pitcher, pour rosé and white wine over them. Then chill.
3. Just before serving, transfer wine/fruit mixture to a punch bowl and pour in a bottle of chilled champagne.

Makes 12 to 16 portions.

Take-It-Along Tips: Follow steps one and 2, and take the pitcher, chilled, along with chilled champagne to the party. Finish the recipe there.

Long Bamboo Drink for a Luau

I like a California Chablis for this and serve it in tall, stemmed glasses.

1 small grapefruit	2 bottles dry white wine
1 slice pineapple	1 egg white, beaten dry
½ lemon	32 ounces lemon soda
10 ounces brandy	20 maraschino cherries
Juice of 1 lemon, strained	1 bunch fresh mint
½ cup superfine sugar	

1. Remove the pulp from the grapefruit, discard the pith and seeds, and dice it. Dice or crush the pineapple. Remove the pulp from the lemon, slice and dice this, too. Soak all the fruit in the brandy for one hour. Add the lemon juice and sugar, and stir well. Add the wine and pour over cracked ice in a punch bowl.
2. Frost the glasses by dipping the rims in egg white and then in superfine sugar.
3. Half-fill each glass with the punch, top with lemonade, and garnish each glass with a cherry and a sprig of mint.

Makes 20 portions.

Take-It-Along Tips: Complete step one, but do not pour over cracked ice till you get to the party. Instead, chill the step one mixture, take it to the party with the remaining ingredients, and complete the recipe there.

Sangria

A cold wine-and-fruit punch traditionally served before, during, and after a Paella dinner. The fruit gives the punch its flavor, and at a Paella dinner, it is often served as dessert—Sangria Fruit Cup.

¼ cup superfine sugar
3 bottles red wine, chilled
Fifth of brandy or cognac
3 navel oranges, peeled, seeded, cubed
1 fresh pineapple, peeled, cubed, or 1 20-ounce can cubed pineapple
4 ripe peaches, peeled, pitted, cubed
4 bananas, peeled, cubed
1 honeydew or cantaloupe, peeled, seeded, cubed

1. Place the sugar and one cup of the wine in a small saucepan and heat, stirring, until sugar is dissolved.
2. Pour this mixture and the rest of the wine and the brandy into a big punch bowl. Turn prepared fruits into the wine mixture and marinate in the refrigerator for 2 hours before serving.
3. Serve the wine with just a few small pieces of fruit in each glass. Dish the remaining fruits into dessert cups and serve after the meal.
Makes 12 generous portions.

Take-It-Along Tips: This is easiest to take along if you complete the recipe, then turn the sangria into wide-mouthed bottles after its chilling period. Or, chill in a punch bowl, wrap the punch bowl closely in heavy duty foil, and keep the bowl level while you travel to the host home.

Spicy Ice Cream Punch

½ teaspoon ground cinnamon
½ teaspoon ground nutmeg
4 whole cloves
2½ cups orange juice
2½ cups ginger ale or Seven-Up
1 cup apple cider
1 pint vanilla ice cream

1. Tie cinnamon, nutmeg, and cloves in a piece of cheesecloth, and soak in the orange juice for one hour. Remove the bag of spices, pour in the ginger ale or Seven-Up and the cider.
2. Just before serving, divide ice cream into 10 even pieces, and float it on top of the punch.

Makes 10 portions.

Take-It-Along Tips: Complete the first instruction in step one, then remove the bag of spices, but don't add ginger ale or Seven-Up or cider till you get to the party. You can get ice cream to a party intact (as long as the trip isn't too long, or the day too hot) by freezing it really hard before you leave, and taking it along in its container, wrapped in foil, and overwrapped in several layers of newspaper. Or, toss ice into an insulated carrying case, and take the ice cream in this improvised refrigerator.

Hot Mulled Wine

4 cups water
¾ cup superfine sugar
Rind and juice of 2 lemons
1 bottle claret, or other light dry red wine
1 cup port wine
1 stick cinnamon
¼ cup cognac, optional

1. Put the water and sugar in a saucepan and boil 5 minutes. Add the lemon rind and juice, the claret, port wine, and stick cinnamon. Heat for a few minutes.
2. Add the cognac, if desired, then strain all into a hot punch bowl in which a large silver ladle is resting.

Makes 12 portions.

Take-It-Along Tips: Make the drink before you leave, take to the party in its cooking kettle, and reheat at the host home.

Rhubarb Rum Punch

Ice cubes with small, whole fresh strawberries frozen inside make a pretty garnish for this gala fruit-and-rum punch. For non-drinkers, omit the rum.

1 pound rhubarb, diced	2 cups grape soda, chilled
2 cups citrus soda, chilled	½ cup rum
½ cup sugar	½ cup lemon juice, strained
2 cups ginger ale, chilled	1 lemon, sliced
2 cups black cherry soda, chilled	

1. In a saucepan, combine rhubarb and one cup of the citrus soda. Simmer over moderate heat for 20 minutes or until the rhubarb is soft. Stir in the sugar and cool. Pour all into a blender. Blend at medium speed for 3 minutes, or until rhubarb is puréed.
2. In a punch bowl, combine the puréed rhubarb, sodas, rum, and lemon juice. Float the lemon slices in the punch.

Serve well-chilled.
Serves 8 to 12.

Take-It-Along Tips: Complete the recipe, combining all the ingredients excepting the sodas. Add these at the host home.

Fruit Punch

For children or those who prefer non-alcoholic drinks. Drinkers like it spiked with gin or vodka.

1 6-ounce can Hawaiian punch	1 6-ounce can frozen pineapple juice concentrate
1 6-ounce can frozen pink lemonade concentrate	6 cups cold water
1 6-ounce can frozen orange concentrate	5½ cups ginger ale, chilled
	Thin slices fresh lime

Mix the frozen juices in a blender. Then mix with cold water in a large pitcher and pour over ice piled in a large punch bowl. Add the ginger ale. Garnish with the lime slices.
Makes 24 to 30 drinks.

Take-It-Along Tips: Complete the recipe, but don't pour over ice till you get to the host home—add the ginger ale after the punch is in the punch bowl.

Glögg

A hot wine cup served in Sweden at Christmas and to warm up skiers and skaters. Saint-Emillion, Beaune, or Beaujolais would be a good choice for this.

2 bottles red wine
10 ounces gin
1 stick cinnamon
5 cardamom seeds, peeled
10 cloves
3 ounces blanched almonds
5 ounces seedless raisins
2 tablespoons clear honey

1. Warm glass mugs in an oven at 250°.
2. Open the wine and pour into an enameled saucepan. Add the gin, cinnamon, cardamom seeds and cloves. The cinnamon can be bruised slightly to bring out the flavor. Simmer gently for 5 minutes, then remove from the heat and stir in the almonds, raisins, and honey.
3. Cool for 3 minutes only, then pour into the glasses. If a spoon is put into each glass as the drink is poured, there is less chance of the glass cracking.

Makes 10 portions.

Take-It-Along Tips: Take to the party in its cooking dish, reheat slightly before serving.

Index

Aïoli Mayonnaise, 222
Angel Food Shortcake, 247
Appetizers and dips
    Artichokes and Mushrooms, 68
    Bagna Cauda, 68
    Brandied Cheese Spread, 71
    Carousel of Stuffed Delights, 65
    Cheese Dip, 75
    Cheese Puffs, 75
    Cheese Straws, 74
    Cheese Toast, 72
    Chopped Chicken Livers, 70
    Danish Open Sandwiches, 50
    Eggplant Relish, 54
    Fiddler's Herring, 51
    Garlic or Herb Cheese Dip, 75
    Guacamole, 67
    Pickled Cucumbers the Old Way, 52
    Quick Pissaladière, 75
    Red Cabbage Salad, 53
    Red Eggs, 52
    Sausage Roll, 54
    scalloped potatoes (Janson's Temptation), 49
    Scandia Herring, 51
    Shrimp Toast, 71
    Stuffed Mushroom Caps, 69
    Stuffed Onion Rolls, 53
    See also Hors d'Oeuvres
Apples
    Stuffed Baked Apples, 252
    in Sweet Potatoes, Vermont Style, 214
    in White Cabbage, 162
Artichokes and Mushrooms, 68
Aspic of Tongue, 122

Avocado dip, 67

Bagna Cauda, 68
Baked Beans the New England Way, 187
Bananas
    Hawaiian Duck with Bananas, 106
    Roast Port Loin with Honey-Baked Bananas, 113
Basket of Fresh Fruit, 255
Bavarian Pork, 166
Bavarian Potato Dumplings, 161
Beans
    Baked Beans the New England Way, 187
    Cassoulet, 144
    See also Green beans
Beef
    Aspic of Tongue, 122
    Beef à L'Estouffade, 138
    Beef-and-Kidney Pie, 192
    Beef-and-Pork Casserole, 168
    Beef Platter, 165
    Boeuf Bourguignonne Marcel's Way, 136
    Bouillon, 20
    Carbonnade de Boeuf à la Flamande, 146
    corned. *See* Sauerkraut Dinner
    drippings, 21
    Elegant Stew by Nona Remos, 139
    ground
        Dolmas (Turkish stuffed vine leaves), 63
        Hamburger Wellington, 189
        Meatballs with Lemon Sauce, 164

Beef, ground (*cont'd*)
  Mrs. Bruzzese's Lasagna, 155
  Mrs. Fearon's Ham Loaf, 118
  Hawaiian Rump Roast, 114
  Pâté Chinois (shepherd's pie), 194
  Paupiettes of Beef, 141
  Rump Roast, 114
  Sukiyaki, 179
Berry Ice Cream, 240
Beverages
  Café Brûlot Diabolique, 260
  Champagne Punch, 260
  Fruit Punch, 265
  Glögg, 266
  Hot Mulled Wine, 264
  Long Bamboo Drink for a Luau, 262
  May Wine Punch, 261
  Peach Champagne, 261
  Rhubarb Rum Punch, 265
  Sangria, 263
  Spicy Ice Cream Punch, 264
Biscuits, Butter, 22
Blanquette de Veau, 132
Boeuf Bourguignonne Marcel's Way, 136
Borscht, 89
Bouillabaisse, 101
Bouillon or broth
  beef, 20
  chicken, 20
Bouquet Garni, 19
Brandied Cheese Spread, 71
Brandied Chicken with Mushroom Sauce, 185
Bratwurst in Sour Cream, 166
Bread and muffins
  Butter Biscuits, 22
  use of mixes, 23
  warming, 22
Butter Biscuits, 22
Butter or margarine, use of, 21

Cabbage
  Chou Farci Catalan, 143
  Cole Slaw, 230
  Holubste (Ukrainian Stuffed Cabbage Rolls), 172
  Red Cabbage Salad, 53
  White Cabbage, 162
Café Brûlot Diabolique, 260

Cakes
  Dick Engelbretsen's Carrot Cake, 249
  Golden Layer Cake, 250
  Joe Bednerz' Christmas Cake, 250
  See also Frosting
Calorie-Counter Dressings, 221
Carbonnade de Boeuf à la Flamande, 146
Carousel of Stuffed Delights, 65
Carrots
  Carrot-and-Raisin Slaw, 230
  Casserole of Root Vegetables, 211
  Dick Engelbretsen's Carrot Cake, 249
Casserole of Root Vegetables, 211
Casserole Poulet Marengo, 157
Casserole Veal Marengo, 157
Cassoulet, 144
Cauliflower, Gratinée of, with Watercress, 210
Celery, Cream-of-Celery Soup, 84
Champagne Punch, 260
Charlotte from the Isles, 248
Cheese
  Brandied Cheese Spread, 71
  Cheese Dip, 75
  Cheese Mousse, 64
  Cheese Puffs, 73
  Cheese Straws, 74
  Cheese Toast, 72
  Green Noodles Baked with Two Cheeses, 149
  Quiche with Cream and Cheese, 59
  Stuffing, 66
Cheesecake with Strawberry Sauce, 242
Chef's Salad, 125
Cherries
  Cherries Jubilee, 252
  Cherry-Brandy Sauce, 198
  Sour-Cherry Ribbon, 246
Chestnut Stuffing for Christmas Goose, 200
Chicken
  bouillon or broth, 20
  Brandied Chicken with Mushroom Sauce, 185
  Casserole Poulet Marengo, 157
  Chef's Salad, 125
  Chicken Breasts, Vermont Style, 188
  Chicken Breasts Chaud-Froid, 135

INDEX

Chicken (cont'd)
   Chicken Livers Islander, 109
   Chopped Chicken Livers, 70
   Chou Farci Catalan, 143
   Coq au Vin, 134
   Creamy Chicken Pie, 193
   drippings, use of, 21
   grilled outdoors, 97
   Indian Chicken Pulao with Shrimps, 176
   Malaysian Chicken Curry, 178
   Paella Valenciana, 159
   Pâté Maison Marcel, 57
   Pilaf Bokhari, 174
   Thick Chicken Soup, 82
Chilled Fruit Mousse, 238
Chinese Mushrooms, Snow Peas, and Bamboo Shoots, 175
Chou Farci Catalan, 143
Christmas Cake, 250
Christmas Duck with Cherries, 197
Christmas Goose with Chestnut Stuffing, 200
Chutney, Pineapple, 225
Cider-Baked Picnic Ham, 119
Clambake for Twenty-Five, 96
Cod of the Sea, 103
Coffee
   Café Brûlot Diabolique, 260
   Coffee Mousse, 238
Cold Meat Salad, 124
Cold Vegetable Salad, 227
Cole Slaw, 230
Coq au Vin, 134
Coquille St. Jacques, 60
Corn
   Corn Pudding, 209
   Country Corn Roast, 97
Crabmeat
   Crabmeat Stuffing, 66
   New Orleans Fresh Crab Gumbo, 183
Cream-Cheese Frosting, 249
Crème Caramel, 236
Cucumbers
   Cucumber Mousse, 231
   Pickled Cucumbers the Old Way, 52
   Raita (cucumber relish), 225
Curries
   Lamb Korma, 177
   Malaysian Chicken Curry, 178

Deer Island Lobster Stew, 99
Desserts
   Angel Food Shortcake, 247
   Basket of Fresh Fruit, 255
   Berry Ice Cream, 240
   Charlotte from the Isles, 248
   Cheesecake with Strawberry Sauce, 242
   Cherries Jubilee, 252
   Chilled Fruit Mousse, 238
   Coffee Mousse, 238
   Crème Caramel, 236
   Dick Engelbretsen's Carrot Cake, 249
   English Trifle, 239
   Fruit in Champagne, 252
   Fruit Mix for a Luau, 254
   Golden Layer Cake, 250
   Indian Pudding, 241
   Joe Bednerz' Christmas Cake, 250
   Lime Meringue Pie, 243
   Mayonnaise au Chocolat des Sables, 237
   Mocha-Brandy Mousse, 238
   New Orleans Pecan Pie, 244
   Pumpkin Pie, 245
   Saffron Fruit Cream, 238
   Sour-Cherry Ribbon, 246
   Stuffed Baked Apples, 252
Diana Walton's Mushroom Pie, 206
Dick Engelbretsen's Carrot Cake, 249
Dips. *See* Appetizers and dips
Dolmas (Turkish stuffed vine leaves), 63
Duck
   Christmas Duck with Cherries, 197
   Hawaiian Duck with Bananas, 106
Dumplings, Bavarian Potato, 161

Eastern and Far Eastern cooking, 171–180
Egg dishes
   Mushroom Quiche, 59
   Quiche with Cream and Cheese, 59
   Red Eggs, 51
   Seafood Quiche, 59
Eggplant
   Italian Rice Salad, 228
   Moussaka, 173
   Ratatouille Niçoise, 147
   Relish, 54
English Trifle, 239

Epaule De Porc à la Normande, 142
Equivalents, list of, 24

Fiddler's Herring, 51
Fish. *See* Seafood
Francesca Bosetti Morris's Risotto alla Milanese, 156
Frankfurters
  Frankfurter Bake-In, 127
  Hot Frankfurter Sandwiches, 126
French bread, warming, 22
French Dressing, 220
French specialties, 131–148
Frostings
  Cream-Cheese Frosting, 249
  decorating with, 10–12
  Maple Nut Frosting, 251
  Party Tube Frosting, 12
Fruit
  Basket of Fresh Fruit, 255
  Berry Ice Cream, 240
  carved fruits, 13–15
  Charlotte from the Isles, 248
  Chilled Fruit Mousse, 236
  Fruit in Champagne, 252
  Fruit Mix for a Luau, 254
  Fruit Punch, 265
  Garden Rhubarb Soup, 92
  Peach Champagne, 261
  Saffron Fruit Cream, 238
  Sangria Fruit Cup, 263

Galantine De Porc Marcel, 121
Game and venison
  Marinade for Game, 224
  New Orleans Marinated Venison, 186
  Partridge in a Pear Tree, 198
Garden Rhubarb Soup, 92
Garlic or Herb Cheese Dip, 75
Garlic Salad Dressing, 220
Garnishes, 9–10
  candied flowers, 10
  carved vegetables and fruit, 13–15
  Gremolata, 154
  pastry decorating, 10–12
Gazpacho Soup, Jellied, 91
German cooking, 161–169
Glögg, 266
Gnocchi, 152
Golden Layer Cake, 250
  Maple Nut Frosting for, 251

Gratinée of Cauliflower with Watercress, 210
Greek dishes, 173
Green beans
  Baked Green Beans, 212
  Green Beans Lyonnaise, 212
Green Goddess Dressing, 223
Green Noodles Baked with Two Cheeses, 149
Green Pea Soup with Ham Bone, 80
Green Peppers. *See* Stuffed Peppers Provençale
Green Salad, 226
Gremolata, 154
Guacamole, 67

Ham
  Chef's Salad, 125
  Cider-Baked Picnic Ham, 119
  Green Pea Soup with Ham Bone, 80
  Ham in Wine Jelly, 120
  Louisiana Ham Pot, 182
  Mrs. Fearon's Ham Loaf, 118
  Salade de L'Île Barbe, 231
  stuffing, 66
Hamburger Wellington, 189
Hasenpfeffer, 163
Hawaiian luau dishes
  Chicken Livers Islander, 109
  Fish Adobo, 112
  Fish Baked in Ti Leaves, 111
  Fruit Mix for a Luau, 254
  Hawaiian Duck with Bananas, 106
  Hawaiian Rump Roast, 114
  Long Bamboo Drink, 262
  Luau Pungent Turkey, 108
  Luau Riblets, 110
  Roast Pork Loin with Honey-Baked Bananas, 113
  Salad for a Luau, 115
  Sweet-Sour Spareribs, 107
Herb Mayonnaise, 222
Herb or Garlic Cheese Dip, 75
Herb Salad Dressing, 220
Herbs and condiments, 18–19
  Bouquet Garni, 19
Herring
  Fiddler's Herring, 51
  Scandia Herring, 51
Hints and tips, 25–27
Hollandaise the Fast Way, 223
Holubste (Ukrainian Stuffed Cabbage Rolls), 172

INDEX

Honey Mayonnaise for Fruit Salads, 223
Hors d'Oeuvres
  Cheese Mousse, 64
  Coquille St. Jacques, 60
  Dolmas, 63
  Mussels Clemence, 61
  Pâté Maison Marcel, 57
  Quiche with Cream and Cheese, 59
  Shrimp in Tomato Aspic, 62
  See also Appetizers and dips

Ice Cream
  Berry Ice Cream, 240
  Spicy Ice Cream Punch, 264
In-the-Bag Potatoes, 209
Indian Chicken Pulao with Shrimps, 176
Indian Pudding, 241
Italian Rice Salad, 228
Italian specialties, 149–160

Janson's Temptation (scalloped potatoes), 49
Jellied Gazpacho Soup, 91
Joe Bednerz' Christmas Cake, 250

Lamb
  Beef-and-Kidney Pie, 192
  Cassoulet, 144
  Elegant Stew by Nona Remos, 139
  Lamb Kabobs, 173
  Lamb Korma, 177
  Lamb Pie, 191
  Luau Riblets, 110
  Navarin Printanier, 133
  Scotch Broth, 83
  Stuffed Peppers Provençale, 208
Lasagna, 155
Leek-and-Potato Soup, 81
Lemon-Butter Sauce the Fast Way, 224
Lemon Salad Dressing, 220
Lime Meringue Pie, 243
Lobster. *See* Seafood
Long Bamboo Drink for a Luau, 262
Louisiana Ham Pot, 182
Luau Pungent Turkey, 108
Luau Riblets (breast of lamb), 110

Macaroni Salad, 229
Malaysian Chicken Curry, 178
Maple-Candied Butternut Squash, 215

Maple Nut Frosting, 251
Margarine or butter, 21
Marinade for Game, 224
Marinade for Vegetables, 224
May Wine Punch, 261
Mayonnaise, 222
  Aïoli Mayonnaise, 222
  Herb Mayonnaise, 222
  Honey Mayonnaise for Fruit Salads, 223
  Mayonnaise Chantilly for Fruit Salads, 223
  Mayonnaise au Chocolat des Sables, 237
Meat. *See* Beef; Lamb; Pork; Veal
Meatballs with Lemon Sauce, 164
Mediterranean cooking, 149–160
Mediterranean Salad, 229
Menus, 29–45
  Boeuf Bourguignonne Dinner for Eight, 33
  Buffet for Sixteen Gourmets, 35
  Christmas Buffet, 30, 31
  Christmas Dinner for Eight, 31
  Clambake for Twenty-Five, 38
  Cold Cup Luncheon, 37
  Easter Menu, 32
  Easy Gourmet Dinner for Eight, 33
  Easy Greek Dinner, 42
  Five-Course Gourmet Dinner for Eight, 34
  Game Catcher's Dinner, 39
  German Specialties, 45
  Gourmet Picnic, 38
  Hawaiian Luau for Sixteen, 43
  Hot Pot for a Multitude, 36
  Hot Pot Skating Party, 36
  Indian Buffet, 43
  Inflation Dinner Party, 40
  Italian Dinner for a Crowd, 44
  Italian Gourmet Dinner for a Few, 44
  Luncheon Parties, 37
  Meat Pie Party for a Crowd, 35, 36
  Mediterranean Dinner, 45
  New England Dinner, 40
  New England Picnic for a Crowd, 40
  New Orleans Dinner, 41
  New Year's Eve Smorgasbord, 30
  Oriental Dinner for Six, 42
  Paella Dinner, 41
  Rhineland Dinner, 46

Menus (cont'd)
  Seashore Dinner, 38
  Six-Course Gourmet Dinner for Eight, 34
  Thanksgiving Dinner, 32
  Try-These Party Menu, 39
Mocha-Brandy Mousse, 238
Moussaka, 173
Mrs. Bruzzese's Lasagna, 155
Mrs. Fearon's Ham Loaf, 118
Mushrooms
  Artichokes and Mushrooms, 68
  Baked Green Beans, 212
  Brandied Chicken with Mushroom Sauce, 185
  Chicken Livers Islander, 109
  Cream-of-Mushroom Soup, 85
  Diana Walton's Mushroom Pie, 206
  Mushroom Sauce, 199
  Quiche, 59
  Spinach-and-Mushroom Salad, 227
  Stuffed Mushroom Caps, 69
Mussels Clemence, 61

Navarin Printanier (lamb stew), 133
New England Clam Chowder, 100
New Orleans Fresh Crab Gumbo, 183
New Orleans Marinated Venison, 186
New Orleans Pecan Pie, 244
Noodle Salad, 228

Oil-and-Vinegar Dressing, 220
Onions
  Cheese Toast Appetizers, 72
  Onion Sambal (relish), 226
  Onion Soup Gratinée, 79
  Quick Pissaladière, 75
  Stuffed Onion Rolls, 53
Oriental cooking, 171–180
Osso Buco, 153
Outdoor cooking, 93–127
Oyster Stew, 98

Paella Valenciana, 159
Parsley Salad Dressing, 220
Parties, 3–7
  beach, 95–103
  carrying food to, 7
  Hawaiian Luaus, 105–115
  menus for, 29–45
  organizing groups for, 6–7
  outdoor, 93–127
  smorgasbord, 49–55
  snacks for, 49–76
  themes for, 3–5
Partridge in a Pear Tree, 198
Pasta
  Green Noodles Baked with Two Cheeses, 149
  Macaroni Salad, 228
  Mrs. Bruzzese's Lasagna, 155
  Noodle Salad, 228
  Spaghetti Salad, 228
  Spinach Ravioli with Salsa Bianca, 150
Pâté Chinois (shepherd's pie), 194
Pâté Maison Marcel, 57
Peach Champagne, 261
Peanut-Butter Soup, 86
Pecan Pie, New Orleans, 244
Pickled Cucumbers the Old Way, 52
Picnic fare, 117–127
Pies and pastry
  Lime Meringue Pie, 243
  New Orleans Pecan Pie, 244
  Pumpkin Pie, 245
  Sour-Cherry Ribbon, 246
  Squash Pie, 245
Pilaf Bokhari, 174
Pineapple Chutney, 225
Pork
  Bavarian Pork, 166
  Beef-and-Pork Casserole, 168
  Cassoulet, 144
  Chou Farci Catalan, 143
  Cider-Baked Picnic Ham, 119
  Epaule De Porc à la Normande, 142
  Galantine De Porc Marcel, 121
  Ham in Wine Jelly, 120
  Mrs. Fearon's Ham Loaf, 118
  Pâté Maison Marcel, 57
  Pork Casserole New York Style, 190
  Roast Pork Loin with Honey-Baked Bananas, 113
  Sweet-Sour Spareribs—Hawaiian Style, 107
  Tourtière Canadienne, 195
Potatoes
  Bavarian Potato Dumplings, 161
  Casserole of Root Vegetables, 211
  Gnocchi, 152
  In-the-Bag Potatoes, 209
  Janson's Temptation (scalloped), 49

INDEX

Potatoes (cont'd)
  Leek-and-Potato Soup, 81
  Potato Salad, 229
Pots and pans, 18
  use of heavy skillets, 21
Poultry, 196–201
  Christmas Goose with Chestnut Stuffing, 200
  Partridge in a Pear Tree, 198
  See also Chicken; Duck
Pumpkin Pie, 245
Punches
  Champagne, 260
  Fruit Punch, 265
  May Wine Punch, 261
  Peach Champagne, 261
  Rhubarb Rum Punch, 265
  Spicy Ice Cream Punch, 264

Quiche
  with Cream and Cheese, 59
  Mushroom, 59
  Seafood, 59
Quick Pissaladière (onion appetizer), 75

Raita (cucumber relish), 225
Ratatouille Niçoise, 147
Ravioli, Spinach, with Salsa Bianca, 150
Red Cabbage Salad, 53
Red Eggs, 52
Relishes
  Eggplant, 54
  Onion Sambal, 226
  Pickled Cucumbers the Old Way, 52
  Raita (cucumber relish), 225
Rhubarb soup, 92
Rice
  Francesca Bosetti Morris's Risotto alla Milanese, 156
  Holubste (Ukrainian Stuffed Cabbage Rolls), 172
  Indian Chicken Pulao with Shrimps, 176
  Italian Rice Salad, 228
  Pilaf Bokhari, 174
Roast Pork Loin with Honey-Baked Bananas, 113
Roquefort or Blue Cheese Dressing, 220
Russian Dressing, 223

Saffron Fruit Cream, 238
Salad Dressings
  Aïoli, 222
  Calorie-Counter I and II, 221
  French or Oil-and-Vinegar Dressing, 220
  Fresh Mayonnaise, 222
  Garlic Dressing, 220
  Green Goddess Dressing, 223
  Herb Dressing, 220
  Herb Mayonnaise, 222
  Honey Mayonnaise for Fruit Salads, 223
  Lemon Dressing, 220
  Mayonnaise Chantilly for Fruit Salads, 223
  Parsley Dressing, 220
  Roquefort or Blue Cheese, 220
  Russian Dressing, 223
  Thousand Island Dressing, 220
  Vinaigrette Sauce, 221
Salads
  Carrot-and-Raisin Slaw, 230
  Chef's Salad, 125
  Cold Meat Salad, 124
  Cold Vegetable Salad, 227
  Cole Slaw, 230
  Cucumber Mousse, 231
  Green Salad, 226
  Italian Rice Salad, 228
  Macaroni Salad, 228
  Mediterranean Salad, 229
  Noodle Salad, 228
  Potato Salad, 229
  Salad for a Luau, 115
  Salade de L'Ile Barbe, 231
  Shrimp in Tomato Aspic, 62
  Smoked Haddock Salad, 123
  Spaghetti Salad, 228
  Spinach-and-Mushroom Salad, 227
Salmon, Poached, with Sauce Verte, 184
Salsa Bianca, 151
Sandwiches
  Danish Open Sandwiches, 50
  Hot Frankfurter, 126
Sangria, 263
Sangria Fruit Cup, 263
Sauces
  Hollandaise the Fast Way, 223
  Lemon-Butter Sauce the Fast Way, 224
  Mushroom, 185, 199

INDEX

Sauces (cont'd)
  Salsa Bianca, 151
  Sauce Verte, 184
  use of leftover gravies and pan drippings, 21
  Vinaigrette Sauce, 221
Sauerkraut Dinner, 167
Sausages
  Bratwurst in Sour Cream, 166
  Cassoulet, 144
  Chou Farci Catalan, 143
  Mrs. Bruzzese's Lasagna, 155
  Paella Valenciana, 159
  Sausage Roll, 54
Scandia Herring, 51
Scotch Broth, 83
Seafood
  Bouillabaisse, 101
  Carousel of Stuffed Delights, 65
  Clambake for Twenty-Five, 96
  Cod of the Sea, 103
  Coquille St. Jacques, 60
  Fiddler's Herring, 51
  Fish Adobo, 112
  Fish Baked in Ti Leaves, 111
  Lobster
    Deer Island Lobster Stew, 99
    Salade de L'Île Barbe, 231
  Mussels Clemence, 61
  New England Clam Chowder, 100
  New Orleans Fresh Crab Gumbo, 183
  Oyster Stew, 98
  Paella Valenciana, 159
  Poached Salmon with Sauce Verte, 184
  Scandia Herring, 51
  Seafood Quiche, 59
  Shrimp
    Cream-of-Shrimp Soup, 90
    Indian Chicken Pulao with Shrimps, 176
    Shrimp in Tomato Aspic, 62
    Shrimp Toast, 71
    Stuffing for Eggs, 66
  Smoked Haddock Salad, 123
Shepherd's Pie, 194
Soups, 79–92
  Beef Bouillon, 20
  Bouillabaisse, 101
  Chicken Bouillon or Broth, 20
  Chicken Soup, Thick, 82
  cold, 87–92

Borscht, 89
Cream-of-Shrimp Soup, 90
Garden Rhubarb Soup, 92
Jellied Gazpacho, 91
Vichyssoise, 88
Cream-of-Celery Soup, 84
Cream-of-Mushroom Soup, 85
Cream-of-Shrimp Soup, 90
Deer Island Lobster Stew, 99
Green Pea Soup with Ham Bone, 80
Leek-and-Potato Soup, 81
New England Clam Chowder, 100
Onion Soup Gratinée, 79
Oyster Stew, 98
Peanut-Butter Soup, 86
Scotch Broth, 83
Vegetable Soup, 82
Vichyssoise, 81, 88
Sour-Cherry Ribbon, 246
Spaghetti Salad, 228
Spicy Ice Cream Punch, 264
Spinach-and-Mushroom Salad, 227
Spinach Ravioli with Salsa Bianca, 150
Squash, Maple-Candied Butternut, 215
Squash Pie, 245
Stuffed Baked Apples, 252
Stuffed Onion Rolls, 53
Stuffed Peppers Provençale, 208
Stuffing, Chestnut, 200
Substitutes and equivalents, 23–24
Sukiyaki, 179
Sweet potatoes or yams
  in Louisiana Ham Pot, 182
  Maple-Candied, 215
  Vermont Style, 214
Sweet-Sour Spareribs–Hawaiian Style, 107

Thousand Island Dressing, 220
Tomatoes
  Baked Stuffed Tomatoes, 207
  Jellied Gazpacho Soup, 91
  Mediterranean Salad, 229
  Shrimp in Tomato Aspic, 62
Tourtière Canadienne, 195
Turkey, Luau Pungent, 108

Ukrainian Stuffed Cabbage Rolls (Holubste), 172

Veal
  Blanquette de Veau, 132
  Casserole Veal Marengo, 157

INDEX

Veal (cont'd)
  Osso Buco, 153
  Stuffed Peppers Provençale, 208
  Veal Fondue, 148
Vegetables
  Baked Green Beans, 212
  Baked Stuffed Tomatoes, 207
  Casserole of Root Vegetables, 211
  Cold Vegetable Salad, 227
  Corn Pudding, 209
  Diana Walton's Mushroom Pie, 206
  dip for (Bagna Cauda), 68
  Gratinée of Cauliflower with Watercress, 210
  Green Beans Lyonnaise, 212
  Green Salad, 226
  In-the-Bag Potatoes, 209
  Maple-Candied Butternut Squash, 215
  marinade for, 224
  Ratatouille Niçoise, 147
  Spinach-and-Mushroom Salad, 227
  Stuffed Peppers Provençale, 208
  Sweet Potatoes, Vermont Style, 214
  Vegetable Soup, 82
  See also name of vegetable
Venison, New Orleans Marinated, 186
Vichyssoise, 81, 88
Vinaigrette Sauce, 221

Watercress. *See* Gratinée of Cauliflower with Watercress
White Cabbage, 162
Wine, Hot Mulled, 264